Together Again

TOGETHER AGAIN

FAMILY REUNIFICATION IN FOSTER CARE

Edited by
Barbara A. Pine
Robin Warsh
Anthony N. Maluccio

CHILD WELFARE LEAGUE OF AMERICA
WASHINGTON, DC

CHILD WELFARE LEAGUE OF AMERICA, INC.
440 First Street, NW, Suite 310, Washington, DC 20001-2085

CURRENT PRINTING (last digit)
10 9 8 7 6 5 4 3 2 1

Cover and text design by Jennifer Riggs

Printed in the United States of America

ISBN # 0–87868–525–1

TOGETHER AGAIN

FAMILY REUNIFICATION IN FOSTER CARE

Edited by
Barbara A. Pine
Robin Warsh
Anthony N. Maluccio

CHILD WELFARE LEAGUE OF AMERICA
WASHINGTON, DC

CHILD WELFARE LEAGUE OF AMERICA, INC.
440 First Street, NW, Suite 310, Washington, DC 20001-2085

CURRENT PRINTING (last digit)
10 9 8 7 6 5 4 3 2 1

Cover and text design by Jennifer Riggs

Printed in the United States of America

ISBN # 0–87868–525–1

Contents

FOREWORD

The public child welfare system has been criticized by policymakers, educators, administrators, practitioners, clients, the media, and the general public, all of whom express a lack of confidence in the ability of federal, state, and local authorities to solve the increasingly difficult family and child problems that come to the attention of child welfare agencies. Seeking to remedy the failure of agencies to adequately address these complex problems, child advocates have filed suits in federal courts, alleging violations of federal law and failure to protect the constitutional rights of vulnerable children.

Some critics argue that the most important problem is the lack of political commitment to allocating and appropriating sufficient funds for an increasingly resource-starved child welfare delivery system. Others blame the system itself for lacking adequate methods to help very troubled children and families. Still others blame the victims—parents and children alike—for creating their own problems. Child welfare professionals and advocates recognize that the problems are complex; that there are no easy solutions; and that without sufficient funds, it is difficult to provide quality services. Given the massive federal deficit and critical budget shortfalls in most states, however, it is likely that child welfare agencies, even those under court-ordered remedies, will continue to struggle for adequate funding, with reducing excessive caseloads a high priority.

Child welfare agencies need to evaluate their methods critically. Poverty-ridden, drug- and crime-infested neighborhoods, coupled with years of official neglect, have seriously compromised the ability of many families to rear their own children successfully. Today's more difficult social and family problems require new solutions. This is particularly true for families already separated by out-of-home placements, the number of which are on the increase.

The American Public Welfare Association compiled data showing that the number of children in out-of-home care rose by 50% from 1985 to 1990. Although many children are eventually reunited with their biological families, the reunification does not work out in a substantial proportion of cases, and the children are returned to foster care, placed elsewhere—perhaps in the mental health system or juvenile justice system—or join the ranks of the homeless. Greater efforts must be made to establish or strengthen programs to reunite placed children with their families and to maintain them there.

Recognizing the need of child welfare agencies for help in their family reunification programs, in September 1988 the Center for the Study of Child Welfare at the University of Connecticut began a two-year project in which a range of training materials was developed. The project was implemented in collaboration with state child welfare agencies in Maine, New Hampshire, Vermont, Massachusetts, Connecticut, and Rhode Island; other schools of social work; Casey Family Services; and other interested agencies and organizations. In addition to this book, the project's staff and faculty produced a monograph that delineates family reunification competencies for social workers, a curriculum sourcebook for use by social work educators and trainers, a newsletter on family reunification, and a chapter in an instructional sourcebook on intensive family preservation services; and hosted a regional conference, from which proceedings were published.

The editors and authors of this book are social work educators, researchers, and practitioners engaged in family reunification work. In focusing on the reunification of families who are separated by out-of-home placement, they address one of the most vulnerable and disempowered groups the child welfare system serves. These families are typically perceived by others as failures, and often experience themselves as lacking in profound ways. Readers will see an emphasis on hope and compassion throughout these chapters, an emphasis that is an essential part of working with families toward lasting reconnections.

Through the publication of this book, the editors—Barbara A. Pine, Robin Warsh, and Anthony N. Maluccio—have made a substantial contribution to our understanding of the complex nature of family reunification policy, practice, and programs. Their work can help agencies to offer our most troubled families a real chance to be together again.

Nancy A. Humphreys, Dean
School of Social Work
University of Connecticut
West Hartford, CT

PREFACE

Attention to family reunification is one expression of the renewed emphasis in child welfare and related fields on preserving families. The unique challenges of preserving families who have been separated through placement, however, require new thinking, informed policy changes, supportive programs, and revised practice strategies.

This book presents material that can aid in establishing and implementing programs in child welfare agencies that promote and maintain reunification of children in out-of-home care with their biological families. Each of its 11 chapters addresses a particular aspect of family reunification, and suggests principles and strategies to guide the work of providers. Case examples are included throughout.

In the introduction, Hartman places family reunification in a historical context, highlighting the turn of societal events that led to the current interest in this specialized field of practice.

Part I (chapters 1 through 4) describes the structures, both conceptual and tangible, that need to be in place to support family reunification. In chapter 1, Maluccio, Warsh, and Pine offer a conceptual framework for rethinking reunification practice as an integral part of permanency planning. The chapter presents an expanded definition of family reunification, delineates the major program components of effective family reunification, and considers selected implications for practice and service delivery. The relationship between the court system and the child welfare agency is the focus of chapter 2; Day, Cahn, and Johnson describe a collaborative approach to reunification that has resulted in improved practice in several communities. In chapter 3, Pine, Warsh, and

Maluccio describe a competency-based approach to training staff members in which family reunification practice is tied to the agency's goals and the supportive agency environment. Boutilier and Rehm, in chapter 4, illustrate how a community mental health center provides an ideal setting to support family reunification work; they delineate the four phases of reunification used by the center, along with guidelines for mounting similar programs within other mental health agencies.

Part II (chapters 5 through 9) focuses on the range of practice methods and approaches that constitute family reunification work. In chapter 5, Fein and Staff examine guidelines for goal-setting with biological families; set forth tools for helping workers in assessment, decision-making, and treatment planning; and discuss policy and practice implications of a goal-oriented approach to service planning. Carlo, in chapter 6, discusses strategies for effective parent involvement in the context of a residential treatment center. In chapter 7, Hess and Proch describe the multiple purposes of visiting, provide guidelines for the development of visiting plans that will facilitate reunification, and identify the agency resources that are essential to an effective visiting program. In chapter 8, Folaron discusses the needs of the child throughout the reunification process; denotes practice activities and strategies for engaging the child, assessing the child's commitment to reunification, improving child and family communication, and developing a plan for the child's protection; and sets forth strategies for maintaining family connections. In chapter 9, Zamosky, Sparks, Hatt, and Sharman discuss how an underlying belief in the potential of all families to care adequately for their children, coupled with a focus on strengths, is uniquely suited to the reunification effort. Putting this approach into practice is examined at four levels of service delivery: those of the individual caseworker, the supervisor, the family, and the larger child welfare system.

Part III (chapters 10 and 11) is concerned with the use of evaluation and research to create a knowledge base on family reunification. In chapter 10, Turner encourages practitioners to consider program evaluation as a necessary aspect of effective family reunification practice. The author offers strategies for undertaking a program evaluation, citing examples of current evaluation efforts in family reunification programs. In chapter 11, Fein and Staff depict the potential benefits of embarking on research in family reunification programs. The Family Reunification Project of Casey Family Services is used as illustration, preliminary findings are made known, and implications of program evaluation for policy and practice are discussed.

This book is intended primarily for use as a reference tool and basic text for in-service training programs for social workers, supervisors, and administrators in public and private child welfare agencies. In addition, it will be useful as either a primary or supplementary text in graduate and undergraduate courses on family and children's services in schools of social work. It is hoped that readers will be encouraged to enhance their current programs and embark on new efforts that can pave the way for more children and their families to reconnect and remain together.

ACKNOWLEDGMENTS

From 1988-1990, the Center for the Study of Child Welfare at the University of Connecticut School of Social Work conducted a project to produce a range of training materials on family reunification.* Its overall purpose was to improve the ability of agency staff members, particularly social workers, to strengthen families so that more foster children could return home following placement and remain home. This book, one of several outcomes of that project, directs staff members to the issues that must be considered when developing and implementing family reunification programs.

We gratefully acknowledge the generous support of the United States Department of Health and Human Services and of Phyllis Nophlin and Beatrice Moore, our Project Officers; The Annie E. Casey Foundation and its director, Douglas Nelson; and Lucille Tomanio, former Executive Director of Casey Family Services. We are also grateful to Nancy Humphreys, Dean of the University of Connecticut School of Social Work, for her support of our work. We owe our deep appreciation to Carl Schoenberg, our editor at the Child Welfare League of America, for his thought-provoking responses to the chapters and his unwavering commitment to excellence, and our sincere admiration to Pamela Harrison, our secretary, for her capacity to keep her wits about her while producing an enormous amount of flawless work; her efficiency and effective-

---

* Funded by the U.S. Department of Health and Human Services, Office of Human Development Services, Administration for Children, Youth and Families (Grant #90–CW–0942/01 and Grant #90–CW–0942/02) and The Annie E. Casey Foundation (1988–1990).

ness continue to make all the difference. To the contributors we are beholden for their insights, thoroughness, patience, and spirit of collaboration.

Finally, we wish to thank the many agency administrators, practitioners, and families who made us keenly aware of the roughness of the road to reunification. We hope that the information contained in this book makes that road a good deal smoother.

INTRODUCTION:

FAMILY REUNIFICATION IN CONTEXT*

Ann Hartman

This volume brings together a variety of in-depth perspectives on the specialized and focused practice of family reunification, as the editors and contributors address the challenge of reuniting children in out-of-home care with their families and the resulting implications for service delivery. First, however, it is important to set family reunification in its multiple contexts: family reunification is a part of child welfare practice, which is a part of social work practice, which is a part of the larger socioeconomic context. It is also important to understand how family reunification evolved and to connect it to the historical development of the systems of service of which it is a part.

The Historical Context

The Revolution in Child Welfare

The past 30 years have seen a major revolution in how child welfare professionals think about the needs of children and how children should be served—a revolution that has changed the definition of good child welfare practice. Unfortunately, most of the changes have been more in thinking and in wishing, rather than in actual programs and service. When people think differently, however, they do begin to act differently as well. Promoting and

---

* This introduction is adapted from the keynote address presented at "Reconnections," a conference on program, practice, and training in family reunification held in Durham, NH, on May 22–23, 1990, under the sponsorship of the Center for the Study of Child Welfare, University of Connecticut School of Social Work, and The Annie E. Casey Foundation.

maintaining reunification of children in out-of-home care with their biological families is a part of the new vision of child welfare.

The child welfare system of the 1940s and 1950s primarily maintained children in foster care or in institutions. Infants in need of care, if they were Caucasian and were clearly developing according to all of the physical and psychological milestones, were placed in adoptive homes. Occasionally, a case of abuse would surface, but these were few and usually handled by a specialized segment of the child welfare system—the Societies for the Prevention of Cruelty to Children.

The "Discovery" of Child Abuse

The "discovery" of child abuse had a major impact on child welfare. When X-rays began to be used in the diagnosis of children, many showed evidence of multiple fractures and other old injuries. Two Denver physicians, Dr. Ray Helfer and Dr. C. Henry Kempe, reporting on their research in 1961, proposed the term *battered child syndrome* to describe the condition of children injured by their parents [Antler 1981].

The publicity that followed brought to the American people an awareness of the extent to which children were being harmed in their own homes. Public outrage led state after state to pass reporting laws that required all professionals to report any suspicion of abuse. The child welfare system responded with a strong emphasis on investigation, protection, and removal, and the number of children in foster and institutional care escalated.

Research

At about the same time, large-scale research studies were examining the experiences of children in out-of-home care. Maas and Engler [1959] documented that placement of children in foster care was not the temporary measure it was initially intended to be, and that children were "drifting" in care, moving from placement to placement. In a longitudinal study, Fanshel and Shinn [1978] found that children in placement for 18 months were likely to remain in care indefinitely and experience multiple placements. These and other studies exposed difficulties in the child welfare system and called into question the value of long-term foster care.

The Civil Rights and Child Advocacy Movements

A third factor influencing the revolution in child welfare was the civil rights movement. Initially this was a social movement to achieve rights for people of color, but it soon spread into a thrust toward increased rights for all oppressed people, including children. The child advocacy movement that began in the 1960s and expanded in the 1970s was an outgrowth of the civil rights movement. Publication of *Children without Homes* [Knitzer and Allen 1978], had a tremendous effect on the field, accomplishing for child welfare, in some respects, what *Uncle Tom's Cabin* did for the abolitionist movement. Professionals, advocates, and the public were horrified by the book's account of what was happening to vulnerable children nationwide. The studies of Mass, Engler, Fanshel, and Shinn, which at first were read only by professionals, began to be widely disseminated. Foster care and the entire child welfare system came under attack, with very powerful demands for change and reform.

Renewed Interest in the Family

Other social developments also had an impact on child welfare practice. After over a decade of criticizing the family and questioning its value and validity, Americans in the mid-1970s felt a new concern about the family. Political leaders were in the forefront, directing national attention to families. President Carter announced early in his 1970 presidential campaign that the American family was his major concern. Popular culture evidenced a fascination with the family. *Roots* was the most widely viewed television program at that time—a story about an African American family that captured the imagination of the nation. *Kramer vs. Kramer*, *Ordinary People*, *Falcon Crest*, and *Dallas* were popular family sagas, tapping people's fundamental sense of the central importance of the family.

Intellectual developments included the increased respectability of family sociology and an expansion of family studies. Family therapy, a way of helping that assumes that human beings are deeply imbedded in their family systems, and that the way to help them is to use the family as both an arena and an instrument for change, was born. Although the 1980 White House Conference on the Family fell into conflict over the definition of *family*, it was further evidence of national interest in this seemingly fragile, varied, and lasting human institution.

Deinstitutionalization

The deinstitutionalization movement also altered the shape of child welfare. This social movement began in the 1950s; by the 1970s it had become the principal guide for social policy on both the state and federal levels. It stressed caring for people in the "least restrictive environment," which, when translated into child welfare, meant "the most familylike." Child welfare policy began to be truly family centered, based on the principle that every child has a right to be with his or her biological family, and if that is impossible, in a caring situation as close in structure to a family as possible.

The Permanency Planning Movement

In child welfare, these social policies were reflected in the growth of the permanency planning movement, which encompassed policy, program, and practice changes. These changes were first focused on adoption, and in particular, on the adoption of children with special needs. The trend to placing children in the least restrictive environment and the growing awareness of what was happening to children in the foster care system led to the belief that every child should be in a permanent family—children who could not remain in their biological families should be in adoptive homes. "No child is unadoptable" became the call to action. This movement was further reinforced by the reality that fewer infants were available for adoption because of readily available and effective birth control methods, the legalization of abortion, and changing social norms that made it easier for single women to keep their children. Adoption grew into a service for children who needed homes rather than one for couples who needed children—a reconceptualization that has completely revolutionized adoption practice [Pine 1991].

Although the permanency planning movement started with an emphasis on adoption, work in this area had an unexpected outcome. Early demonstration projects, such as those in California and in Oregon [Maluccio et al. 1986], were set up to free children for adoption and place them in adoptive homes. When workers sought out long-absent parents, however, they found that a great many biological families wanted their children at home and were in a position to care for them. They discovered that the parents, feeling growing alienation, loss, and guilt about being separated from their children, and powerlessness in relation to the agency, had finally withdrawn. Many of the children in these projects were able to go back home, even though they had been out of their homes for years. The emphasis in modern child welfare practice quickly shifted to include as facets of permanency planning not only special-needs adoption and foster care, but, even more important, family preservation and family reunification.

Outcome of the Revolution: Landmark Legislation

These many events and changes led at last to the passage of the Adoption Assistance and Child Welfare Act of 1980 (Public Law 96-272), which codified this new vision of services to children [Pine 1986], and to the halcyon days of child welfare, when service to people was a top national priority. To celebrate the passing of the bill and to gain support to for its funding, the National Child Welfare Training Center, located at the University of Michigan, organized a conference in Washington and invited all of the members of the U.S. Senate and House of Representatives. Child welfare people gathered from all over the country—and Rosalynn Carter invited them all to the White House for tea.

Implications of P.L. 96-272

When P.L. 96-272 was enacted in 1980, it achieved a very important step by defining, on a federal level, good child welfare practice and child welfare philosophy. There followed a period during which permanency planning was expanded and refined, calling for practice that included the following considerations:

1. *Intensive, in-home services* to maintain children in their own homes and prevent placement. Family preservation programs have since spread across the country.*

2. *Reconceptualization of foster care* as a temporary service to parents. New kinds of services developed from this major shift. In Michigan, for example, several child welfare agencies adopted a new approach to foster home recruitment: they advertised with the slogan, "Help a family get back together." A different population of foster parents emerged when the need for caregivers began to be phrased in that way rather than "Do you want to parent a little child in your home?"

3. *Careful assessment* of every child who does come into care and of the child's family.

4. A *permanency plan* with clearly defined time limits.

5. *Contracting* with the parents and others so that everyone is absolutely clear about plans and expectations.

A New Administration

Public Law 96-272 put good family-centered child welfare practice into law. Soon after the law was passed, however, the Reagan administration took office. Almost immediately, the social programs that needed to be in place for the support of families began to be systematically dismantled. The trickle-down

---

* The term *family preservation* is reserved for intensive and short-term services in families whose children would have to be placed if such services were not available [Cole and Duva 1990; Whittaker et al. 1990].

theory of economics was operationalized, but resources, defying the law of gravity, did not trickle down—they rose to the top. In the last decade, the rich have become richer, the poor have become poorer, and the gap between them has grown steadily wider.

The landmark law that was passed in one political administration was undermined almost at once by the new political administration, which made it impossible to achieve the goals established by the law. Social workers and the whole child welfare system were put in a major double bind. On the one hand, they were mandated to support families, to keep children at home, and to return children to their families. At the same time, the resources available for the support of these families disappeared. The child welfare system can operate effectively only as part of a network of supportive services, and in a relatively healthy socioeconomic climate. During the early 1980s, as unemployment increased and benefits decreased, the buying power of a welfare allowance was sharply diminished. Yet at the same time that the services needed to support families were disappearing, the potential client population was growing larger and larger.

In this connection, it is instructive to recall that one of the earliest social initiatives in this country, the initiative that may be considered the beginning of the "welfare state," was the development of mothers' pensions in the early 1900s. Although these allowances were an expression of the philosophy that children should not be separated from their families because of poverty, a careful examination of the child welfare population makes clear that in the largest proportion of cases, children *are* out of their homes because of the grinding effects of prolonged poverty and stress. As Pelton [1989] has so eloquently demonstrated, poverty, abuse, and neglect are directly connected.

Family Reunification: Essential Work in Impossible Times

Finding the Resources

It is in this context that social workers are challenged to provide family reunification services. The first challenge is to find the resources and the support for families that make reunification possible. Individual social workers must negotiate, advocate, and broker in a continual effort to get resources in place so that families can be supported. This work takes enormous energy, and in time, burns social workers out, especially when it is continuously aggravated by high caseloads. The burden of creating something out of almost nothing cannot be left with the individual worker.

What can social workers and others who help children and their families do? First, we must bear witness. No one knows the havoc wrought by public neglect and indifference better than do social workers. All social workers and social agencies should gather information about what is actually needed to reunify families and make this information available to lawmakers, legislators, advocates, and professional organizations. We must campaign to get better services for families. We must tell the stories of these families. We must let people in power know what these families are like, the painful losses they have sustained, how they have suffered. As Zamosky and her colleagues point out elsewhere in this volume, everyone knows these families' failings, but no one seems to care about the challenges they face or the strengths they show.

As long as our national resources go into unbelievably costly military equipment and into bailing out corporations that have violated the trust of the American people, rather than into the people themselves, social workers will continue to be like the Dutch boy with a finger in the dike. Clients and social workers are struggling with overwhelming and destructive socioeconomic problems. We must join with clients in the struggle, rather than blaming them for the failings of the system. Social workers and clients, as social work pioneer Bertha Reynolds knew, are on the same side.

Maintain Rather Than Reunite Families

The second challenge is for family reunification to cease to exist—the ultimate goal of child welfare services. If resources were available for families, and if permanency planning were really in place, family reconnection and family reunification would no longer be necessary. The focus would instead be on how to maintain family connections and how to preserve family unity. There would be no "re" in front of "unification" and "connection." The "re" speaks of repair, it implies that these connections have been broken and that families have been torn asunder.

Family reunification and reconnection are often efforts to undo iatrogenic damage that has been done to families and children by a failing socioeconomic system and by a child welfare system that has found it difficult to follow the principles of permanency planning. The child welfare system is faced with families destroyed by poverty, deprivation, poor education, underemployment or unemployment, apathy, alienation, drugs, and violence. Many children are placed in out-of-home care because needed resources are lacking. Overburdened workers are unable to work with families toward rehabilitation or even help them maintain the connections that are so essential.

In a perfect world, with a perfect child welfare system free to use the knowledge we have, family reunification and reconnection would not be necessary. In this imperfect world, however, it is necessary to give special attention to family reunification and reconnection. Agencies must avail themselves, as much as possible, of the knowledge and skills necessary for this important service. Maintenance or reestablishment of family connections is a bottom line. The principles embodied and the knowledge and skills required in the work of family reunification should guide practice from the first day the client comes into contact with the agency until the end of that contact.

References

Adoption Assistance and Child Welfare Act of 1980. P.L. 96-272 (June 17, 1980).

Antler, S. "The Rediscovery of Child Abuse." In *The Social Context of Child Abuse and Neglect*, edited by L.H. Pelton. New York: Human Sciences Press, 1981.

Cole, E., and Duva, J. *Family Preservation: An Orientation for Administrators and Practitioners*. Washington, DC: Child Welfare League of America, 1990.

Fanshel, D., and Shinn, E. *Children in Foster Care: A Longitudinal Investigation*. New York: Columbia University Press, 1978.

Knitzer, J., and Allen, M.L. *Children without Homes: An Examination of Public Responsibility to Children in Out-of-Home Care*. Washington, DC: The Children's Defense Fund, 1978.

Maas, H., and Engler, R. *Children in Need of Parents*. New York: Columbia University Press, 1959.

Maluccio, A.N.; Fein, E.; and Olmstead, K.A. *Permanency Planning for Children: Concepts and Methods*. New York: Routledge, Chapman, and Hall, 1986.

Pelton, L.H. *For Reasons of Poverty*. New York: Praeger, 1989.

Pine, B.A. "Child Welfare Reform and the Political Process." *Social Service Review* 60, 3 (September 1986): 339–359.

Pine, B.A. Special Families for Special Children: The Adoption of Children with Developmental Disabilities. Unpublished doctoral dissertation, Brandeis University, 1991.

Whittaker, J.K.; Kinney, J.; Tracy, E.M.; and Booth, C., eds. *Reaching High-Risk Families: Intensive Family Preservation in the Human Services*. Hawthorne, NY: Aldine de Gruyter, 1990.

PART ONE

Creating the Context

Family Reunification:
An Overview*

Anthony N. Maluccio, Robin Warsh, and Barbara A. Pine

The growing emphasis in the field of child welfare on preserving families has led to renewed attention to reunification of children in out-of-home care with their families. This attention is a crucial development, since each year many children in family foster care, group homes, or residential treatment centers are reunited with their families.

In the United States in 1986 (the most recent year for which comprehensive national data are available), 103,000 (nearly 59%) of the 176,000 children who left care were discharged to their biological families [Tatara 1989: 16]. This number has since increased, as a result of expanded efforts to reduce the duration of foster care placement. Sooner or later, however, a substantial proportion of children who are returned to their families reenter some form of out-of-home placement or another helping system, such as juvenile justice or mental health [Fein et al. 1983; Goerge 1990; Rzepnicki 1987]. In addition, many others await reunification indefinitely [Fein et al. 1990]. Delivery of services to these children and their families must be examined and refined.

As noted by Hartman in her introduction to this book, attention to family reunification is part of the major revolution in child welfare services that has taken place in the last two or three decades. The rapid development of family preservation services to prevent out-of-home placement has been one feature of that revolution. But much less attention has been paid to the services that help to reunite families *after* they have been separated by a foster care placement,

---

* An earlier version of this chapter appeared in Tracy, E.M.; Haapala, D.A.; Kinney, J.; and Pecora, P.J., *Intensive Family Preservation Services: An Instructional Sourcebook* (Cleveland, OH: Case Western Reserve University School of Applied Social Sciences, 1991).

even though the Adoption Assistance and Child Welfare Act of 1980 (Public Law 96-272), stresses the rehabilitation of biological families [Maluccio et al. 1986].

To fill this gap, this chapter offers a conceptual framework for rethinking reunification practice. Following a brief comparison of family preservation and family reunification services, the chapter redefines family reunification, delineates the major program components of effective family reunification, and considers selected implications for practice and service delivery.

Family Preservation and Family Reunification

In response to the needs and experiences of children in out-of-home care and their families, increasing efforts have recently been made to apply principles and strategies of family preservation, particularly intensive family preservation services (IFPS), to cases involving family reunification. The intensive efforts needed to reconnect families separated by out-of-home care placement and keep them together are similar in many ways to the services designed to prevent placement. Foremost among these similarities is a common purpose: strengthening and enhancing families. Other similarities include the provision of concrete as well as intangible services and supports in the family's own home by accessible staff members who work flexible hours. The family is viewed as a system in order to strengthen family bonds, help families use formal and informal resources, and help parents improve their child care skills [Kinney et al. 1991; Whittaker et al. 1990].

Services aimed at reunifying families differ significantly, however, from those designed to prevent placement. First, workers seeking to reconnect and reunify a family must address the typically traumatic impact of loss and separation on the placed child as well as on the parents and other family members. Second, for some families, contact between children and parents may have to be reestablished before family bonds can be strengthened. Third, both the practitioner and the family face special challenges in teaching and learning parenting skills when children are out of the home, as there will be fewer opportunities to observe and intervene in parent-child interactions. Fourth, motivation for change is not always as strong in a family that has adjusted to separation as it is in one that faces the immediate crisis of the imminent removal of a child. Fifth, a family whose child has been placed may be perceived by family members and others as a "failed" family; therefore, fostering hope and a belief in competence and the potential for success presents a greater challenge in work with families who have experienced placement than with those who have not. Finally, during placement a child may form a relationship with a caregiver, such as a foster parent, that will need to be recognized and dealt with by parent and child.

In addition, efforts to prevent placement presume that parents are willing and able to be daily caregivers for their children. An essential aspect of reunification practice as presented in this book is the assessment of the optimal degree to which children can and should be reconnected with parents and/or other family members. Such an assessment may show that, while it is not possible for children to live full-time with their biological parents or relatives, family bonds can be preserved by less extensive forms of contact.

Finally, another significant difference between intensive family preservation services and family reunification services is the length of service provision. Although reunification services may be intensive at times and less so at others, such services typically are provided for a much longer term than is true in most IFPS models. Some families may need services indefinitely if they are to stay together.

These differences pose special challenges for child welfare staff members and administrators, as well as foster parents, therapists, attorneys, judges, and others involved in reunifying families. Agency staff members and foster parents must recognize the importance of family visiting as an opportunity to assess family functioning and promote positive change. Administrators and judges must create policies that support forms of family reconnection other than return home. Therapists must be particularly attuned to opportunities to promote family functioning. And all service providers are, in a sense, specialists, that is, they must be trained to meet the special needs of families on the path to reunification [Maluccio et al. 1990].

Rethinking Family Reunification

As a first step in changing service delivery to meet contemporary needs and challenges, it is important to rethink family reunification. Traditionally, family reunification practice has been based on the premise that children in out-of-home care should be either returned to their families of origin or placed permanently elsewhere. This either-or orientation has long been supported—and in some ways required—by a framework of policy and law. For example, termination of parental rights has at times been sought inappropriately, in cases in which there are reasons to continue the parent-child relationship even though the family is unable to care for the child fully.

Redefinition

It is time to challenge this all or nothing premise as too simplistic, and to view family reunification as a flexible, dynamic approach to meeting the needs of children and their families in an individualized and carefully thought-through way—as a response to the unique qualities, needs, and situations of each child and family. Accordingly, the authors propose that family reunification be redefined as follows:

> *Family reunification is the planned process of reconnecting children in out-of-home care with their families by means of a variety of services and supports to the children, their families, and their foster parents or other service providers. It aims to help each child and family to achieve and maintain, at any given time, their optimal level of reconnection—from full reentry of the child into the family system to other forms of contact, such as visiting, that affirm the child's membership in the family.*

This expanded view of family reunification underscores the value of maintaining and enhancing connectedness between children in out-of-home care and their families and of reconnecting children and their families when possible. At the same time, it recognizes that not every parent can be a daily caregiver and that some families, though not able to live together, can still maintain kinship bonds. In short, reunification can take place in a variety of ways besides physical reconnection.

Underlying Principles

This redefinition leads to a number of guiding principles for family reunification policies, programs, and practices, including, in particular, the following:

1. Family reunification is an integral part of the philosophy of preserving families and of permanency planning, with their emphasis on ensuring continuity of care for children. Family reunification should be systematically considered and planned for as early as possible in a child's out-of-home placement.

2. Family reunification is a dynamic process based on the child's and family's changing qualities, needs, and potential. It should be viewed as a continuum, with levels or outcomes ranging from full reentry into the family system, to partial reentry, to less extensive contact, such as visiting, phoning, writing, and other affirmations of the child's membership in the family. At any point during the child's out-of-home placement, the most appropriate or optimal level of reconnection should be identified and actively pursued. At the same time, it should be recognized that reconnection is not possible or desirable in some situations, which may appropriately require termination of parental rights. Even in those cases, however, older

children should at the least be helped to move into new permanent families with some tangible tie to their past in the form of pictures, a lifebook, or other family memorabilia.

3. As a form of preserving families, reunification encompasses (a) a conviction that the biological family is the preferred child-rearing unit whenever possible; (b) a belief that most families can care for their children, if properly assisted; and (c) an attitude that welcomes the involvement, as appropriate, of any and all members of the child's family, including extended family members or others who, while not legally related, are considered by the child and themselves to be "family."

4. Family reunification practice is guided by an ecologically oriented, competence-centered perspective that emphasizes such aspects as improving the interaction between people and their environments, promoting family empowerment, engaging in advocacy and social action so as to achieve societal conditions and structures that enhance family functioning, reaching for—and building on—the strengths and potential of parents and other family members, involving parents as partners in the helping process, and providing needed services and supports.

5. Children in care, their biological families, foster families, other caregivers, social workers, and other service providers should establish an ongoing partnership, promoted by effective teamwork, in which the different roles of all parties are clearly spelled out and understood.

6. Human diversity—cultural, racial, ethnic, and other forms—should be respected. Lifestyles and child-rearing methods that might be considered different or unusual should be accepted so long as they promote a child's health and safety. This principle is especially crucial because a disproportionate number of children in care come from minority families, while most practitioners do not.

7. A commitment to early and consistent contact between the child and family is an essential ingredient in preparing for and maintaining reunification of children with their families. Child-family contact can serve as a laboratory in which both work on the problems that may have contributed to the need for placement, and learn new, constructive ways to be together.

8. Family reunification services should be offered for as long as they are needed to maintain the reconnection of children with their families. For many families, intensive family reunification services may need to be

followed by less intensive services. For a few families, some level of service may be necessary until the children are ready for independent living.

Issues and Dilemmas

In rethinking family reunification, one must take into account recurring issues and dilemmas in child welfare. Social workers and others engaged in family reunification practice face a major challenge: deciding *whether* children—who have already been deemed to be at such significant risk as to necessitate their placement—can return home, and *when*. This challenge raises a number of matters that must be considered in developing family reunification programs and practices:

- How can practitioners deal with the tension between the value of preserving families and the imperatives of child protection?

- What guidelines are needed or already in place for assessing the risk of returning children to their families versus the risk of prolonging their stay in foster care?

- What is a minimum adequate level of care and parenting for family reunification? What constitutes "good-enough" parenting?

- How can practitioners implement the concept of degrees of reconnection in practice? How will practitioners know if a child and family have achieved their greatest degree of reconnection? What does reconnection mean when parental rights are terminated and children are placed for adoption?

- Where is the line between providing continuing supports to reunited families and perpetuating their dependence?

- What elements influence the ability and willingness of practitioners to care for families for extended periods?

- How can practitioners apply reunification competencies differentially with different target populations (such as young children versus adolescents), or in different settings (such as family foster care versus group residential care)?

- How can practitioners deal effectively with differences between the legal and social services systems, in relation to such questions as whether, when, and how families should be reunited?

- How can practitioners help families to change when their environments remain so harsh?

- How can practitioners maintain or restore optimism and belief in the potential of even the most difficult families to do what is best for their children, while also accepting that some parents cannot care for their children?

Despite these unanswered questions and continuing dilemmas, progress has been made in helping families to reunite and to remain together once reunited, as agencies develop programs that reflect the eight guiding principles delineated earlier. Many public agencies are purchasers of services from voluntary agencies in such fields as child welfare, mental health, and family counseling; increasingly, these public agencies are also incorporating family reunification services directly into their own programs.

Program Components

Various exemplary projects throughout the country, including those described later in this book, are seeking to operationalize the principles discussed earlier in this chapter. These projects vary in agency auspices (public, voluntary, or a combination); primary service context (family foster care home, residential treatment center, or community mental health setting); target population (e.g., families with young children); and duration of service (three months to two years). A review of these projects suggests that the reunification of children and their families is more likely to be successful when an agency articulates and carries out its mission through a comprehensive framework of policies, strategies, and resources. This framework requires a supportive agency that incorporates program components such as those outlined below.

Family-Centered Orientation

The first and foremost component of a reunification program is a family-centered orientation to service delivery; that is, the family should be the central unit or focus of attention and decisions should be made in the best interests of the family. Underlying this component is the assumption that human beings can be best understood and helped within their significant environments, and that the family is the most intimate environment of all [Hartman and Laird 1983; Maluccio and Whittaker 1988].

As in all efforts to preserve families, intervention is directed as much as possible toward strengthening the family. The family's own environment can be employed as the arena in which practitioners intervene to help strengthen tangible resources, such as those related to housing and employment, as well as intangibles, such as communication, parenting skills, and parent-child relationships.

Partnership with Parents and Other Family Members

A second component, which flows from the first, is an ongoing partnership among practitioners, foster parents and other caregivers, and parents, as well as other family members. Effective family reunification programs are those that involve family members—especially parents—as much as possible as partners in the helping process. This idea is widely accepted in theory, but it is especially difficult to put into practice in reuniting a family after a child has been removed from the home. A variety of organizational and service impediments exist, including inflexible work schedules, insufficient or unavailable client transportation services, limited fiscal resources, and insufficient worker time to visit families in their homes. Involving parents and children as decision makers in a continuing partnership with foster families, child care workers, social workers, and other service providers is a continuously difficult task.

Although various tools and strategies, such as the contract or service agreement, are available to effect the concept of partnership, the reality calls for major attitudinal changes toward parents on the part of social workers and others. In particular, this involves shifting from a view of parents as carriers of pathology to a belief that many of them can change and grow, if given adequate supports and opportunities to realize their potential and demonstrate their strengths. In family reunification, as in intensive family preservation, parents can be viewed as colleagues in the change process [Kinney et al. 1990).

In this connection, the importance of viewing foster parents and child care workers as partners in the provision of services should also be emphasized; they are truly members of the service team. This view underscores the necessity of clarifying their respective roles, offering varied opportunities for professional development, and providing adequate supports and financial rewards.

Empowerment of Social Workers

Social workers must be trained, supervised, and given the authority to make decisions in family reunification practice. Specifically, agencies empower their staff members by creating a climate and structure that promote professional skill attainment and permit the exercise of decision-making authority; agencies must recognize that the ability of staff members to empower families is linked to the degree to which staff members themselves feel empowered.

It stands to reason that social workers who are helping children and families to take charge of their lives must practice within an environment that recognizes, sustains, and enhances their own professional identity. Above all, if family reunification is to be planned and carried out, social workers have to feel—and be—supported in the difficult decisions they are required to make. Flexible schedules, opportunities to work in teams, creative and flexible supervision or consultation, and other organizational supports make this possible [Kinney et al. 1990].

Comprehensive Services and Supports

Given the multiple and complex needs of families with respect to their basic life conditions, providing a variety of supports and services is another major component, as illustrated by practice examples throughout this book. Research to date strongly indicates that successfully reuniting children and families calls for a combination of "soft" services, such as counseling and parent training, and "hard" services, such as income assistance, housing, and day care. Parents need both expanded knowledge and strengthened tangible resources to be able to provide developmentally sound parenting for their children. Informal supports, such as parent aides, volunteers, and recreational opportunities for parents, have been found to be especially useful [Haapala 1983; Levine 1964; Polansky et al. 1981].

At the same time, it is important to avoid giving rehabilitative or therapeutic services in a way that tells parents that they are defective; practitioners should avoid the typical tendency to blame the victim. The range of societal or systemic problems that lead to out-of-home care in the first place—problems such as racism, poverty, and homelessness—call for advocacy and social action in addition to direct practice with families [Pelton 1989].

Collaboration and Case Management

Successful programs recognize that family reunification practice requires the services of several systems, such as law, health, mental health, and education; such programs regularly convene interagency, interdisciplinary teams for training, service planning, and service implementation. Coordinating the interactions of the child welfare, judicial, mental health, income maintenance, and other systems in behalf of each family continues to be a serious concern.

Providing the kinds of services that are required is no simple task, even when services are adequate and accessible. As in the human service field in general, and permanency planning in particular [Maluccio et al. 1986], one person must orchestrate the whole plan and its implementation with and in behalf of the family. Given the many difficulties involved in both formulating and effecting a service plan in the complex situations that come to the attention of agencies, the case manager has a crucial role to play in any family reunification program. In addition to negotiating for the families with service providers such as those noted above, the case manager helps parents learn to work with these systems in their own behalf.

Therapeutic Use of Out-of-Home Placement

Another component of reunification is the therapeutic use of out-of-home placement. With but a few exceptions, care away from home can no longer be viewed as an end in itself, as a full substitute for the biological family, or as custodial care. Out-of-home placement is a means to an end—the rehabilitation of the family or child and the reconnection of the child with the family to the extent possible. For example, parent-child visiting can be used therapeutically for a number of purposes, including maintaining or enhancing the parent-child relationship, assessing the parent's functioning as a parent, and teaching parents and children to relate to each other more constructively [see Hess and Proch 1988; chapter 7 of this book].

Even in cases in which the family cannot care for a child fully, efforts should be made to teach the parents how to relate at least in part to their children. This is especially important for adolescents who move into an independent-living situation. Research has disclosed that many of these young people resume contacts with their parents upon discharge from care and entry into independent living [Fanshel et al. 1990; Jones and Moses 1984]. But even though they may want it, both the adolescents and their parents are often unprepared for such a relationship. Both need help to develop the necessary skills for living together, whether permanently or intermittently [Maluccio et al. 1990].

Specialized Training

Last, but not least, social workers, foster parents, and others should receive specialized training for family reunification practice, with emphasis on the values of preserving families and on the knowledge, attitudes, and skills necessary in work to reunite a family that has experienced the trauma of separation and placement and to help the family remain together.

As delineated in detail in chapter 3 and elsewhere [Maluccio et al. 1990], practice requires that social workers possess not only generic or core competencies in child welfare but also family reunification competencies in relation to:

- valuing the preservation of family ties;

- assessing the readiness of child and family for reunification;

- planning to actively involve parents in decision-making in behalf of their placed children;

- implementing the family reunification plan;

- maintaining the reunification; and

- ending the service.

Implications for Practice

The principles and program components delineated in regard to family reunification clearly have much in common with intensive family preservation efforts, but the unique aspects of family reunification have many implications for practice and service delivery. For example, Fein and Staff [1991; chapter 5] discuss practice issues such as goal-setting, use of service agreements, and work with substance-abusing families. Other practice and program implications unique to reuniting or reconnecting families are considered below.

Continuum of Reunification Outcomes

Families as well as service providers need help to recognize that reunification represents a continuum of outcomes, from return home to less extensive forms of contact. Various principles and strategies can contribute to supporting connectedness of children with their biological, extended, foster, or adoptive families.

In particular, ambivalent parents can be helped to maintain a relationship with their child by deciding on the degree of reconnection that they and the child can and wish to have, and to prepare for it through such means as trial visits. In identifying each child's and family's optimal degree of reconnection, consideration should be given to helping the child rejoin with family members, including not only parents and siblings, but also relatives and significant others who constitute a family for a particular child. It should also be recognized that in some cases no contact is appropriate or desirable, or even possible.

Mobilizing Motivation

Various approaches may be employed to take advantage of the motivation that family members often have to become reconnected. If a threat of termination of parental rights exists, clarification of this possibility can help parents to become more focused and involved in reunification activities. In most cases, however, a great deal of outreach is required on the part of the worker to support and encourage family members' interest in relating to the child. Unless contraindicated, aggressive efforts to maximize the family's involvement with the child should begin during the preplacement phase and continue through the placement itself.

As noted earlier, placement can be used as a therapeutic tool not only to promote changes in the child and family, but also to maintain and improve their sense of connectedness with each other. One pertinent strategy encourages the use of claiming behaviors by both parents and children, such as sharing photographs, using the children's nicknames, celebrating birthdays, and reinitiating healthy family rituals practiced in the past [Fahlberg 1979; Hartman and Laird 1983].

Perhaps an even more important element in bringing about lasting reconnections is the social worker's attitude toward the family. Social workers are most apt to be helpful when they believe fully that families are growth-promoting units with a powerful urge to survive. When social workers look for ways in which the families they work with are motivated, caring, and interested in better caring for themselves, they can encourage family members to believe in themselves and change in positive ways [see Zamosky et al., chapter 9].

Readiness for Reunification

One of the major challenges in family reunification practice is working with family members to assess whether and when they are ready to be reunited. Family members and service providers must balance the risks of returning a child home with those of prolonging the child's stay in foster care. Above all else is the necessity of ensuring the child's safety while respecting family integrity and autonomy. Workers and family members must also assess whether the conditions that originally brought about placement have been satisfactorily relieved.

Practitioners must be well-versed in assessing the risk factors associated with all aspects of child maltreatment. Especially pertinent in this regard is an ecological framework for assessment that considers at least the following elements:

- Child-related risk factors and strengths;

- Parent-related risk factors and strengths;

- Family-related risk factors and strengths;

- Type and nature of past maltreatment; and

- Availability of necessary treatment services and family supports, as affected by the family's ability or willingness to use them to address the most critical risk factors [Holder and Corey 1986].

Additionally, evaluation of readiness for reunification is likely to be based on interactions that take place during visits between the child and family in the care setting or the home, as well as subsequent reactions to the visits. Practitioners must use the visiting experience as a unique, experience-specific source of much-needed information that can be derived in no other way [Hess and Proch, chapter 7].

Workers should also appreciate that the risk assessment instruments currently available, while useful for guiding practice in certain circumstances, are imperfect and are not a substitute for professional interviewing skills, analytical skills, and clinical assessment [Pecora 1991; Wald and Woolverton 1990]. A thorough evaluation includes assessing, with the family, the family's and child's willingness to reunite, the parents' ability to meet the child's changed or changing needs, the family's conflict-resolution and other problem-solving skills, the strengths and potential that make reconnection possible, and the supports available to maintain the reconnection [Maluccio et al. 1990].

Parents' Emotional Readiness

Parents have to develop an intangible yet vitally important personal resource if they are to care for their children competently: psychological readiness to live differently than they have in the past. Oftentimes, families need help to separate emotionally from a legacy of family dysfunction—a culture of defeat—which requires that participants be fraught with problems, and where, in fact, competence is suspect. "The true primary goal of all behavior is to find a sense of belonging and significance" [Nelsen 1987]. Will the parents' steps toward achieving competence and self-sufficiency put them at risk of becoming outcasts in their world, of losing a sense of significance and belonging with their friends, family, and larger community? For many, it feels safer to remain stuck in dysfunctional patterns, often with their children placed in out-of-home care, than to develop the readiness to move on to more productive lives.

It is the practitioner's task to help parents find new arenas from which to derive a feeling of belonging. Many parents who have been reunited with their children point to the one single aspect that made the reconnection possible: a special someone who kept hope alive, forgave them for their mistakes, and made them feel important for their efforts and accomplishments. Practitioners should be diligent in their search for people who can give this sense of belonging to parents as they experience the separation, anxiety, and loss associated with leaving familiar people and behaviors behind.

Reentry into a Changed Family System

In each case, it is also essential that workers appreciate the ways in which the family system has changed since the child's removal and assess what needs to be done to facilitate that child's reentry. For example, parents often have to be helped to cope with the lack of privacy, frequency of visitors, telephone calls, and financial responsibilities that can accompany a child's return home.

Workers should help family members to identify perceived differences or changes in family rules, patterns, and behaviors on the part of each family member. This understanding can then be used to plan for cognitive and behavioral changes that might help family members to cope with the impact of the child's reentry. In some situations, the family can be helped to expect certain problems or pressures as one of its members, who has also changed, returns home. The impact of separation and placement on a particular child and family also has to be understood, and the child or other family members may need help with their feelings of loss, grief, anger, and so on.

As Hess and Proch discuss in chapter 7, family-child visiting can be used to help heal separation trauma, to help parents learn or relearn parenting skills, and to prepare everyone for reconnection. Even when it becomes clear that the highest level of reconnection—return home—is not attainable, parents can sometimes be helped to take on caregiving roles that strengthen bonds with their children. Visiting can be planned to yield opportunities for parents to recognize and appreciate their children's achievements, find ways to help their children to feel positively about themselves and other family members, and join them in cultural rituals and family celebrations.

Finally, foster parents can be a valuable resource to children and parents on their path toward reunification by promoting and supporting visiting efforts, sharing sensitively with parents what they have learned about the child, and collaborating effectively with other service providers in behalf of the family. At the same time, foster families must also be supported throughout the process of reunification, lest their reaction to their own separation and loss negatively affect the child's transition to her or his home. Many children are sensitive to, and easily upset by, the messages of guilt and sorrow directly or indirectly conveyed by even the most competent foster parents.

Duration of Services

Many of the families to whom children return are likely to be crisis-ridden and to have continuing needs in multiple areas such as health, housing, income assistance, and family functioning [Jenkins et al. 1981; Polansky et al. 1981; Shyne and Schroeder 1978]. Most family reunification programs consequently incorporate long-term follow-up services or plan for a longer service period than is typical of intensive family preservation services. The duration of services must be flexible, and this presents a number of challenges for workers:

- identifying the intensity as well as the types of service required during each phase of the reunification process;

- providing concentrated services, especially during the initial phase of reentry, when the family system is likely to be in a state of crisis and thus amenable to change;

- linking the family with informal and/or formal supports;

- ensuring that service providers work in concert to meet the needs of children and families;

- providing services as long as they are needed to maintain the reunification, including knowing when to contact families to provide interim supports; and

- balancing the concern for protecting the child and supporting the family with the risks of perpetuating dependency and intruding into the family.

Conclusion

Attention to family reunification is one expression of the renewed emphasis in child welfare on preserving families, and part of the contemporary revolution in child welfare services. Effective family reunification practice requires extensive resources and commitment on the part of administrators, policymakers, practitioners, foster parents, and other service providers. It should not remain the province of a few exemplary or demonstration projects here and there; rather, it should become an integral, regular component of the services provided in each community for all young people in care and their families. Additionally, family reunification should be considered as soon as it is determined that a child should be placed in out-of-home care, given intensive and persistent attention throughout the placement, and reinforced through follow-up services that maintain the reconnection. Above all, the unique challenges of preserving families that have been separated through placement require new thinking, revised practice strategies, and an attitude of hope and compassion for even the most vulnerable families.

References

Fahlberg, V. *Helping Children When They Must Move*. Lansing, MI: Michigan Department of Social Services, 1979.

Fanshel, D.; Finch, S.J.; and Grundy, J.F. *Foster Children in a Life Course Perspective*. New York: Columbia University Press, 1990.

Fein, E.; Maluccio, A.N.; Hamilton, V.J.; and Ward, D.E. "After Foster Care: Outcomes of Permanency Planning for Children." *CHILD WELFARE* LXII, 6 (November–December 1983): 485–562.

Fein, E.; Maluccio, A.N.; and Kluger, M. *No More Partings: An Examination of Long-Term Foster Family Care*. Washington, DC: The Child Welfare League of America, 1990.

Fein, E., and Staff, I. "Implementing Reunification Services." *Families in Society* 72, 6 (June 1991): 335–343.

Goerge, R.M. "The Reunification Process in Foster Care." *Social Service Review* 64, 3 (September 1990): 422–457.

Haapala, D. *Perceived Helpfulness, Attributed Critical Incident Responsibilities, and a Discrimination of Home-Based, Family System Treatment Outcome: The Homebuilders Model*. Report prepared for the U.S. Department of Health and Human Services, Administration for Children, Youth and Families, OHDS (Grant #90-CW-626). Federal Way, WA: Behavioral Sciences Institute, 1983.

Hartman, A., and Laird, J. *Family-Centered Social Work Practice*. New York: The Free Press, 1983.

Hess, P.M., and Proch, K.O. *Family Visiting in Out-of-Home Care: A Guide to Practice*. Washington, DC: The Child Welfare League of America, 1988.

Holder, W., and Corey, M. *Child Protective Services for Risk Management: A Decision-Making Handbook*. Charlotte, NC: ACTION for Child Protection, 1986.

Jenkins, S.; Schroeder, A.G.; and Burgdorf, K. *Beyond Intake: The First Ninety Days*. Washington, DC: U.S. Department of Health and Human Services, DHHS Publication # OHDS–81–0313, 1981.

Jones, M.A., and Moses, B. *West Virginia's Former Foster Children: Their Experiences in Care and Their Lives as Young Adults*. Washington, DC: Child Welfare League of America, 1984.

Kinney, J.; Haapala, D.; Booth, C.; and Leavitt, S. "The Homebuilders Model." In *Reaching High-Risk Families: Intensive Family Preservation in Human Services*, edited by J.K. Whittaker, J. Kinney, E.M. Tracy, and C. Booth. New York: Aldine de Gruyter, 1990, 31–64.

Kinney, J.; Haapala, D.; and Booth, C. *Keeping Families Together*. New York: Aldine de Gruyter, 1991.

Levine, R.A. "Treatment in the Home." *Social Work* 9, 1 (January 1964): 19–28.

Maluccio, A.N.; Fein, E.; and Olmstead, K.A. *Permanency Planning for Children: Concepts and Methods*. London and New York: Routledge, Chapman, and Hall, 1986.

Maluccio, A.N., and Whittaker, J.K. "Helping the Biological Families of Children in Out-of-Home Placement." In *Troubled Relationships* (volume three in the *Families in Trouble* series), edited by E.W. Nunnally, C.S. Chilman, and F.M. Cox. Newbury Park, CA: Sage Publications, 1988, 205–217.

Maluccio, A.N.; Krieger, R.; and Pine, B.A. *Reconnecting Families: Family Reunification Competencies for Social Workers.* West Hartford, CT: Center for the Study of Child Welfare, University of Connecticut School of Social Work, 1990.

Nelsen, J. *Positive Discipline.* New York: Ballantine Books, 1987.

Pecora, P. "Investigating Allegations of Child Maltreatment: The Strengths and Limitations of Current Risk Assessment Systems." *Child and Youth Services* 15, 1 (1991): 73–92.

Pelton, L.H. *For Reasons of Poverty: A Critical Analysis of the Public Child Welfare System in the United States.* New York: Praeger Publications, 1989.

Polansky, N.; Chalmers, M.A.; Buttenweiser, E.; and Williams, D.P. *Damaged Parents: An Anatomy of Child Neglect.* Chicago: University of Chicago Press, 1981.

Rzepnicki, T.L. "Recidivism of Foster Children Returned to Their Own Homes: A Review and New Directions for Research." *Social Service Review* 61, 1 (March 1987): 56–70.

Shyne, A.W., and Schroeder, A.G. *National Study of Social Services to Children and Their Families.* Washington, DC: U.S. Department of Health, Education, and Welfare, DHEW Publication #OHDS–78–30150, 1978.

Tatara, T. "Characteristics of Children in Foster Care." *Newsletter of the Division of Child, Youth, and Family Services* (American Psychological Association) 12, 3 (Summer 1989): 3 and 16–17.

Wald, M.S., and Woolverton, M. (1990). "Risk Assessment: The Emperor's New Clothes?" *CHILD WELFARE* LXIX, 6 (November/December 1990): 483–511.

Whittaker, J.K.; Kinney, J.; Tracy, E.M.; and Booth, C., eds. *Reaching High-Risk Families: Intensive Family Preservation in Human Services.* New York: Aldine de Gruyter, 1990.

2

Building Court-Agency Partnerships
to Reunify Families

*Pamela Day, Katharine Cahn, and Paul Johnson**

Children need permanent, safe, and nurturing families in which to live and grow. Children who are separated from their families are often confused about who they are and where they belong. They lack the certainty of family ties, the continuity of having the same important people in their lives over time, and a sense of history and identity.

The Adoption Assistance and Child Welfare Act of 1980 (Public Law 96-272) was framed to encourage reunification of children in out-of-home care with their families. The act addresses a number of systemic problems that have historically prevented timely reunification, as well as the role of the juvenile and family courts in reunification and permanency planning.

This chapter focuses on the interagency aspects of family reunification practice, giving particular attention to the relationship among judicial personnel, legal counsel, and child welfare agency professionals. A collaborative approach to reunification and permanency planning in the Northwest** has

* The authors wish to thank the many court and agency professionals and advocates in the northwestern states of Idaho, Oregon, and Washington, U.S.A., who have contributed their time, talents, and leadership to this effort. Major funding for the projects described in this chapter was provided by the U.S. Department of Health and Human Services, Administration for Children, Youth and Families, Child Welfare Training Grants #10CT0036 and #90C00395.

** The approaches and methods described were used at the Northwest Resource Center for Children, Youth and Families (NWRC) at the University of Washington School of Social Work. The NWRC, working closely with a team of consultants from three states, developed an interagency seminar to help court personnel, agency professionals, and advocates for children improve the system's capacity to serve children and their families.

resulted in improved reunification practice in several communities and has demonstrated that interagency collaboration is not only possible, but also effective in promoting timely and successful reunifications.

This chapter begins with a discussion of the context of family reunification practice, including the impact of Public Law 96-272 and the changing role of the courts. It continues with a discussion of the relationship between the courts and the child welfare agencies, followed by an overview of the development of an interagency seminar as a catalyst for improved coordination and a description of the seminar's effect on the participants' day-to-day reunification practice. The chapter closes with an examination of the potential for and the limits of interagency efforts to improve practice.

The Changing Role of the Courts

The passage of Public Law 96-272 significantly increased the role of the judicial system in child welfare at several critical case decision points. P.L. 96-272 also introduced the use of legal structure and process as an integral part of child welfare practice, limited the use of professional discretion by social workers, and made decision making more public and accountable by establishing procedural standards to aid professional judgment in casework decisions.

The law's mandating of court involvement was intended to serve as a check on the process, to ensure that reasonable efforts were being made to prevent placement, to reunify the child and family, or to proceed with another permanent plan. Related developments, notably the establishment of Court-Appointed Special Advocate (CASA) programs and citizen review boards, were also designed to improve the decision-making process by monitoring case activity and advocating for permanency planning and reunification efforts.

Although the intent of P.L. 96-272 is laudable and some positive results have been documented, the law has never been fully implemented. States have never received the level of funding authorized in the act and the courts have not received the resources they need to carry out the requirements imposed on them. In addition, the federal administration has failed to provide the leadership to implement the law [General Accounting Office 1989; Hartman in this volume; Kammerman and Kahn 1990; Select Committee 1989].

Given the limitations courts and agencies face in implementing P.L. 96-272, the increased involvement of the courts mandated by the law has not always resulted in improved reunification practice. All too frequently, the court hearing process has become a paper process devoid of useful deliberations. Recent reports suggest that any positive impact court monitoring and involvement could bring about has been greatly undermined by the sheer volume of cases that must be handled by an understaffed legal and judicial system [Hardin 1989].

Inadequate staffing of child welfare agencies and a lack of trained agency counsel have also contributed to the problem. Overburdened workers lack the time and resources to be prepared for court or to make timely reports. Because of the additional court involvement, staff members report having to spend increased time preparing for, waiting for, and making presentations in courts and to review boards.

In some parts of the country, where legal counsel is unavailable to agencies, workers themselves must represent their agencies as best they can. This is problematic for two reasons: legal representation is not available at key decision points, and workers spend even less time than before doing the critical work of reunification.

Other court-related elements also may interfere with reunification—poor judicial case management, outdated court rules and procedures, and a lack of training on permanency planning for judges, attorneys, workers, and guardians *ad litem*.

Even setting aside the resource deficits experienced by all parts of the system, however, a major obstacle remains: the lack of coordination among key players in the permanency planning process.

In the fall of 1985, a consortium of child welfare training managers met with the NWRC staff to discuss training needs and a training proposal. The discussion quickly focused on permanency planning and reunification practice. The managers felt that permanency planning had not been successfully accomplished in their respective states, due in part to a lack of training for judges, attorneys, and social workers on how to work effectively together. Following the meeting, funding was obtained for a regional project to provide interdisciplinary training to judicial, legal, and child welfare professionals, and to improve the prospects of permanency for children by enhancing the capacity of court officials, attorneys, child welfare professionals, and CASA program managers to collaborate.

The Court-Agency Relationship:
A Central Ingredient in Successful Reunification

In 1986, the Northwest Resource Center for Children, Youth and Families (NWRC) conducted a telephone survey of court and agency staff members in three states on the quality of their relationships with each other. Respondents pointed to the tensions among judicial personnel, legal counsel, and child welfare professionals as a source of major difficulty in achieving reunification.

According to the respondents, professionals representing the agencies, the courts, and the legal system lack a common framework for carrying out their responsibilities. They have conflicting notions about what their respective roles should be and fail to appreciate the financial and legal constraints placed upon their colleagues in other disciplines.

Respondents also reported that reunification is often delayed or made increasingly difficult because someone else "won't carry the ball," because parties seem to be working at cross-purposes, or because an "institutional inertia" has overtaken all parties. At worst, court and agency professionals were described as being "at war" with one another, blaming another part of the system for everything that was not working. These professionals—and the systems they represent—were mired in a negative pattern of interaction that was delaying the thoughtful and timely resolution of child and family service cases.

The survey results underscored the importance of collaboration to successful reunification. Court and agency professionals need to be clear about what they are trying to accomplish and why. They need to understand each other's roles and establish a healthy respect for the different perspective, expertise, and style each brings to the process. Such collaboration is most likely to develop when people have an opportunity to work together outside the courtroom, when they have clear avenues for communication and problem solving, and when they share a commitment to the best possible future for children and their families.

Fostering Collaboration: The Interagency Seminar

At the outset, seminar planners recognized that to inspire the participants and teach team skills, the project had to do more than tell people how to collaborate; it had to provide, at every step in the process, an opportunity for them to learn by doing.

The resulting interagency seminar, replicated 17 times throughout the Northwest, was a collaborative effort. Key steps in creating the seminar, carrying it out, and evaluating its effectiveness are described below.

Creating a Permanency Planning Training Model

A tristate planning team comprising key decision-makers from the judicial, legal, social work, and CASA sectors was established. Team members were selected for their knowledge of the issues, commitment to improving practice, leadership capability, and ability to represent a professional and organizational point of view. The team's goals were:

- to assist in the development, testing, and refinement of a training
  seminar model to help judges, lawyers, social workers, and child

advocates work together to achieve reunification or other permanent plans for children and their families;

- to create techniques for fostering interagency problem-solving at the local level; and

- to develop plans for conducting interdisciplinary training sessions in each of the three participating states.

Team members first met in state groups to familiarize themselves with the project, identify state-specific issues relating to reunification and permanency planning, and suggest training content and resources. The tristate team then came together to field test the seminar training model. Five team members from each state attended the seminar field test, which was staffed by NWRC staff members and the state training managers. Participants provided useful feedback on the training content and format, and began planning to conduct training seminars in their states.

Planning the In-State Seminars

Team members met again in individual state groups to advise project staff members on how and where to conduct the in-state seminars, and whom to invite to participate. Team members identified as potential participants representatives from the judiciary, the parents' and agency counsel, the child welfare agency, and CASA programs; court staff members; and in some cases, an even broader representation of professionals and advocates in the community. The team envisioned a mix of participants in terms of knowledge and commitment, including at least one judge who already understood the importance of permanency planning and who could influence his or her peers.

Team members were instrumental in recruiting seminar participants. As previous efforts have demonstrated, judges are more likely to attend training if they are invited by other judges, attorneys by other attorneys, and so on. A leading judge and a leading attorney from each state team wrote a cover letter to be enclosed with the invitation directed to their professional colleagues. Leading judges also made personal contact with certain invitees to urge their attendance. As much as possible, seminars were scheduled on dates that were convenient for key judges.

Seminar Objectives and Key Features

The objectives of the seminar were to build strong working relationships among colleagues from key disciplines serving children and families, to identify impediments to good reunification practice, to share techniques for fostering interagency problem-solving, and to establish a state or local agenda for achieving permanent families for children.

The seminar included the following key features:

- *A participatory training approach that modeled mutual respect and problem-solving.* State team members representing the courts, the legal community, and the agency served as presenters. Seminar participants were given an active role through group discussion, small group exercises, and finally, by being called on to develop a plan for their own state or county.

- *Attention to the central aspects of the interagency relationship.* The seminar included content and exercises on goals and values, roles, and professional norms and behavior.

- *Attention to the historical nature of interagency relationships and recognition of progress already made.* Participants came to the seminars with some old wounds and prejudices. Many also wondered if they had been singled out because they were viewed as a problem. A nondeficit, blame-free training environment was therefore established, emphasizing the importance of leaving old baggage and organizational history behind and concentrating on common goals. Humor was used to normalize differences and help everyone recognize that the different orientation others bring is not only acceptable but desirable for thorough work.

- An emphasis upon the systemic nature of reunification and the importance of working together to make the system work. There were opportunities for successful problem-solving so that participants could leave feeling supported by one another and hopeful about what might be done.

Seminar Content

The seminar began with an introduction of the participants and staff members, a brief history of the project, a statement of purpose, and an overview of the training. This was followed by what was informally called "the conversion piece." State or community leaders talked about why they were there, including information on trends affecting children in out-of-home care in their states and localities. This information dispelled the myth that everyone else was pleased with the outcome of their efforts, and pointed up how the system was not working. At one seminar, for example, presenters revealed significant differences in placement and length-of-stay rates among the three counties participating in the seminar.

A section entitled "Where Are We with Permanency Planning?" continued the focus on participants' attitudes and knowledge. A video presentation based on a *60 Minutes* story, "Karen's Kids," illustrated the systemic nature of permanency planning and how efforts can fail when all parts of the system do not work in concert; it also stimulated discussion on whether the failures depicted in the video could happen in the participants' communities.

Values and Roles

The seminar included a section on values and roles. Participants first met in small groups, by discipline, and agreed upon a list of professional values related to permanency planning. They were asked to define their role in the process and, as a large group, discussed common values and points of difference, then role differences and how they can create tension and misunderstanding among key players.

Attention to Obstacles

Facilitators also engaged participants in a discussion of the *yes buts*, inviting them to express any feelings of discomfort or to say what part of the presentation was not working for them. Impediments to competent reunification practice, which most often centered on resources, staffing, management, and training, were listed and referred back to as participants proceeded through the session.

The Case Analysis Exercise

The heart of the seminar was the case analysis exercise, in which participants met in small interagency groups and reviewed a written synopsis of a reunification case. By having participants practice staffing a case, seminar leaders sought to develop a consensus on competent practice with children and families and to highlight the role that each professional must play in order to achieve it. The exercise helped increace participant comfort in working as an interagency team.

Each small group staffed two different cases and reported back to the larger group. The material was based on actual reunification cases provided by the participating state agencies. Two of the cases featured common systemic problems: failure to provide services to prevent removal and facilitate reunification, a lack of coordination among professionals who were involved with the family, and unclear legal and judicial involvement. These cases forced participants to ask hard questions regarding the importance of the family to the child, how best to serve parents who have long histories of mental health difficulties or chemical dependency, and when to move forward with an alternate plan for a child.

In the small groups, participants were asked to suggest potential case outcomes and what each could do to move the case toward resolution. This emphasized the fact that participants can come up with the best possible plan for a child and his or her family by sharing different perspectives while seeking agreement. Much discussion took place among the participants as local biases and differing professional points of view came into play. Some groups reached relatively early consensus, while others struggled to agree. Although agreement on case recommendations is desirable, too early agreement can close off a healthy exchange of opinions and fail to elicit people's real feelings about a case and about broader systems issues.

Group Dynamics

The dynamics of the groups reflected status, role, and professional cultural differences between legal professionals and social workers that can contribute to the latter's reluctance to counter a strong judge or attorney who is a group member. The win/lose mentality of an attorney in the group may prevail over the judgment of social service professionals who have strong feelings about moving a case toward termination. Conversely, court professionals may go along with agency members to avoid conflict or because they lack strong opinions about the case.

As the small groups reported back to the group as a whole, the facilitators helped group members describe how they reached agreement. Differences in goals, values, and professional norms were raised. Staff members invited discussion from the larger group as well, and summarized points of agreement and difference.

Staff members also helped participants to underscore the important role each party must play. For example, agencies were encouraged to do an early and comprehensive assessment of the child and family, to promote early involvement of the parents in case planning and decision-making, and to use visiting purposefully. Attorneys were urged to become familiar with cases, talk with children they are representing, and consult with social workers throughout the history of a case. Judges were asked to instruct the parties clearly, to insist upon clear timelines, to increase court involvement as a means of promoting progress on a case, and to resist requests that unnecessarily delay court action.

Following the recommendations for competent practice, the participants and the staff suggested how they could work on obstacles and improve reunification practice. They developed a list of family reunification practice strategies. Participants were asked to describe what each party could do, based on its role, with regard to the strategies. The emphasis was on how each party in the reunification process can play a part in improving it.

Improving Practice

The final section of the seminar dealt with improving practice at the state, regional, and local levels. Participants were grouped together on the basis of their geographic region. Each put into words the conditions in their state or community that were stumbling blocks to reunification and permanence for children, and developed interagency strategies for improving those conditions.

Each group developed at least one action plan to take back to its community, specifying responsibilities of each participant, time frames, and anticipated outcomes. Each group described its action plans to the larger group, and participants wished each other well in their efforts to improve practice in their communities. The accent in this last section was on working together to improve practice at home. The message was, "You can work together and you can make a difference."

The interagency action plans created by participants fell into three categories:

- Resolving specific inter- or intra-agency procedural obstacles;

- Clarifying roles, attitudes, or philosophies associated with permanency planning; and

- Expanding or combining resources to support children and families requiring a reunification plan.

Evaluating the Seminar

Written evaluations completed by participants at the conclusion of each seminar measured the extent to which seminar objectives were met; they also provided useful feedback on content, format, and exercises. Participants felt that the seminar gave them an enhanced family reunification competency by strengthening relationships with colleagues from other agencies and disciplines, improving interagency problem-solving, and creating an ongoing mechanism for working together.

As a second form of evaluation, participants were followed up after they had returned to their states and communities to see how successful they were in carrying out their interagency plans. It was thought that the best test of the usefulness of the seminar would be the participants' ability to mount reunification agendas in their states and communities. Although it was not possible to follow up with all seminar participants, the project staff did make contact with two-thirds of the participants from around the region and offered them continuing consultation and encouragement. The seminar participants contacted were able to follow through with a number of activities for promoting permanency planning in general, and family reunification in particular, as the following examples illustrate:

- Court and agency professionals concerned with the disproportionate number of children of color spending long periods of time in foster care sought ways to increase the cultural responsiveness of the system. They formed an interagency task force to improve the recruitment of minority foster and adoptive families and the recruitment and development of more minority professionals who could facilitate reunification.

- In County A, participants were handicapped by a lack of funding for reunification staffing, training, and services. They formed an interagency group that developed a fact sheet of service needs, is seeking grants to augment services, and will advocate for increased funding.

- In County B, participants conducted educational events to offer judges and attorneys information on children and reunification. They also facilitated training sessions for agency workers, foster parents, community professionals, and CASA personnel on court procedures and expectations. Judges and attorneys served as presenters and trainers for these sessions. The same county also formed a multidisciplinary task force to advocate for the resources to provide better reunification and permanency planning services.

- In County C, participants found a lack of parenting classes to be an obstacle to returning children to their families. Their interagency plan sought to improve these classes and related services and provide greater access to them. Shortly after the seminar, the group reported that it had already met with representatives from key agencies to develop a needs assessment, to identify available programs, and to create new programs for parents.

- In County D, participants were concerned that the parties in a reunification case often did not find out what progress was being made until the review hearing. They agreed to hold a planning conference four weeks after the filing of every dependency petition for all parties to decide together on the plan of action. Only contested issues would then be heard in court. Representatives from all parties in the court process have been meeting regularly since the seminar to establish this procedure.

- Counties E and F worked on plans to more clearly define the federally mandated *reasonable efforts* standard for their respective communities. They hoped to reduce the time it takes to process a case through the court and to reduce the number of cases with undetermined permanency planning goals. The county committees have researched case law and surveyed court and agency professionals in their communities in preparation for developing guidelines.

- In an effort to gain a clearer definition and understanding of the roles and responsibilities of each member of the reunification team involved in the court process, participants from County G designed a cross-training conference for judges, court administrators, agency workers, attorneys, CASA personnel, and others. Before the conference, the agency hosted a walk-around session at which the two juvenile court judges and all of the juvenile court referees toured the local children's services office and observed its workings.

Conclusion

When does a planned intervention, such as the interagency seminar, make a difference? In communities where people have a history of working together, interagency projects are conceived and carried out without the impetus of outsiders. In communities where parts of the system hold onto differences in status and professional orientation, however, and especially where there is a history of conflict or lack of coordination, a planned interagency experience such as the seminar described in this chapter can be a vehicle for building more productive interagency relationships.

This project demonstrated certain key considerations:

1. Collaboration works best in settings where people have already begun, at some level, to work together. Even in these settings, it helps to bring key people on board in advance of the seminar. Establishing a local planning

group, meeting with people individually, and having key judges or attorneys meet with their colleagues are some of the ways to build readiness for an interagency intervention.

2. Inclusion fosters collaboration. Through their participation in the planning and presentation of the seminar, key judges, attorneys, and agency personnel began to experience collaboration and to model it for their colleagues. This seemed to inspire them to tackle problems beyond the original scope of the project.

3. The participatory approach does not come easily for everyone. Judges and attorneys, for example, are accustomed to attending training sessions in a lecture style. Care has to be taken to emphasize throughout the seminar why a participatory approach is being used. Participants must be asked to withhold judgment until they see the results.

4. Attending to the interagency relationship means accepting that there will be differences, and building on the strengths that each profession brings to the relationship. This may be the most difficult aspect of interagency intervention. Project planners felt that more could be done before and during the seminar to help participants become comfortable with their differences and appreciate the contributions each can make to the reunification process.

5. Improving collaboration means changing people and the way they do things. The interagency seminars demonstrated that change can come from a number of different directions and that collaboration can be contagious. For example, when key administrators or judges were not immediately responsive, line staff members and middle managers, once they felt clear about what they wanted to accomplish, were often able to convince them that their initiatives had merit, and thus gain their support.

6. Creating a reunification agenda for children and families takes people who care and people who feel empowered to act on their caring. It involves overcoming inertia: challenging hopelessness, standing up for what one believes in, and having confidence in one's ability to effect change. It involves risk-taking: being willing to stick one's neck out, to try something that has never been tried before or that has been tried and did not work the first time. It involves others: knowing that one is not alone in this, that others will join the effort.

Improving the systems of which we are a part is no small undertaking. The results of this project suggest that it can be done and that enabling the professionals in the system to work together is a key ingredient in success. Our experience indicates that systems can correct themselves, that people who are different by virtue of their organizational auspices and training can find ways to solve problems and move forward with a common purpose. We can help by attending to the interagency relationships that are so vital to successful reunification practice.

References

Hardin, M. Improving the Performance of the Courts in Implementing P.L. 96-272: Improving Child Protection Litigation. Draft document prepared for working group concerned with programs of grants to the courts. Washington, DC, November 22, 1989.

Kamerman, S.B., and Kahn, A.J. "Social Services for Children, Youth and Families in the United States." *Children and Youth Services Review* 12, 1 and 2 (1990): 1–183.

Select Committee on Children, Youth, and Families. *No Place to Call Home: Discarded Children in America.* Washington, DC: U.S. House of Representatives, 1989.

U.S. General Accounting Office. *Foster Care: Incomplete Implementation of the Reforms and Unknown Effectiveness.* Gaithersburg, MD: U.S. General Accounting Office, GAO/PEMD–89–17, 1989.

3

Training for Competence
in Family Reunification Practice

Barbara A. Pine, Robin Warsh, and Anthony N. Maluccio

Reunifying children in out-of-home care with their families is most likely to be successful when an agency articulates this goal within a comprehensive and integrated framework of policies, practices, and resources. Competent social workers are an essential element of this framework. This chapter describes a competency-based approach to educating and training staff members in which performance and practice outcomes are tied to the agency's goals and to a supportive agency context; it also delineates the knowledge, attitudes, and skills needed for family reunification practice. Finally, it illustrates this competency-based approach through training activities concerning certain key concepts described in chapter 1 and elsewhere in this book.

A Competency-Based Approach to Education and Training in Family Reunification

Competency-based—or performance-based—training is among the most important developments in education for child welfare practice today. It consists of designing and delivering training that ties worker performance to the goals of an organization and its deployment of resources, and evaluating the results. In competency-based programs of social work education, teaching and learning are outcome-focused and defined in performance terms [Arkava and Brennen 1976]. The competency-based approach comprises the following major components:

- A thorough job analysis defining the knowledge, skills, and attitudes or values required of staff members throughout the agency;

- An accurate assessment of each person's individual learning needs, and a plan for meeting them;

- A standardized curriculum based on a set of requisite knowledge, skills, and attitudes;

- A training delivery system emphasizing the conditions that foster adult learning. The system should be learner-centered rather than trainer-centered, take into account different trainees' learning needs and learning styles, and have feedback mechanisms that enable students to monitor their own development and continue to learn and improve performance;

- An evaluation of learning outcomes in relation to both job performance and the achievement of agency goals and objectives; and

- A process for identifying obstacles to competent performance, such as workload, work environment, lack of resources, and policy limitations [Boyer 1981; Arkava and Brennen 1976; Sims et al. 1989; Blostein and Ryan 1988; Hughes and Rycus 1989].

A competency-based approach goes well beyond education and training aimed at enhancing social workers' skills and knowledge; it encompasses the range of factors influencing their application in practice and the achievement of service outcomes. Both child welfare agencies and schools of social work benefit from this approach.

Benefits to Child Welfare Agencies

For managers of child welfare programs, a competency-based training system offers the potential for increased effectiveness and efficiency in a climate of rapidly shrinking resources. Effectiveness—the extent to which intended results are achieved—and efficiency—the extent to which results are achieved using the least amount of resources—are increased in a number of ways.

Because the learning needs of each worker—derived from a set of standardized performance criteria as well as a specification of the learning outcomes—are clearly delineated, workers attend only trainings targeted to their needs. Thus, time and money are not wasted on training staff members who do not need the content offered. Moreover, the learner-centered focus of a competency-based approach, in which staff members participate in identifying their own needs and selecting training to meet them, increases motivation to learn and the likelihood that new knowledge and skills will be applied on the job.

Proponents of a competency-based approach emphasize its relevance for selecting appropriate instructional methods. In addition to the typical group-training sessions, these methods include use of self-instructional materials, coaching, use of learning contracts, and small-group interactions. Because they are targeted to individual learning needs, these methods may be more cost-effective than traditional in-service training programs [Boyer 1981]. Moreover, agencies using a competency-based approach limit expenses and eliminate extraneous content by organizing curriculum development around what learners need to know. Thus, training is directed at the highest priorities for effective practice.

Standards for worker competence help define job descriptions, aiding in recruiting and retaining the most qualified staff members. Measurable standards for performance—competencies—can also guide supervisors in their coaching/teaching roles. This is critical because much of the learning in child welfare agencies takes place in the worker/ supervisor conference [Hughes and Rycus 1989].

Finally, "sending the worker to training" for all the staff problems that seem to be endemic to child welfare practice—everything from worker burnout to low morale or lack of motivation—is a major source of both inefficiency and ineffectiveness. A competency-based approach identifies and addresses in appropriate ways those performance problems that are not related to worker competence, and uses training as a solution only for those that are [Hughes and Rycus 1989].

Benefits to Schools of Social Work

A competency-based curriculum yields a number of benefits to schools of social work. Among them are consistency with curriculum policy standards for accreditation, increased clarity about the classroom objectives and practicum learning activities, increased practice relevance of the educational offerings, and perhaps, increased employment opportunities for the school's graduates in the field of child welfare.

Recently revised standards for social work curricula issued by the Council on Social Work Education [CSWE 1982] require specification of learning objectives and expected outcomes for each course in a curriculum. Thus, using an explication of all of the practice competencies in the child welfare field as a framework, a school offering a child welfare specialization could plan a series of courses aimed at student achievement of the competencies. Stating course content in terms of practice competencies leads quite naturally to the development of particularized learning outcomes for each course. Moreover, this approach to curriculum development results in greater clarity about what is considered core, or foundation, content in social work and what is unique to a given field of practice [Public Children Services 1990].

The competency-based approach contributes to greater clarity about the relationship between education and practice. Since the ultimate purpose of the profession is practice, and that of professional education to teach practice behaviors, schools of social work must provide opportunities for learning both theory and skills [Arkava and Brennen 1976]. When a curriculum is competency-based, the artificial dichotomy between classroom and field learning is lessened, possibly leading to more opportunities in each arena for students to develop practice competence [Blostein and Ryan 1988].

Finally, of much recent concern is the decline in the number of professionally trained social workers in the field of public child welfare [Lieberman and Hornby 1986; Public Children Services 1990]. This has occurred for a number of reasons, including a devaluing of professional training as irrelevant for the work and negative perceptions by students and graduates concerning the demands of child welfare and the work environment in public agencies. Curricula organized around practice competencies have the immediate advantage of demonstrating practice relevance, particularly when the set of competencies has been developed in a careful process with information from credible sources—the professional literature, accepted practice standards and legal mandates, and experts in the field [Public Children Services 1990]. Moreover, when the full range of child welfare competencies—basic and specialized—is delineated [see for example, Hughes and Rycus 1989; Public Children Services 1990; Children's Services, n.d.], social work educators at both the baccalaureate and master's level are able to show how much better prepared their graduates are for jobs in child welfare.

The Supportive Agency Context

Preparation for competent practice, whether in agency-sponsored training programs or in more formal social work education programs, is only part of what is needed to reunify families successfully. A competency-based approach requires a supportive agency context in which the social worker is able to effectively use his or her knowledge and skills.

Although competent social workers constitute a key element in any successful program to reconnect children in out-of-home care with their families, a comprehensive framework of policies, practices, and resources must support their work. For example, an agency must have a working definition of family reunification, ideally one that is incorporated in its mission statement as well as in its policies. The agency's policies should also set forth the principles of permanency planning and family preservation, such as those delineated in chapter 1. The agency's philosophy about the services it provides may be implemented in several ways:

- Agency policy ensures adequate time following family reunification to provide needed services to families before cases are closed. Moreover, the agency has practice guidelines for ensuring the family's access to service after case termination.

- Roles and tasks are assigned in such a way that practitioners working to reunify children and families have adequate time and training to carry out the wide range of activities required for competent family reunification practice. The agency emphasizes professional discretion, team-building, and the general empowerment of social workers.

- The agency recruits staff members whose race and ethnicity reflect those of the groups served by the agency.

- The agency uses supervision and consultation to enhance workers' skills and reinforce workers' learning.

- Program funding ensures that resources are available to purchase services needed to effect and maintain reunifications.

- The continuing development of resources and supports needed for effective family reunification is an integral part of the agency's operations.

- The agency has clear guidelines for deciding when family reunification services will be purchased, as well as from whom. In addition, workers are given clear responsibilities with respect to obtaining, negotiating for, coordinating, and evaluating purchased services.

- Agency procedures ensure that practitioners can convey information about needed resources to program planners and decision-makers.

- To obtain the community supports needed by practitioners and the families they work with, the agency regularly convenes interdisciplinary, interagency teams for service planning.

- Adequate linkages and collaboration with the court system and legal personnel are in place to ensure that the legal aspects of family reunification are facilitated.

- The agency works with the legislative system to develop statutory directives that support family reunification.

- The agency uses a uniform and integrated approach to assessment and case planning with all of the families it serves. Thus, the process of reunifying a family is directly related to the problems that caused the original family separation.

- The agency has a system of evaluation to monitor and promote its effectiveness in accomplishing family reunification.

Staff Development

Staff development in this supportive agency context would be consistent with elements of the competency-based approach to training. An agency would provide regular in-service training in basic child welfare practice, with attention to varying levels of expertise. Specialized training in family reunification would build on past training experiences and the skill level of each participant. In addition, staff members would regularly be involved in assessing their own learning needs. Training can best model partnerships and enhance collaboration among parents and other family members, foster parents, social workers, and service providers when all members of the service delivery team are involved in joint training activities.

Finally, a competency-based approach to staff development ties learning events directly to performance: what will the trainee be able to do differently as a result of taking part in the training? Performance—in this case, successfully reunifying children with their families—is broken down into a set of family reunification competencies, that is, the specific knowledge, attitudes, and skills needed to do the job.

Family Reunification Competencies

Social work practice that follows the expanded definition and principles delineated in chapter 1 requires a range of specialized practice competencies for social workers. These are outlined in this section and described more fully elsewhere [Maluccio et al. 1990].

It should be stressed that although these competencies are specific to family reunification practice, they build on generic or core, as well as specialized, child welfare competencies in such areas as assessment, case planning, and the psychological impact of separation and placement [Hughes and Rycus 1989]. Family reunification practice also requires specialized competencies in related areas, such as family therapy, child abuse, and legal issues in child welfare. In short, the competent family reunification practitioner is a specialist equipped with the full range of generic child welfare competencies as well as reunification-specific competencies. These latter are presented below in the order in which they are needed in the process of family reconnection: valuing families; assessing readiness for family reunification; planning goals for family reunification; implementing the family reunification plan; and maintaining the reunification/ending the service.

Valuing Families

Practitioners must be guided by a set of values and attitudes, including, among others:

- Possessing an ecologically oriented, competence-centered perspective;

- Appreciating and dealing with one's own experiences of separation and loss;

- Valuing the biological family as the preferred child-rearing unit, with the conviction that most families, if properly assisted, have the potential for positive change and can care for their children;

- Viewing family reunification as a process, with a continuum of outcomes or goals;

- Recognizing the wide range of symbols of family membership;

- Recognizing the importance to some children in out-of-home care of primary caregivers other than the biological parents, including adoptive parents, grandparents, and other members of the extended kinship system;

- Being committed to family reunification efforts that respect family integrity and promote empowerment of children and families; and

- Valuing human diversity, particularly diversity of family styles, lifestyles, and child-rearing methods.

Assessing Readiness for Family Reunification

A practitioner evaluating the family's readiness to be reunified should make use of competencies such as the following:

- Entering the biological and foster family systems in a manner that promotes trust and confidence;

- Using assessment approaches that are congruent with the family's heritage and that recognize the ways in which cultural variables can affect an assessment;

- Identifying any persons beyond the immediate family whose involvement in the reunification effort is essential or helpful;

- Assessing the child's and family's functioning and situation;

- Appreciating the psychological impact of the out-of-home placement on children, parents, and other family members, paying particular attention to feelings of loss and separation;

- Recognizing environmental barriers, obstacles, and other potential threats that may affect reunification; and

- Determining an optimal degree of connection that the family and child can be helped to establish or reestablish and maintain when return home is not possible.

Planning Goals for Family Reunification

On the basis of the assessment, practitioners engage in goal planning toward family reunification. This involves competencies such as the following:

- Helping children, parents, and other family members to form a partnership that works to establish agreed-upon goals;

- Helping the family to identify the optimal level of reconnection that is possible, from actual reunification of the child with the family to visiting or other kinds of contact;

- Helping the family to develop priority goals that must be achieved in order to effect a reunification;

- Helping children, parents, and family members to cope with loss and separation, and their related feelings and behaviors;

- Taking into account the laws and policies that affect reunification, and incorporating the requirements of the legal system into goal planning with the family;

- Helping biological parents, foster parents, children, and service providers to develop a service agreement for carrying out the reunification plan; and

- Involving biological parents, children, and other significant family members in making plan-related decisions.

Implementing the Family Reunification Plan

Implementation of the plan requires direct work with children and parents and collaboration with other service providers. This involves competencies such as the following:

- Working directly with children, parents, and other family members toward the desired form of family reunification;

- Helping children, parents, and other family members to cope with the psychological impact of loss and separation, in a way that prepares them to reestablish their ties;

- Helping parents to accept the ways they and their children may have changed while living apart;

- Helping children to cope with feelings of loss, anger, or grief that may be reactivated as departure from the foster family approaches;

- Using visiting to prepare for reunification;

- Promoting the foster family's collaboration and participation in family reunification;

- Maintaining accurate and complete records of service activities and the progress of the child and family.

Maintaining the Reunification/Ending the Service

In the postreunification period, practitioners help the family to stay together and also to evaluate and end the service, employing competencies such as the following:

- Continuing to provide needed services and supports to the family;

- Engaging the foster family in the postreunification phase as appropriate;

- Preparing a family to remain together once the service is terminated;

- Holding a closing session with the family and others to summarize accomplishments, elaborate on family strengths, establish priorities for the work that remains, and review the supports that can help the family carry out the tasks ahead;

- Dealing effectively with the disruption of a reunification plan that sometimes occurs; and

- Building on their own experiences as practitioners by assessing and analyzing what was learned in each family reunification case and evaluating the program's implementation as well as its impact.

Training Activities

Specification of learning outcomes is a central feature of the competency-based approach to training. In family reunification, training is designed for the particular skills, attitudes, and knowledge to be attained, selected from a set of competencies such as those described above. Workers attend only those training offerings targeted to their own learning needs. Moreover, the learner-centered focus of the competency-based approach, in which staff members participate in identifying their own needs and selecting training to meet them, increases their motivation to learn and the likelihood that new knowledge and skills will be applied in their work with families. A related feature of this approach is the emphasis on developing practice skills that can be attained only in experiential learning activities.

This section offers examples of learning activities to help students better understand and apply to their practice certain key themes and concepts that are discussed throughout this volume: an expanded definition of family reunification; multiple levels of family reconnection; the central place of visiting in successful reunifications; collaboration among service providers; and a strengths approach to working with families.

The examples described below are sample exercises discussed elsewhere in greater detail, and with accompanying resource materials [Warsh et al. 1993]. These learning activities are aimed primarily at values and attitudes and should serve to introduce a more comprehensive plan for competency-based training designed around the knowledge, skills, and attitudes outlined earlier.

Expanding the Definition of Family Reunification

A new way of thinking about family reunification helps providers and families shift from the narrow, traditional view—a child's return home to live with his or her family—to the broader view that is presented in chapter 1 and repeated below:

Family reunification is the planned process of reconnecting children in out-of-home care with their families by means of a variety of services and supports to the children, their families, and their foster parents or other service providers. It aims to help each child and family to achieve and maintain, at any given time, their optimal level of reconnection—from full reentry into the family system to other forms of contact, such as visiting, that affirm the child's membership in his or her family.

As noted in chapter 1, this expanded definition underscores the value of maintaining and enhancing connectedness between children in foster care and their families. It recognizes that even when parents cannot assume daily care of their children, they have an important role to play as family members. Moreover, the term *family* is broadened to include the child's kinship network, as well as others who may be significant in a child's life. This definition also allows for individual family needs to be identified and met in a range of ways. And perhaps most important, it allows service providers to feel hopeful about families.

In training, this definition of family reunification could be the centerpiece of a lively discussion of workers' values and attitudes about family reunification and of implications for policy and practice. Some of the discussion-focusing questions might include:

- How does this expanded definition reflect or contrast with your own concept of family reunification?

- Using an actual case of a family whose child is currently in out-of-home care, what might be the value of considering this expanded definition in relation to efforts to reunify this family?

- Currently, what is your agency's capacity to provide services in line with the expanded definition?

- What would be the implications for policy and/or practice of implementing the expanded definition in your agency?

Levels of Reconnection

The definition hinges on the concept of levels of reconnection between a child and his or her family. It enables social workers to view family reunification as a continuum, with levels of connectedness among family members that range from living together to lesser forms of contact, such as visiting, phoning, and writing.

Students can use a case example, perhaps one from their own work, to consider the following questions:

- How is the potential for the child and family to maintain a relationship influenced by a consideration of forms of reconnection other than return home?

- What would be some initial steps toward helping the family to make some form of reconnection?

- What family strengths could be built upon? What are the needs to be addressed?

- How can family visits be used to achieve the optimal level of reconnection?

- What are the possible risks to the child if the identified level of reconnection is sought?

- How can the child's foster parents best support the reunification goal?

- What policies and programs would the agency have to develop to delineate levels of reconnection for its family reunification efforts?

- How could the court system in a particular state or county be helped to recognize and act on this expanded definition?

The Centrality of Visiting

As detailed by Hess and Proch in chapter 7, family and child visits are central to successful reunification. Visits and other positive contacts are the means by which children and families are helped to work toward case goals. Thoughtfully planned visits give children and parents the reassurance that their relationship is still viable, and that the agency supports it; visits allow progress to be assessed, offer opportunities to learn and practice new behaviors, and give families and providers a chance to document progress.

Despite its importance, visiting is perhaps the most difficult dimension of family reunification practice. Visits can be time-consuming and complicated. Social workers may experience considerable stress in dealing with safety issues, family distress around visiting, and inadequate resources to sustain family visits. Training can design activities to target negative attitudes that social workers may have about visiting, and provide opportunities for developing visiting-related skill and knowledge. For example, working in small groups, students could be asked first, to brainstorm a list of activities that children and families can do during visits, and second, to consider how they and foster parents can help parents to identify and respond to the children's needs through these activities. This exercise can help social workers to think more creatively about planning for visits as well.

Another activity, involving a group of students working in pairs, is also aimed at improving family visiting. Each pair is asked to generate a list of six strategies, as follows:

- In what two ways can social workers demonstrate empathy for parents in planning and carrying out visits?

- In what two ways can foster parents or other caregivers support positive visits?

- What are two policies an agency should have in place to promote positive visits?

Recording each pair's six strategies produces an extensive list of conditions that promote positive visiting. These introductory activities should be followed by other experiential techniques using case examples and role-play to further develop and enhance social workers' skills in planning, carrying out, and evaluating family visits.

Collaboration

Family reunification typically involves competing perspectives, which derive from the different values, ideas, needs, and recommendations of those involved in it. Yet collaboration—and sometimes partnership—among social workers, legal personnel, foster parents, and biological parents are key to the success of reunification efforts. Training can address this in terms of both content and process.

For example, a training activity could involve a panel consisting of a biological parent, a foster parent, a judge, a social worker, and perhaps an agency administrator. Using a vignette of a case typical of the agency's foster care caseload, panelists might each discuss issues such as the following:

- What do you see as your primary obligation in this case?

- What do you think is the biggest challenge this case presents in relation to family reunification?

- What are the obstacles to meeting case goals?

- What policies or programs would you change to improve this family's chances of being reunified?

Because extensive collaboration and teamwork are required in family reunification, joint training involving foster parents, social workers, and other service providers can be quite effective. Training of this kind models the practice ideal, provides the environment for relationship-building, influences social workers' attitudes about collaboration, and also offers opportunities to develop skill in building partnerships. Chapter 2 describes an innovative training approach to improve collaboration among social workers and court personnel.

A Focus on Family Strengths

Family strengths are the key to solving the problems that necessitated placement. As detailed in chapter 9, a focus on strengths is both a philosophy and an approach to practice with families. Empowerment of families is necessary for family members to change in positive ways and to manage their own lives. A strengths approach teams the biological family, the foster family, and the helping system to accomplish reunification goals; assumes an inner competence and logic behind everyone's behavior; assumes that a focus on strengths activates them as resources for solving family problems; and acknowledges that a family's own constructive solutions to problems are likely to be the most effective and long-lasting.

To consider implications of a strengths approach for their work with families, students could participate in the following sentence completion exercise: "I imagine that one of the biggest obstacles to families on the path to reunification is..." Responses should reflect extrafamilial obstacles such as lack of resources and negative attitudes of service providers, as well as intrafamilial problems such as substance abuse and domestic violence. The instructor can then highlight the importance of responding to these obstacles with a strengths approach, detailing the components listed above. The exercise helps students to be more empathic about the wide range of hurdles facing such vulnerable families, and can enhance their belief in the strengths approach, both as a philosophy and a way of working.

Students can practice a strengths approach to family reunification with a prepared case example or with cases from their own caseload. A case in which family problems are extensive and seemingly unsolvable, such as one where termination of parental rights is being considered, is one way to illustrate the power of the strengths approach. Students can be asked to identify the family's strengths and needs and to consider, in light of the strengths, whether an alternative to terminating parental rights seems possible.

Conclusion

Training of social workers is often selected as the first (and sometimes only) solution to improving child welfare programs. Isolated training events, or training that is not integral to all other aspects of a program, will not result in the desired outcomes—enhanced family functioning, fewer children in out-of-home care, and permanent families for all children. A competency-based approach to training social workers can improve the outcomes and increase the incidence of reunification for families whose children are in out-of-home care. This approach begins with setting standards for social worker competence that aid in recruiting the best qualified staff. Training is targeted to particularized learning needs of staff members and thus increases the likelihood that their ability to reunify families successfully will improve. Moreover, a competency-based approach places the ability of staff members to work effectively within a broader context of agency supports they need to do their work.

References

Arkava, M.L., and Brennen, E.C., eds. *Competency-Based Education for Social Work.* New York: Council on Social Work Education, 1976.

Blostein, S. and Ryan, R.M. "A Competency-Based Approach to the Education of Social Work Administrators." *Journal of Continuing Social Work Education* 4, 3 (Summer 1988): 13–17.

Boyer, C.M. "Performance-Based Staff Development: The Cost-Effective Alternative." *Nurse Educator* 6, 5 (September–October 1981): 12–15.

Children's Services Training Needs Assessment, Ohio-Wisconsin Project Report. Columbus, OH: Ohio State University, College of Social Work, n.d.

Council on Social Work Education. *Curriculum Policy Statement for the Master's Degree and Baccalaureate Degree Programs in Social Work Education.* New York: Council on Social Work Education, 1982.

Hughes, R.C., and Rycus, J.S. *Target: Competent Staff—Competency-Based Inservice Training for Child Welfare.* Washington, DC: The Child Welfare League of America, and Columbus, OH: The Institute for Human Services, 1989.

Leiberman, A.A., and Hornby, H., eds. *Professional Social Work Practice in Public Child Welfare: An Agenda for Action.* Portland, ME: Center for Research and Advanced Study, University of Southern Maine, 1987.

Maluccio, A.N.; Krieger, R.; and Pine, B.A. *Reconnecting Families: Family Reunification Competencies for Social Workers.* West Hartford, CT: Center for the Study of Child Welfare, University of Connecticut School of Social Work, 1990.

Public Children Services Association of Ohio. *An Analysis of the Activities, Knowledges and Skills of County Children's Protective Services Workers*. Public Children Services Association of Ohio, 1990.

Sims, R.R.; Veres, J.G.; and Heninger, S.M. "Training for Competence." *Public Personnel Management* 18, 1 (Spring 1989): 101–107.

Warsh, R.; Maluccio, A.N.; and Pine, B.A. *Teaching Family Reunification: A Sourcebook*. Washington, DC: The Child Welfare League of America, 1993.

**4**

FAMILY REUNIFICATION PRACTICE IN A
COMMUNITY-BASED MENTAL HEALTH CENTER

Linda Boutilier and David Rehm

A community-based mental health center (CMHC) is an unusual and, in some ways, unlikely agency to undertake a family reunification project. Traditionally, CMHCs are committed to the care of chronically mentally ill adults. Yet the commitment of CMHCs to the deinstitutionalization of the chronically mentally ill does set the stage for such centers to appropriately extend their services into the child welfare field in the form of family reunification services.

This chapter describes the critical features of a CMHC that support family reunification work, suggests an effective staffing pattern and work environment, describes the program's four phases of reunification, and provides guidelines for mounting similar programs within other mental health agencies. It is based on the experiences of the staff of a model family reunification program that was developed at a community mental health center under contract with a state child welfare agency, from which it receives referrals.*

The Setting: A Critical Component

A CMHC that is committed to offering child and family services can adapt the expertise gained in serving chronically ill adults to the development of family reunification services. Most CMHCs have:

- Experience with an aggressive case management technique based on outreach into home and community settings;

---

* Kent County Mental Health Center, Warwick, RI, provides a wide range of services, including emergency services, outpatient services, in-home intervention, and day programs for chronically ill adults and behaviorally disordered children and adoles-

- Twenty-four-hour emergency and crisis intervention services that help to prevent clients and families from entering the state system;

- A willingness to advocate for socially unpopular clients;

- A philosophical committment to enabling clients to function in the most normal and least restrictive environment possible;

- An orientation toward maximizing strengths as well as remedying pathology;

- A focus on using existing resources and natural social supports to maintain successful community functioning; and

- A rehabilitation model incorporated into the system of care.

Many of these features are consonant with the values and strategies associated with family preservation services [Whittaker et al. 1990]. To maximize the potential of a CMHC as the setting for a family reunification project, however, several ideological and administrative issues have to be resolved. CMHCs usually focus on individual clients rather than families as the unit of intervention. (It is interesting to note that the parenting needs of chronically mentally ill clients who are also parents are often overlooked.) In addition, difficulty in identifying reunification referrals may mean that clients will have to be sought from noncatchment areas, which can drain agency resources. These potential problems aside, CMHCs, as compared to public child welfare agencies, often prove to be more flexible and able to take risks, less encumbered by state bureaucracy and collective bargaining units, and more credible to family courts for their capacity to engage in case planning and resolution.

Staffing Considerations

Having the flexibility to adapt to changing program needs is crucial. In this agency, the staffing of the family reunification program evolved over a six-year period. Initially, the program coordinator was a master's-level social worker who also carried a full caseload. This quickly proved unworkable, and after the first

---

cents. The Rhode Island Department for Children, Youth, and Families (formerly the Rhode Island Department for Children and Their Families) provides family foster care, children's mental health services and residential group care, and emergency response to child abuse and neglect. The Department contracts with local mental health centers to provide family preservation programs and intensive community-based treatment for children at risk of placement in out-of-home care.

six months, the program coordinator's caseload was reduced by one-half. Since this put an undue burden on the rest of the staff, the following staffing pattern evolved:

- One half-time program manager;
- Two full-time master's-level clinicians who provide individual, group, and family therapy to parents, are responsible for treatment planning, and teach parent education classes;
- Two bachelor's-level case managers, who, teamed with the clinicians, carry a caseload of six to 10 families; they focus primarily on advocacy, services to children, and outreach;
- One half-time child care worker who provides transportation for children to and from visits with their parents; and
- Two part-time foster grandparents who, along with the child care worker, assist case managers in supervising parent-child visits at the center.

Number of Families Served

The contract with the state at first required a yearly caseload of 60 families. This contract assumed that the families referred were ready to be reunified and that aftercare services would be minimal. Both of these assumptions proved to be inaccurate; the staff soon realized that reunifying families could take up to a year. Aftercare services became central to the success of reunification efforts. Since these efforts were more time-consuming than originally expected, the number of families accepted into the program was reduced, first to 40 families a year and later, with the addition of the reunification phase, to about 24 families a year. Each team of staff members serves six families at a time; each has some families in the aftercare phase as well. The two teams run their groups concurrently and overlap in picking up new cases, so that six families enter the program about every three months.

The Importance of Case Management

No one agency can provide all the services that reunifying families need. Because service coordination can be complex and time consuming, the case manager role is central in working with families. Professionals themselves often have a difficult time negotiating the social service system; for families, the system often presents an impossible maze with new obstacles at every turn. The case manager must first learn to use the service network, then teach families to do the same. Concrete services are as important as therapeutic services, and tangible assistance helps to form an alliance between staff members and clients. When there is no food in a client's house and the heat has been turned off, staff members cannot focus on building the client's self-esteem or teaching new skills until they address the basic needs. *How* a case manager helps a family obtain food and heat, however, can be an empowering process that ultimately builds self-esteem and teaches new skills. Staff members learn that their job is to help families help themselves, while at the same time educating the social service community about how it can better support healthy family functioning.

Qualities Required of Staff Members

The relationship between staff members and clients—which is intense, given that they are often together for five hours a week, with part of the time in the families' homes—calls for a special set of personal and professional characteristics. Staff members have to have boundaries loose enough to let them enter into a family's system, but clear enough to let them disengage as needed. They may often feel as if the best they can do is to stay one step ahead of the families. Case managers and clinicians must have clear goals and keep families focused on what needs to be done for children to return home, rather than colluding with a family or merely creating an unhealthy dependency of the families upon the workers. This focus requires good clinical skills, effective supervision, and constant monitoring.

Loss, separation, and mourning are central to the work and can be as painful for staff members as for clients. A common theme for staff members seems to be the working through of their own experiences with separation and loss. These personal experiences usually enable staff members to empathize with the families. Staff members, however, must learn to be aware of how their past experiences may affect the present, and be helped to distinguish between their own feelings and those of the families. This has to be addressed gently but firmly in supervision, so that boundaries are maintained and families are seen as objectively as possible. As Reynolds-Mejia and Levitan [1990] point out:

> *Any and all emotional responses of the therapist to a client family may prove to be of crucial significance in the treatment process. The professional in the child abuse field functions daily within the deepest layers of human disturbance, working with traumas of others as well as coping with events that can traumatically alter the professional's own views of human life. The therapist, no less than the victims, faces a loss of innocence by virtue of simple empathy with all the family members and*

the family's pathological system—an empathy necessary to rendering effective treatment.

Empowerment of Staff Members

People who are attracted to family reunification work are a special group committed to respecting clients' rights and empowering families. The sense of uniqueness, innovation, and being on the cutting edge that characterizes involvement with these programs is part of what attracts practitioners to the work. Staff members should have enough autonomy to impact administrative decisions regarding program design and services. The CMHC models the philosophy of empowerment, which is then carried over to work with families.

> *Workers can overcome the feeling and reality of powerlessness by learning how power and powerlessness operate in human systems and acquiring skill in using power in behalf of clients, creating mutual support groups, developing an entrepreneurial spirit, engaging in political advocacy, and implementing interventions based on principles of adult learning. [Hegar and Hunzeker 1988]*

The importance of empowering the staff calls for a strong commitment to staff development on the part of the program and the sponsoring agency (see Pine et al., chapter 3). Planning-days and retreats should be scheduled as frequently as feasible. Further, since the staff will be using such an eclectic array of skills, outside consultants are often helpful. Staff members can also learn from other members of the team; opportunities for staff members to share knowledge and experience regularly should be a component of staff development.

Support for the reunification program staff must be strong, consistent, and built into the program design. Reunification is a risky undertaking that can turn into an emotional roller coaster for everyone involved. Team building is essential to prevent the staff from becoming overstressed. Staff member feelings of isolation and overload are constant dangers to be guarded against. It is helpful to have the full teams meet twice a week for peer supervision and team building. The smaller teams that share a caseload should meet almost daily to check in and plan for meetings with client families.

The Four Phases of Reunification

The CMHC's family reunification program draws on a behavioral paradigm that involves modeling behaviors, providing opportunities to practice newly learned skills, and giving direct feedback. Services are given in four phases: assessment, intensive treatment, reunification, and aftercare.

CMHC staff members believe that "reparenting" benefits their clients and helps clients become better able to nurture and protect their own children. Reparenting is achieved by education, the provision of concrete services, and the establishment of therapeutic relationships. Staff members try to meet parents' needs without creating a dependency that reinforces family members' view of themselves as failures. The staff conveys the expectation that each family is capable of learning to eradicate the conditions that led to placement [see Zamosky et al., chapter 9].

Families need specific, clear, and time-limited behavioral objectives to guide their progress in relearning [see Fein and Staff, chapter 5]. Expectations are quantified and timelines are set for measuring progress. A "graduation date" is proposed at the time that a family enters the program. Rites of passage are built into the program so that families graduate from intensive treatment to a less intensive level of service as they are ready to do so. The message conveyed is that the parents are believed in and expected to succeed. Both staff members and parents are prevented from indulging their ambivalence and prolonging place-ment limbo for children by the requirement that within a specified—albeit somewhat flexible—period of time, families either achieve reunification or move out of the program.

Assessment Phase

Families referred for reunification services enter the assessment phase of the program, which lasts about four weeks and involves evaluating an individual family's ability and willingness to participate in the full range of services. Most families are accepted into the program. Many parents see the program as their final and only hope of being reunited with their children; they have already been told by their state caseworkers that they are in serious jeopardy of losing their rights as parents. Staff members do not attempt to assess the prognosis for actual reunification during this phase. Recommendations regarding reunification, based on direct observation of families' participation in program activities, are made later. Therefore, assessment of the appropriateness of reunification for a given family actually goes on throughout all phases of the program.

During the assessment, families are observed in at least one center-based visit and one home visit. Transportation arrangements for parent-child visiting are also discussed. Parents, program staff members, and state workers review and sign the program contract, which outlines expectations in terms of participation and service provision from each party. Staff members review materials sent to them by the state caseworker and set parameters for treat-ment, such as the stipulation that active substance abusers participate in substance abuse treatment before and during their participation in the program. Families are told that the program will last up to 18 months and that they will move through the different phases of the program as reunification progresses. Parents may expect to be reunited with their children within six to 12 months, and will be expected to remain in the program for six months after their children return home.

Intensive Treatment

Intensive treatment is the central phase of the reunification process. During this phase, which typically lasts for 16 weeks, families have up to five hours a week of contact with the program staff. Six families meet in group sessions twice a week at the center and are seen at least every other week at home. The group sessions are run by a team of staff members that includes a master's-level clinician, a case manager, two foster grandparents, and a child care worker.

One of the weekly group meetings involves a supervised visit between children in care and their biological parents. The children are transported from their foster homes by the staff, and structured activities are planned for each family. After about an hour of supervised play, the children meet for an activity group and the parents have a parent education class.

Services for parents and children together are critical. The unit of service is the family, and the program staff members use visits between children in care and their parents as an opportunity to teach new skills [see Hess and Proch, chapter 7]. Parents are expected, however, to take responsibility for themselves and their children. Staff members intervene only when necessary, and with the goal of teaching new skills. Mistakes are expected and seen as opportunities for growth. Parents and children often have to be supported in play with each other because it may not come naturally. Staff members are available to help families practice new behaviors in a safe, nonjudgmental atmosphere. As a parent who was successfully reunified with her two sons explains:

> *Before the program, I saw my boys once a month for two hours. When I started the program, I got 2 ½ hour weekly visits plus my monthly visits. Visiting at the state agency is very uncomfortable. It's like they are waiting for you to do something wrong. At the program, the staff is not watching to hurt the parent but to help the parent. You don't feel that the staff are trying to take your kids. You're always afraid the state agency will accuse you of abusing your kids if you discipline them. The program made me feel like a parent again, like it's okay to correct kids. Anyone can be a mother; it's a lot of work to be a parent. [Boutilier 1989]*

Groups for Empowering Parents. When the parents meet for their parent education class, staff members have the chance to discuss with parents the visits that have just taken place and to reinforce new behaviors. Immediate feedback is critical to relearning. The curriculum of the class is flexible, including child development, discipline techniques, and any other topics that seem pertinent to a particular group of families. [See Carlo, chapter 6, for a discussion of parent education approaches in a residential treatment center for adolescents.]

Invariably, a group of families has a number of concerns in common. Once these have been assessed by the staff, learning activities can be structured around particular issues. For example, when substance abuse is a common concern in a group of families, parents and children are encouraged to discuss their feelings about their family's misuse of substances and to learn healthier ways of coping. The group's size (six families) is small enough to allow staff members to individualize the approach and arrange activities according to what families need to learn, the ages of the children, and the skills that parents already possess.

The last hour of the parent-child visit each week is given over to a group supper and a closing activity. Parents bring food for themselves and their children and sometimes work cooperatively on a potluck supper. The format of the parent-child group allows staff members to observe children and parents in a variety of different activities. Groups are open enough to allow the families to be themselves. Meeting regularly becomes a routine that parents and children come to count on.

The second group meeting each week is a therapy group for the parents in the same six families. This meeting deals with individual goals and histories and helps establish a support network. Parents are encouraged to work through their feelings about their children's placements and are helped to learn new behaviors.

The group approach to treatment is essential. Individuals with personality disorders often respond best to group treatment and many of the parents carry this diagnosis. The effectiveness of working with families in groups, however, goes beyond individual needs. There is strength in numbers, and the group experience is a strong source of empowerment for parents who have been labeled failures. The joint experiences of the families increase the impact of services and accelerate the process of relearning. As one parent for whom reunification was successful said:

> The groups helped me realize that I wasn't alone, others are in the same situation. There are other people you can talk to. This was different than other groups. This was more like a small family than a group. I can call friends from the group as well as staff, which helps me feel supported. Even after the group ends I will not be alone. [Boutilier 1989]

Services to Children. Although the program's services emphasize rehabilitation of parents, it is recognized that the children involved also need services. Shuttling back and forth between two families can be agonizing for children in care, particularly for children under five years of age, who often do not have the verbal ability to express themselves. It has been a challenge to work with these younger children within a group setting and to find creative ways to help them express their feelings. The program has used puppets, art materials, storybooks, and role-plays. For the older children, the group sessions can work well as an opportunity to discuss hopes and fears about reunification.

As a parent in the program said:

I feel that the kids' counseling groups were very important. Kids learn to trust adults again, that they are not alone, that not everybody is out to hurt them. The case manager did a really good job of getting the kids to trust her and to talk. [Boutilier 1989]

The program does not try to be all things to all people, and has been active in linking children with therapeutic and educational services in the community that are not provided by the program. For example, when a child has been sexually abused, the child is referred to a therapy group designed for child victims. The program has been able to assess children's needs and facilitate referral to appropriate services in a way that the state agency may not have the time for. Caseworkers from the public agency are often quite pleased to have a clearer idea of the emotional and educational needs of an individual child as a result of the child's participation in the CMHC program.

Reunification Phase

Those families who have successfully completed the intensive phase and are being recommended for reunification move on to the reunification phase, which may last up to 12 weeks. During this phase, staff members continue to provide intensive phase services, including group sessions twice a week and frequent home visits. Those families who are not recommended for reunification are referred back to the public child welfare agency for consideration of other permanency planning options.

Aftercare Phase

The program's final phase involves six months of post-reunification services. Parents continue to attend one group meeting a week. Child care is provided, so those children who are not in school come with their parents. Home visits gradually decrease over this period and case conferences continue as needed. As families move out of the program, networking becomes vital. Successful reunification usually means that the family has a social support network in place and feels comfortable using it for assistance.

Aftercare services, or services provided once reunification has taken place, have been increasingly emphasized as the program has evolved. At first, services began to decrease shortly after the family was reunified, but it soon became apparent that this was a critical mistake. The first three months after a family is reunified are often fraught with the difficulties and stresses of learning to be together again, and require monitoring to help prevent the need for re-placement of the child.

Families naturally assume that their problems will be resolved once they are reunified. Resistance to continuing with services at that point has to be countered firmly: each family must continue receiving services. Previously reunified families can help to convince newly reunified families that the parents will need assistance in adjusting to having their children home. The children themselves, of course, are making a difficult change, during which separation anxiety tends to increase. It is very important to gently help parents become aware of what they and their children are feeling. Parents often want to cover over uncomfortable feelings at this time for fear that revealing them will cause others to see the reunification as unsuccessful.

This is a critical time for staff members as well as families since the practitioner's anxiety regarding a child's safety in the home increases. It is easy to question the wisdom of having recommended reunification in the first place. Since many families fear that they will fail again, the staff's faith in a family's potential to relearn is vital. One parent in the program described her feelings about continuing the relationship between her sons and their foster parents after reunification. During aftercare, she said:

> The case manager was a mouthpiece between me and the foster mother. The program helped me resolve some of my feelings about my children's foster parents. The foster parents' bonding with my boys was very intense. The foster mother was the mother I couldn't be. My boys went through a big thing breaking away from their foster parents and foster brother. At first I was real resentful. The foster parents had the love and respect of my kids. The program helped me learn how to earn the love and respect of my boys back again. Now, I follow through on what I say that I want to do. The program also showed the foster parents that they could trust me. [Boutilier 1989]

Additional Considerations

The Role of Foster Parents

Foster parents are visited at their homes and given a written description of the program's services and an explanation of how they are expected to participate in the reunification effort. Working with foster families' ambivalence about reunification is a delicate task. Foster parents should be empowered to advocate for children in their care but not to sabotage the building of relationships between children and their biological parents. Ideally, the foster parents become an important resource for reunifying families because of their investment in and knowledge of the children's needs. In one case, the foster parents became the child's godparents and were a baby-sitting resource for a single parent.

Termination

Helping families leave the program is a delicate and gradual process. Social isolation is a key factor in failed reunifications. Since successful reunification may depend on a healthy social support network, much of the work associated with terminating program services involves making sure that families are able to use their network. Program staff members do not assume that families will be able to function without social services upon discharge. Families will continue to experience conflict and will at times have crises. It is important to prepare families to successfully manage these expected events. Successful client families will become involved with social service providers as they feel the need and before problems reach a catastrophic stage. They will trust themselves to make good choices and will be able to accept assistance as needed. Program staff members model this by developing relationships with other service providers and teaching clients how to access and use appropriate services in their communities. Ideally, staff members gradually move out of clients' lives once adequate support networks are in place.

Case Conferences

Monthly case conference meetings are held during all phases of the reunification process to keep communication open, evaluate progress, and reassess goals. They are attended by program staff members, families, and public agency workers, and are open to foster parents, lawyers, school personnel, family court advocates, church officials, friends, and extended family members, all of whom are seen as partners with the family in working toward reunification. Discussions include visiting schedules, recommendations for additional services, obstacles to reunification, and projected reunification dates.

State caseworkers must be an active part of the reunification team. Too often, they feel that they can turn their cases over to the program staff and wait for recommendations regarding reunification. It is important to make clear that state caseworkers continue to have responsibility for case outcomes; this is usually signified during the assessment when all parties sign a contract that outlines their working relationship. State caseworkers are expected to continue any parent-child visits that have been taking place before acceptance into the program, to follow up on recommendations for outside services such as counseling for children or parents, and to assist in resolving crises that may arise. Case conferences are used to discuss any disparities in how state workers and program staff members may be viewing a family's progress. It is important to keep lines of communication open to state workers, even if this entails several phone calls a week as well as monthly meetings, so that members of the team can avoid working at cross-purposes. State workers generally find the program of great assistance in formulating treatment plans and in reporting to the family courts.

Making It Happen: Guidelines for Action

Once the model program had proven itself and moved beyond the experimental stage, the staff formed an advisory council to enlist support in maintaining the program. The council was made up of client families, public agency workers, family court staff members, child advocates, foster parents, and other service providers. The council's respect and enthusiasm for the program strengthened the staff, and the council's involvement helped the program through a rocky funding period by reassuring both the state and the mental health center that the program was valuable and vital to the interests of the child welfare community. The council has been discussing ways to expand the program into other geographic areas.

Administrators and others interested in creating a family reunification project within a CMHC might consider the following suggestions for establishing broad-based support:

1. Establish strong support for the program, both within the host agency and in the larger community. Key people whose support can ensure the program's viability should be invited to shape the mission statement and policies. The media should be used to educate the community about family preservation.

2. Everyone involved with the program must be constantly mindful of the need to market the concept of reunification to the appropriate state agency,

which often sees reunification efforts as counter to its mandate to protect children. Marketing will result in referrals to the program.

3. Every effort must be made to ensure the program's cost effectiveness. The array of intensive services required to bring about reunification and sustain it is expensive, but the cost of keeping children in continual care is higher still. Using volunteers (such as foster grandparents) creatively and locating free or low-cost meeting space can reduce costs.

4. Program competence and credibility must be proven to family court judges. Judges have come to rely on the model program's recommendations because its staff members have demonstrated excellent assessment, analytic, and writing skills. Judges learned quickly that this model provides intensive, community-based services, not just typical CMHC outpatient services.

5. The respective responsibilities of state agency workers and reunification staff members should be clearly set forth. Role confusion creates tension and compromises the family's capacity to work.

Conclusion

Family reunification can be a demanding and difficult undertaking, requiring much skill, adequate time, flexible hours, service options, staff development, and good relations with the full range of service providers helping families reunite. Public agencies are so often constrained by budget woes and staff shortages that they require the backup of a voluntary project such as the one described here. What is most important for families on the path to reunification is that they feel they are in charge of their own lives and not responding to the dictates of overburdened agencies. Staff members of the public agencies have appreciated the program's support and collaboration, and have reinforced the program staff's belief that a community mental health center can be an excellent setting for a viable family reunification project.

References

Boutilier, L. "Families, Workers Successful in Permanency Planning." *A Common Ground for Children and Families* IV, 5 (May 1989): 21.

Hegar, R.L., and Hunzeker, J.M. "Moving Towards Empowerment-Based Practice in Public Child Welfare." *Social Work* 89, 6 (November–December 1988): 499–502.

Reynolds-Mejia, P., and Levitan, S. "Countertransference Issues in the In-Home Treatment of Child Sexual Abuse." *CHILD WELFARE* LXIX, 1 (January–February 1990): 53–61.

Whittaker, J.K.; Kinney, J.; Tracy, E.; and Booth, C., eds. *Reaching High-Risk Families: Intensive Family Preservation in Human Services*. Hawthorne, NY: Aldine de Gruyter, 1990.

PART TWO

Creating the Methods

5

GOAL-SETTING WITH BIOLOGICAL FAMILIES

Edith Fein and Ilene Staff

"Goal-setting is one of the critical tasks of the social work problem-solving process" [Anderson 1989]. Goal-setting encourages procedures that give a clear picture of problems, support treatment planning and assessment of progress, and facilitate review and evaluation of outcomes.

This chapter presents policy and practice in setting goals with biological families whose children have been removed because of abuse or neglect. Using the experience of a demonstration program in operation since 1989 as illustration, the authors examine guidelines for the goal-setting process; set forth tools for helping workers in assessment, decision-making, and treatment-planning; discuss policy and practice aspects; and consider the application of results and conclusions from this example to family reunification practice in general.

The Family Reunification Project

Casey Family Services is a voluntary long-term foster care and permanency planning agency founded in 1976 in Connecticut, currently serving over 200 children in six New England states. This chapter draws from the agency's experience with its Family Reunification Project, which assists families whose children are in foster care primarily because of abuse or neglect and who need a broad range of intensive or special services if the family is ever to be reunited. The program offers families case management and clinical intervention services in their own homes. Unlike most time-limited, crisis-oriented family preservation programs, family reunification services may be provided for periods as long as two years. Professionals assigned to the families have low caseloads and are able to give sustained attention to the families.

Each family is assigned to a reunification team consisting of a social worker and a family support worker. The team provides such services as training in parenting skills; mental health counseling; respite care; group support; and assistance with housing, job training, transportation, and legal problems. Services begin before the child returns home, when the reunification team and the biological family create a service agreement setting forth treatment goals and plans, and continue after reunification for as long as needed, up to a two-year total.

Referrals to the program come from state agency workers who determine that reunification should be the permanent plan for an abused or neglected youngster, but who are not optimistic that it can be achieved unless intensive services are provided. The biological family must be willing and able to participate in formulating a service agreement and to work with the reunification team. In addition, the foster parents or residential care facility staff must be willing to work with the team, and the child must have been removed from the home within the previous 18 months. To protect children and ensure the safety of workers, cases are not accepted if a sibling has died because of abuse or neglect or if life-threatening abuse has taken place in the past; if the child's safety would be jeopardized by reunification; if sexual abuse has taken place and the perpetrator lives in the home or is an active member of the family; if violence has taken place (or a potential for violence exists) toward people outside the family; or if caregivers are substance abusers with no willingness to participate in treatment.

Goal-Setting in Child Welfare

Since the 1970s, goal-setting has found expression in several areas of practice, including the development of task-oriented casework [Reid and Epstein 1972], time-limited therapy [Mann 1973], and goal-attainment scaling [Garwick and Lampman 1972]. The child welfare field has benefited from this emphasis on goals. Permanency planning—the mainstream movement in delivering child welfare services—stresses explicit formulation of problems, treatment planning, identification of permanent placement options, case management, review of plans, and timely decision-making based on the implementation of service agreements [Maluccio et al. 1986]. Permanency planning thus epitomizes goal-setting.

Functions

Service planning for family reunification using a goal and plan orientation, as Maluccio et al. [1986] suggest, fulfills the following functions:

- Encourages systematic thinking about many areas of family needs;

- Structures service delivery activity so workers, supervisors, and clients are fully aware of what is occurring;

- Aids in case planning and management, allowing for timely decision-making and corrective action when necessary;

- Helps clients participate in what is happening to their families in achieving reunification;

- Ensures program accountability; and

- Documents case progress for possible court testimony.

In the child welfare field, intensive family preservation programs have given further impetus to the goal-setting orientation. Intensive family preservation programs typically are in-home, time-limited, crisis-oriented services, and are designed to prevent foster care placement of children at risk of removal from their homes [Whittaker et al. 1990]. Various family preservation training courses and handbooks underscore the usefulness of focus and goal-setting in delivering these services [Lloyd and Bryce 1985; Tracy et al. 1991; Whittaker et al. 1990].

Some family preservation program advocates believe the family preservation model might make family reunifcation efforts more timely and more successful than they are at present [Maluccio et al. 1991; Nelson 1990]. Many family reunification programs are superficially similar to family preservation services, having developed from the same roots. As discussed in chapter 1, however, there are important differences. Most important, in intensive family preservation programs a family's motivation to develop and achieve goals and to work with service providers is tied to the fear that children will be removed from the home—a strong authoritative mandate. Families of children already in foster care, however, have different concerns.

First, family reunification readily occurs two-thirds to three-fourths of the time in the course of normal service delivery by state agencies [Fein et al. 1983; Tatara 1989]; parental motivation is not necessarily an issue. Second, those children not reunified with their families are typically victims of one or more unfortunate circumstances: the state agency may not be able to deliver the kind or depth of services the family needs; the children present almost insurmountable problems in adjusting to family life; or the families are too troubled to make use of the services available. Third, even children who are quickly reunited with their families face difficulties [Turner 1984]. When children stay out of the home for long periods, families achieve a new equilibrium without them, and parents may feel ambivalent about having the children return. As a result, reunification programs, which by their nature work with many families in situations such as those described above, are forced to deliver services without the motivation and authoritative mandate that family preservation programs command.

For all these reasons, goal-planning is an essential feature of family reunification practice and was made an integral part of the Casey program model. Family members and social workers alike can use the focus and structure that goal-planning provides, particularly when reunification aims at a level of reconnection short of living in the same household. In those cases, the goal-planning process enables the family and the social worker to identify the appropriate level of reconnection and achieve some success in attaining the selected level despite the family's inability to live together.

The Service Planning Process

The process of service planning requires that workers and clients together (1) identify appropriate goals, (2) build on existing strengths and resources, and (3) create action plans to help the clients' progress toward the goals. Of the three, identifying and explicitly stating the goals is probably the most difficult, but all are crucial for a successful case plan.

Identifying and Stating Goals

To create a goal statement, the worker must consider what problems the family is facing (see figure 1), what must change about the family's functioning to allow reunification to take place, and what the family will be like if the goals are achieved. Goals are statements of positive family functioning, as illustrated in figure 2.

Building on Strengths and Resources

While goals are positive statements about changes the family can achieve [see Zamosky et al., chapter 9], strengths and resources are abilities, ways of functioning, personal characteristics, environmental conditioning, social connections, or any positive aspects of the family's life that are present or that can be found or mobilized in behalf of the family (see figure 2).

Creating Action Plans

Particular actions must be taken by the reunification team and the family, separately and together, to achieve progress toward the family's goals. The plans should be specific, indicate a date by when they will be accomplished, and

FIGURE 1—PROBLEM AREAS

In creating goals and plans, each of the following problem areas should be considered for families whose children are in care because of abuse or neglect:

1. Parents' feelings toward selfs
2. Parents' relationship, including sexual relations
3. Parents' recognition of problems
4. Parents' capacity for child care
5. Parents' approval of children
6. Discipline of children
7. Supervision of children
8. Incidence of sexual abuse
9. Child's behavior
10. Relationship between parents and child
11. Child's relationship to family
12. Child's feelings toward self
13. Child's disabling condition
14. Child's developmental lags
15. Child's relationship to peers
16. Child's relationship to foster family
17. Child's educational needs
18. Health care
19. Home management (nutrition, clothing, sanitation, hygiene, physical safety)
20. Money management
21. Housing and transportation needs
22. Employment needs
23. Social networks

FIGURE 2–GOALS AND STRENGTHS

Goals	Strengths and Resources
Ms. Parker and Mr. Vega will not abuse drugs or alcohol.	Mr. Vega has enrolled in a drug rehabilitation program. Ms. Parker has already completed Phase 1 of day treatment and has been regularly attending AA meetings.
Ms. Parker and Mr. Vega will have enough money to pay for the basic needs of life, including housing, clothing, food, and utilities, and will manage their money carefully.	Ms. Parker currently has a stable job. Mr. Vega is actively looking for a job.
Ms. Parker and Mr. Vega will set limits and teach Jacob right from wrong.	Ms. Parker and Mr. Vega want very much to learn better ways to be good parents.
Ms. Parker and Mr. Vega will have a good understanding of Jacob's needs.	Ms. Parker and Mr. Vega intend to visit Jacob regularly and will provide their own transportation.
Ms. Parker and Mr. Vega will develop a good relationship, free from abuse.	Mr. Vega and Ms. Parker are involved in counseling to improve their communication with each other.

identify who will be working on each plan. For example, consider goal #1 in figure 2: Ms. Parker and Mr. Vega will not abuse drugs or alcohol. Plans for them might include the following actions:

- Ms. Parker will no longer associate with the drug dealers she knew in the past, beginning immediately. *Responsibility:* Ms. Parker.

- Weekly until May 1, Ms. Parker and the social worker will discuss Ms. Parker's drug cravings, how she feels about herself, and how she is managing her new life. *Responsibility:* Social worker and Ms. Parker.

- Mr. Vega will continue attending AA meetings. *Responsibility:* Mr. Vega.

Guidelines for Setting Goals and Creating Case Plans

The following guidelines should be applied in developing an effective service plan.

Goals

A. A goal should state how the family situation will be different, not what the reunification team or family will do to make it happen.

> Confusing goals and plans is the problem most frequently encountered in writing goal statements. The goal is the end-state that is sought; details of the work that needs to be done will be written in the plans. They are related as strategy and tactics are related.

> *Not a goal: Mother will visit with her two sons.*
> *Goal: Mother will give her children the affection and attention they need.*

B. Each goal should be explicit and germane to the family's functioning and ability to cope. The language should be direct and informal.

> To participate productively in their plans, client families have to understand the concepts and language of their goal statements. Technical jargon is not helpful. The goals should define what the clients' life situation must be to have their children live with them.

> *Unclear goal: Mother will have a responsive support network.*
> *Clear goal: Mother will be close to other people she can talk to and get help from them when she needs it.*

C. Goals should be formulated to balance explicit and assessable expectations with the family's social and emotional needs.

> The goals must specify the changes necessary for the family to attain reunification. Goals that define a better state but are irrelevant to the original reason for placement should not be identified.

Irrelevant goal: Mother should volunteer her time to help others.
Relevant goal: Mother will locate and use community resources.

D. Family members should be able to make progress on some goals in a fairly short time period so that a feeling of success can emerge from their interactions with the worker.

> Long-term goals should include more easily attainable short-term goals, to encourage the confidence that family members must have to work toward their larger achievements.

Long-term goal: Mother will earn sufficient money from employment to support her children on her own.
Short-term goal: Mother will obtain services to have enough to pay for such basic needs as housing, clothing, food, and utilities.

E. Goals should be stated in such a way that progress toward their achievement can be assessed.

> Progress toward a goal is an important concept. Some of the goals will never be fully reached—improvement is always possible in such areas as understanding a child's needs or providing needed affection. Goal achievement, moreover, is not always easily measured. Sufficient progress toward the goal, however, can be evaluated through the social worker's observation of parent-child interactions.

Limited goal: Mother will interact with her children.
Assessable goal: Mother will give her children more of the affection and attention they need.

Strengths and Resources

F. Family strengths and resources should be articulated so workers and family members begin to think positively about the family's potential.

Strengths may be dispositional attributes such as motivation, biological predispositions such as intellectual capacity, or positive events. They should always be the focus when formulating goals. As Zamosky et al. stress in chapter 9, strengths should be germane to the particular case and explicitly stated.

Strength: Mother has had her own apartment in the past. Mother has begun to look at classified ads for affordable housing.
Goal #1: Mother will provide a home with space, furnishings, appliances, utilities, and so forth, adequate for essential household functions and for meeting the personal needs of family members.

Strength: Mother already receives food stamps and has dealt with state and local welfare offices.
Goal #2: Mother will have enough money to pay for basic needs, such as housing, clothing, food, and utilities, and will manage her money carefully.

Action Plans

G. Each action plan should be explicit, doable in a specified time period, and assessable.

The plans proposed to achieve each goal, that is, the work to be done, should be reasonable and specific enough so that the worker's and the family's actions can be monitored and measured.

Goal: Mother will give her children more of the affection and attention they need.

Plans: (A) Mother will visit children once a week at the agency office; (B) Social worker will bring children to mother's home once a week starting June 1st; (C) Mother will attend parent support group.

Supportive Record-keeping

Effective goal-planning requires a systematic recordkeeping procedure that is consonant with a program's philosophy and practice. The procedures suggested here are based on earlier work in goal-planning [Jones and Biesecker 1980; Miller et al. 1984; Maluccio et al. 1986], and incorporate concepts and techniques developed in permanency planning work in child welfare. The recordkeeping system is a logical extension of the service-planning process and guidelines discussed above, and was developed by the staff of the project on which this chapter is based.

The recordkeeping system uses a variety of forms to establish goals with the family, outline the plan of action, define responsibilities, document case activity, and monitor and evaluate case progress. The forms are described briefly below, and in the following section their use is illustrated with a case example.

The Case Plan Form

The case plan form (figure 3) is the central document upon which most of the others depend. It defines what the case is about and what planning will lead to progress toward specified goals. The case plan requires that workers consider a multitude of potential problems, define applicable goals with the client, delineate resources and strengths that may be brought to bear, create plans that will help the client progress toward the goals, and identify responsibility for completion of the plans.

The Monthly Goal and Plan Rating Form

The monthly goal and plan rating form (figure 4) allows for monthly review of goal and plan progress. It tracks changes in the amount of effort expended, monitors continuance or completion of the plan, and evaluates the past month's efforts. The form is completed by the reunification team and reviewed with the family. The monthly evaluation enables both team and family to be supported in the successes they have had and to be aware of the work that remains.

Other Forms

Additional forms include a referral sheet (see figure 5), containing information provided by the state agency; a face sheet, with full demographic information; an assessment, using the Family Risk Scales [Magura et al. 1987], at several key points in case progress; a status change form, documenting milestones in case progress; narrative recordings, comprising an intake summary, periodic case updates, and case notes; an expense form; and the service agreement described above. The following case example illustrates the use of some of these forms for service planning and goal setting and for case documentation.

Five-year-old Josh has been in family foster care for the past three months. Months before, he was admitted to a hospital clinic along with his two-year-old brother, Philip. Both had bruises, head lice, and scabbed sores around the hairline severe enough for the clinic to refer them to state care. Josh was not yet toilet trained, Philip seemed to be developmentally delayed, and both boys were poorly socialized.

This was not the first time the two boys had been removed from their family. Earlier in the year they had been placed in family foster care and later returned home. But now their mother was not keeping medical appointments and was known to be associating with drug dealers. In light of this information, social workers from the public child welfare agency were pessimistic about the outcome of a second effort to reunite the family, but they referred the family to a private agency for intensive reunification services.

Josh and Philip's case plan contained seven goals, three of which are illustrated in figure 3. The mother was involved in the creation of the goals and for each goal, family strengths were defined and plans made. The case plan identifies the date each goal and plan was established, as well as who is responsible for the plan. Note that for goals 1 and 3, additional plans were made a month after the original plans.

The Monthly Goal and Plan Rating Form (figure 4) illustrates the first month's rating of progress on goal 1. (A rating form is normally completed for each goal.) The social worker and family support worker team complete the form together. This form is shared with the mother or can be completed with her participation. The rating form charts progress, shows where more work needs to be done, and keeps the goals and plans in everyone's consciousness.

Program and Practice Issues

As discussed above, the goal-setting process is a familiar, if not completely comfortable, procedure for social workers. When it is used systematically, benefits for clients and staff members are well documented [Klier et al. 1984; Miller et al. 1984]. Agency reunification programs, however, have not generally directed themselves to the particular fit between their reunification objectives and a goal-setting orientation [see Fein and Staff, chapter 11]. For goal-setting (or goal-oriented service planning) to be an integral feature of family reunification programs, a number of factors must be considered.

Workers' Skills and Attitudes

Social workers are often uncomfortable at first with formulating goals and plans. "We were struck by the meager reporting we found in most of the case records about the social worker's definition of clinical tasks and description of ongoing therapeutic work. A well-articulated service plan was often not present in the records" [Fanshel et al. 1989: 477]. Indeed, many programs are not clear about their continuum of goals [Videka-Sherman 1988]. Even training courses

FIGURE 3–SAMPLE CASE PLAN

Family Name: Smith

Workers: J. Jones

Case #: 01

Use as many pages as needed to identify all goals and plans to be worked on. Add new goals and plans as they emerge. In the right-hand columns, please indicate the date each goal and plan was identified and who will be working on each.

	Date	*Who*
GOAL #: 1		
Mother will give her children the affection and attention they need.	2/10/90	
Strengths and Resources		
Mother loves to play with the boys when they visit.	2/10/90	1
Mother likes to read magazine articles about child care.	2/10/90	2
Plan A.		
Mother will visit children once a week at the agency office.	2/10/90	1

Plan B.

Worker will discuss discipline and other child-rearing problems

at each home visit.

2/10/90   2   ___   ___

Plan C.

Social worker will bring children to mother's home

at each home visit.

3/10/90   3   ___   ___

Plan D.

Mother will attend parent support group.

3/10/90   1   ___   ___

Codes: 1–Family, 2–Family Support Worker, 3–Social Worker, 4–Other (specify)

FIGURE 3—SAMPLE CASE PLAN (CONT.)

Family Name: Smith
Workers: J. Jones

Case #: 01

Use as many pages as needed to identify all goals and plans to be worked on. Add new goals and plans as they emerge. In the right-hand columns, please indicate the date each goal and plan was identified and who will be working on each.

	Date	Who
GOAL #: 3		
Mother will not abuse drugs or alchol.	2/10/90	
Strengths and Resources		
Mother has been free of drugs for extended periods in the past.		
Mother is determined to stay clean in the future.		
Plan A.		
Mother will no longer associate with the drug dealers she knew in the past.	2/10/90	1

Plan B.

Mother will attend AA meetings each Wednesday evening.   2/10/90   1

Plan C.

Mother and social worker will discuss mother's cravings, how she feels about herself, and how she is managing her new life.   2/10/90   1, 3

Plan D.

Mother will attend parent support group at the agency.   3/10/90   1

Codes: 1–Family, 2–Family Support Worker, 3–Social Worker, 4–Other (specify)

FIGURE 3–SAMPLE CASE PLAN (CONT.)

Family Name: Smith

Workers: J. Jones

Case #: 01

Use as many pages as needed to identify all goals and plans to be worked on. Add new goals and plans as they emerge. In the right-hand columns, please indicate the date each goal and plan was identified and who will be working on each.

	Date	Who
GOAL #: 2		
Mother will have enough money to pay for the basic needs of life, including housing, clothing, food, and utilities, and will manage her money carefully.	2/10/90	
Strengths and Resources		
Mother already receives food stamps and has dealt with state and local welfare offices.		
Plan A.		
Worker will help mother draw up a budget.	2/10/90	2

Plan B.

Worker will go with mother to open a bank account.   2/10/90   1, 2

_____   _____   ____

_____   _____   ____

Plan C.

Mother will not buy anything on layaway or credit.   2/10/90   1

_____   _____   ____

_____   _____   ____

Plan D.

Worker will help mother with shopping to take advantages of   2/10/90   1, 2

coupons, sales and bargains.

_____   _____   ____

_____   _____   ____

Codes: 1–Family, 2–Family Support Worker, 3–Social Worker, 4–Other (specify)

FIGURE 4—SAMPLE MONTHLY GOAL AND PLAN RATING FORM

Family Name: Smith

Workers: J. Jones, O. Doe

Case #: 01

Rating Date 2/28/90

INSTRUCTIONS: At month's end, list all goals and plans by describing them briefly in the space provided. Rate goals and plans on focus and status; indicate this month's progress for goals, and an evaluation for plans, in the third column. The codes and scales are listed on the bottom of the form.

	Focus	Status	Goal Progress
GOAL #: 1 Mother will give her children the attention and affection they need.	1	C	2

Plan	Focus	Status	Eval.
A. Mother will visit.	1	C	3
B. Worker will discuss discipline, etc.	1	C	2
C.			
D.			
E.			
F.			
G.			
H.			

I. _____
J. _____
K. _____
L. _____

Codes:

Focus:
Over the past month, how much time has been spent by the family or the team on this plan? Toward achieving this goal?
1. A major amount of time.
2. A minor amount of time.
3. Goal or plan not worked on this month.

Goal Progress
How much progress, if any, has there been this month in approaching this goal?

0	1	2	3	4	5
Regress from goal	None	A litte progress	Moderate progress	A lot of progress	Goal achieved

Status:
At this time this goal or plan is:
C. Continued
D. Discontinued

Plan Evaluation
Over the past month, how well was this plan working?
1. Not at all.
2. Working a little.
3. Working very well

FIGURE 5–SAMPLE REFERRAL FORM

Case # _____ Refferal Date _____ Taken by _____ Team Assigned _____

State Worker _____ Phone # _____

Child Information

Name _____ DOB _____

Current Placement: Type _____ Name _____ Removal Date _____

Address _____

_____ Phone # _____

Sex _____ Race _____ Grade _____ School _____

Previous Placements: ☐ No   ☐ Yes   How many? _____

To be reunified with

Name _____ Relationship to child _____

Address _____

_____ Phone # _____

Biological Parents   Mother   Father

Name _____ _____

Address _____ _____

_____ _____

Phone # _____ _____

Comments (mention siblings to be reunified)

designed to teach the procedure can add to the confusion—some define goals as the most general of the plans, others equate goals with mission statements, and still others confuse the workers' efforts with the clients' needs [Anderson 1989].

Despite training and the availability of written guidelines, staff members may vary widely in their ability to articulate goals. Some workers may write goals that are action-oriented, rather than ones that describe new situations for the client. Consensus may not exist on the degree of specificity that differentiates a goal from a plan. Moreover, in some cases goals may correctly describe an improved family situation but their relationship to reunification may not be clear. A client's goal, for example, might be to become self-supporting, but having a job might not result in managing money well enough to achieve reunification.

To assist workers in the goal-setting process—in effect, to come to agreement on the proper scope for goals in relation to plans—the authors examined all the early goals and plans in the family reunification project being presented in this chapter. These goals and plans fell into fairly clear categories, addressing financial stability, child care, substance abuse treatment, and educational and vocational attainment. These categories were congruent with factors in the Family Risk Scales [Magura et al. 1987], already used in the project to assess families at intake, reunification, and case closing.

From this examinations, a list of representative goals was created, amalgamating the workers' experience and the Family Risk Scale factors (see figure 6). Workers and family members can select a pertinent goal from the list or use one as a guide or model. This procedure, used in other goal-oriented programs [McCroskey and Nelson 1989], can smooth out variations in specificity of goals and plans, and help to create goals that are germane to the reunification effort.

Role of Supervisor

The supervisor's importance in formulating, documenting, and monitoring goals and service delivery plans cannot be overestimated. Although an evaluation component within a program can help with monitoring and assuring consistency, it does not replace the supervisor. Service quality and oversight are managed by monitoring responsibility. For example, the case plan sets forth a clear overview of expected action for each case, indicates who is responsible for the action, and often provides a timeline. The supervisor can use the case plan to determine whether appropriate planning is taking place.

Supervisors also can use the Monthly Goal and Plan Rating form (figure 4) as a summary of progress and a basis for case conferences with workers and families. The goal concentration minimizes the sometimes rambling nature of presentations based on narrative recordings.

FIGURE 6–REPRESENTATIVE GOALS

The (parents) (family):

1. Will have and keep a clean, safe home, without physical dangers.

2. Will provide a home with space, furnishings, appliances, utilities, and so forth, adequate for essential household functions and meeting the personal needs of family members.

3. Will have enough money to pay for the basic needs of life, including housing, clothing, food, and utilities, and will manage their money carefully.

4. Will keep themselves and their children healthy by eating healthy, balanced meals and by getting medical and dental care when needed.

5. Will be close to other people they can talk to and get some help from when they need it.

6. Will get and use community services.

7. Will have a good relationship, free of abuse, with other adults in the home.

8. Will each feel that he or she is a good person and deserves to be treated well.

9. Will not abuse drugs or alcohol.

10. Will give their children the affection and attention that they need.

11. Will make sure that their children are safe from harm at all times, and that they are not left alone or left with someone who is not able to take care of them.

12. Will set limits and teach their children right from wrong without hurting them physically or with words.

13. Will have a good understanding of their children's needs.

14. Will make sure their children attend school regularly.

Number of Goals

As discussed elsewhere by Fein and Staff [1991], various issues arise in goal-oriented reunification services that are not readily dealt with by extra effort or training. In particular, how many goals should be set at the beginning of service? Some workers believe that it is most respectful of families if family members know from the beginning of service all they will need to do to have their families reunited. These workers advocate starting with as complete a list of goals as is necessary to effect reunification, with the understanding that other goals can be added if the situation changes during the course of the case. They reason that beginning with only a few goals and then adding others as early successes occur makes families feel they will never achieve the ultimate reunification.

Other workers fear that a complete list of goals will dishearten a family, that a few goals will lead to early successes, and that the original goals can easily be amended because the family will have had that understanding from the beginning. Some writers suggest that developing a complete list of goals is important; clients then rank goals and the most pressing receive attention first [Pomerantz et al. 1990].

No evidence documents that one method is superior to the others. Examination of various questions about goal-setting as a client motivator is sorely needed, particularly for neglectful families [Videka-Sherman 1988].

Conclusion

The project described in this chapter is part of a small, financially healthy, voluntary agency that can afford the small caseloads, specialized programs, and individualization of clients good case management and effective casework for reunification require. How well would the method apply to large, publicly funded reunification services in public agencies? If a public agency has the resources, it can implement a goal-oriented intensive service. Alternatively, it can contract for such services from voluntary agencies. The principles of goal orientation and careful and systematic documentation, however, can be used to support any agency's reunification efforts.

References

Anderson, S.C. "Goal Setting in Social Work Practice." Presented at the 1989 Annual Meeting of the Profession, National Association of Social Workers, San Francisco, CA, October 1989.

Fanshel, D.; Finch, S.J.; and Grundy, J.F. "Foster Children in Life-Course Perspective: The Casey Family Program Experience." *CHILD WELFARE* LXVIII, 5 (September–October 1989): 467–478.

Fein, E.; Maluccio, A.N.; Hamilton, V.J.; and Ward, D. "After Foster Care: Outcomes of Permanency Planning." *CHILD WELFARE* LXII, 6 (November–December 1983): 485–558.

Fein, E., and Staff, I. (1991). "Implementing Reunification Services." *Families in Society* 72, 6 (June 1991): 335–343.

Garwick, G., and Lampman, S. "Typical Problems Bring Patients to a Mental Health Clinic." *Community Mental Health Journal* 8, 4 (April 1972): 271–280.

Jones, M., and Biesecker, J. *Goal Planning in Children and Youth Services.* Washington, DC: U.S. Department of Health and Human Services. DHHS Publication # OHDS–81–30295, 1980.

Klier, J.; Fein, E.; and Genero, C. "Are Written or Verbal Contracts More Effective in Family Therapy?" *Social Work* 29, 3 (May-June 1984): 298–299.

Lloyd, J.C., and Bryce, M.E. *Placement Prevention and Family Reunification: A Handbook for the Family-Centered Service Practitioner.* Iowa City, IA: The University of Iowa National Resource Center on Family Based Services, 1985.

Magura, S.; Moses, B.S.; and Jones, M.A. *Assessing Risk and Measuring Change in Families.* Washington, DC: The Child Welfare League of America, 1987.

Maluccio, A.N.; Fein, E.; and Olmstead, K. *Permanency Planning for Children: Concepts and Methods.* London and New York: Routledge, Chapman and Hall, 1986.

Maluccio, A.N.; Krieger, R.; and Pine, B.A. "Preserving Families Through Reunification." In *Intensive Family Preservation Services: An Instructional Sourcebook*, edited by E.M. Tracy, D.A. Haapala, J. Kinney, and P.J. Pecora. Cleveland, OH: Mandel School of Applied Social Sciences, Case Western Reserve University, 1991, 215–235.

Mann, J. *Time-Limited Psychotherapy.* Cambridge, MA: Harvard University Press, 1973.

McCroskey, J., and Nelson, J. "Practice-Based Research in the Family Support Program: The Family Connection Project Example." *CHILD WELFARE* LXVIII, 6 (November–December 1989): 573–587.

Miller, K.; Fein, E.; Howe, G.; Claudio, C.; and Bishop, G. "Time-Limited, Goal-Focused Parent Aide Services." *Social Casework* 65, 8 (October 1984): 472–477.

Nelson, D. "Recognizing and Realizing the Potential of Family Preservation." In *Reaching High-Risk Families: Intensive Family Preservation in Human Services*, edited by J.K. Whittaker, J. Kinney, E.M. Tracy, and C. Booth. Hawthorne, NY: Aldine de Gruyter, 1990, 13–30.

Pomerantz, P.; Pomerantz, D.J.; and Colca, L.A. "A Case Study: Service Delivery and Parents with Disabilities." *CHILD WELFARE* LXIX, 1 (January–February 1990): 65–73.

Reid, W.J., and Epstein, L. *Task-Oriented Casework*. New York: Columbia University Press, 1972.

Tatara, T. "Characteristics of Children in Foster Care." *Division of Child, Youth, and Family Services Newsletter* (American Psychological Association) 12 , 3 (Summer 1989): 16–17.

Tracy, E.M.; Haapala, D.A.; Kinney, J.; and Pecora, P.J., eds. *Intensive Family Preservation Services: An Instructional Sourcebook*. Cleveland, OH: Mandel School of Applied Social Sciences, Case Western Reserve University, 1991.

Turner, J. "Reuniting Children in Foster Care with Their Biological Families." *Social Work* 29, 6 (November/December 1984): 501–505.

Videka-Sherman, L. "Intervention for Child Neglect: The Empirical Knowledge Base." Presented at the National Center on Child Abuse and Neglect Research Symposium on Child Neglect, Washington, DC, 1989.

Whittaker, J.K.; Kinney, J.; Tracy, E.M.; and Booth, C., eds. *Reaching High-Risk Families: Intensive Family Preservation in Human Services*. Hawthorne, NY: Aldine de Gruyter, 1990.

6

FAMILY REUNIFICATION PRACTICE IN
RESIDENTIAL TREATMENT FOR CHILDREN

Paul Carlo

Developing a family reunification program in a residential treatment center requires a competency-based model of practice. Such a model assumes that the parents of children in care have strengths that, with help, they can build upon to the point where they can resume care of their children. This chapter discusses strategies and tactics for implementing an effective parent involvement program and suggests its didactic and experiential components. The experiential is emphasized, however, in the context of planned change and the needs of children, parents, staff members, and agency administrators.

Toward a Competency-Based Model of Reunification Practice

In the late nineteenth century, services for families and services for children emerged as separate fields of social work practice. The Children's Aid Societies were essentially orphanages that housed not only orphaned or abandoned children, but also those being "rescued" from "bad"—and therefore immoral—parents. A pejorative, punitive attitude was established toward parents who were unable to provide an adequate, nurturing home for their children. Even today, this attitude sometimes prevails, as the temporary caregivers of these children may fall into the role of "good parents" and find themselves viewing the children's own families as fundamentally inadequate.

The severely disturbed children in out-of-home care, who typically require residential treatment because they have failed in family foster care placements, have often been separated from their families for extended periods. Such long separations, coupled with the severe emotional/behavioral problems these children may have, can frustrate the possibilities of reuniting them with their families. To counter this separation, agencies must incorporate parents as true partners in the helping process [Maluccio and Sinanoglu 1981].

Professionals in tune with the ecological perspective guiding this volume see clients as inherently capable of helping themselves once their capacity to interact with the environment has been improved. They see adaptation and competence as strongly affected by the goodness of fit between personal abilities and environmental supports and demands. They view clients as resources rather than as carriers of pathology, as human beings with potential and with assets that can be mobilized in their own behalf [Maluccio 1981].

What Do Parents Need?

The serious problems of these parents have multifarious sources, but close attention must be given to parent education and socialization. To improve their child-management skills, achieve a sense of adequacy and competence, and increase their commitment and willingness to resume full-time child-rearing responsibilities, parents must receive both didactic and experiential structured learning opportunities. Didactic learning opportunities (the passing on of information) are provided through parent education/support groups. Experiential learning opportunities are provided in programs that invite, encourage, and help parents to participate with their youngsters in placement (e.g., in birthday parties, field trips, exercise classes, holiday celebrations, meal preparations, conferences with houseparents and school personnel) and provide opportunities to observe how houseparents or child care workers manage children.

Didactic learning is more effective if accompanied by experiential opportunities—chances to experience changes in feelings and attitudes by becoming involved in planned doing [Towle 1954]. A more positive approach to learning can result when the learner understands connections between organized knowledge and personal experience [Knox 1978]. Knowles [1972] has written extensively on the differences between the teaching of children (pedagogy) and the art and science of helping adults to learn (androgogy). He views the transmittal techniques of traditional teaching, wherein the teacher or socializing agent is a leader and the learners are dependent recipients of lectures, audiovisual presentations, and assigned readings, as typical of the subject-centered pedagogic approach. Androgogy, in contrast, is problem-centered learning that is tied to experience, wherein the teacher is a facilitator who helps to provide and analyze the experience through action-learning techniques.

Model for Family Reunification Practice

The model suggested here for family reunification practice in residential treatment has both of the components indicated above: it offers a parent education/support group for the parents of youngsters in residential treatment, and it weaves the parents into the everyday life of the residential milieu, affording them a variety of possibilities for being together with their children.

The goals of this treatment model are neither to "cure" or "fix" the troubled child, nor to "cure" or "fix" the troubled family, but to achieve family reunification in a safe environment where the child will not be reabused or allowed to act out. The approach centers on helping parents to learn the behaviors, emotional responses, skills, and values they need to fulfill their parental roles more successfully than in the past, and therefore, to gain more satisfaction from those roles. As parents experience and understand the daily realities of living with children, they develop more realistic expectations about their children's performance than they previously held. Frequent interactions with their child, in both fun activities and more demanding routines such as homework or household chores, allow the parents to gain increased comfort and confidence in their ability to rejoin with their child in a mutually helpful family unit.

Parent Education/Support Group

The parent education/support group provides a basic understanding of children's behavior and introduces parents to an array of behavior-shaping and relationship-building techniques employed by the agency. In developing this part of the program for a particular agency, the author drew upon the literature [Ginott 1965; Gordon 1970; Dinkmeyer and McKay 1976] as well as knowledge gained from the experiences of parents and other agency staff members.

Topics for discussion in parent education/support groups should include, but not be limited to, self-awareness, values clarification, parents' and children's rights, negative aspects of guilt over causation, purposes and goals of both positive and negative behavior, behavior management techniques, building feelings of self-confidence and self-worth, differences between punishment and discipline, the application of natural and logical consequences, and aspects of daily routines for living with children. Specific topics may also arise from within the group, such as how to handle allowances, sex play, and sibling rivalry. At the end of the last meeting, parents should be encouraged to exchange phone numbers and to create an ongoing support network.

The format and conduct of the group are extremely important. Arnold et al. [1978] characterize parent education groups as supportive but caution that such groups are not group therapy. They see the distinction as a hazy one, with many overlapping areas, including practical aspects of dealing with children and exploration of parents' feelings about their children, each other, themselves, their own parents, and how these feelings affect their relationships. Organizing the group in a time-limited, well-structured manner and maintaining focus on the agenda topics help to keep the distinction clear.

A decision will have to be made about the number of sessions and the number of weeks the group will last. Timing will vary according to the needs and goals of each agency. In the setting described here,* a structured 10- to 12-week course, meeting one and one-half hours per week, was offered.

In the pregroup phase, an agency worker who knows the parents contacted them by phone or in person to inform them of the group's availability and its purpose. Once they agreed to come to the first session, a welcoming follow-up letter with exact date, time, and location of the group was sent to the parents by the coleaders of the group.

The group is led by a social worker experienced in group dynamics and a child care worker experienced in child behavior management. Preferably, one leader should be male and one female. Having two leaders gives the participants an opportunity to relate well to at least one group leader and gives them an opportunity to see group leaders role-play and model issues such as resolution of differences. It also gives each leader another person to confer with before and after each session.

This group method of learning effective behavior management techniques encourages the parents to share their experiences and feelings and to receive support and encouragement from others in a forum that allows them to ventilate anger, frustration, disappointment, fears, and guilt, and to share joys, successes, accomplishments, and growth. For suggestions on designing and conducting a parent education/support group, readers are referred to the notes for group leaders in Appendix A (page 111) and the annotated bibliography on parent education in Appendix B (page 116).

Parental Involvement in Residential Treatment

Finkelstein [1974] links parental involvement to shorter stays for children in residential care. She offers a prescription in which both the child and family

---

* Five Acres Boys' and Girls' Aid Society of Los Angeles County, located in Altadena, CA, is a private, nonprofit multiservice agency for neglected and abused children (ages 2 to 18) and their families. The setting for the parent involvement program described in this chapter is the agency's residential treatment center, which serves severely emotionally disturbed children ages 4 to 13.

hear and see at intake that they are participating members of the team, that they have responsibilities, and that they are important to the decision-making process. She sees frequent parental participation in the cottage milieu, and the opportunity for parents to observe that adults and children can have fun together, as essential elements in a program aimed at reuniting placed children with their parents.

Krona [1980] advocates involving parents from intake all the way through the treatment process, citing the need for frequent contact between staff members and parents, discussion of all major disciplinary actions, frequent home visits and, perhaps most important, weekly family counseling and parent education sessions on behavior management as key elements for a successful outcome. He states, "Child care programs without parental involvement are unlikely to effect lasting change."

Jenkins [1981] discusses the concept of "filial deprivation" and advises practitioners in residential settings to be aware of the sadness, worry, and anger that parents feel about their child, themselves, the worker, the agency, or society in general, when they find themselves unavoidably separated from their troubled child. She recommends frequent parental visits and work with parents to enhance their capability to provide for their child.

Some youngsters who go into out-of-home placement come from adoptive homes. It is important to note that not all children who enter residential placement from their adoptive homes represent disrupted adoptions. The interruption of an adoption may signify a temporary critical juncture in the life of that family that can be ameliorated or resolved if workers provide the same reunification services to the adoptive family and child as they would to those who are biologically related.

For those children who have no available biological relatives and who come to residential treatment centers after foster and/or adoptive placements have failed, workers can try to bring in former caregivers to help both worker and child understand what went wrong in previous settings and how to begin planning for future living that will not repeat the errors of the past. The plan should take into account both intrapsychic and environmental elements in order to find optimal matches for these multiple-placement youngsters. Although these youngsters may have no previous caregivers with whom they can be reunified, they may be able to move on to permanent homes by joining new caregivers who start out as "special friends." These caregivers gain the comfort level and skills they need by participating in the parent involvement program before taking the child home to live. At the same time, as indicated in chapter 1, it is important to consider the optimal level of reconnection with the child's own family in each case. Occasional contact between parents and child may be possible even when reunification is not.

Once the decision to have an on-campus parent participation program has been reached, the details of implementation are relatively straightforward. Child care personnel must first be trained to welcome parents as partners in the helping process and to facilitate and oversee parental involvement. Frequent meetings should be held with the child care staff to discuss successes and disappointments and to further the implementation of the program.

Initially, parents may be invited to come in and meet the child care staff at a prearranged time, and observe some relaxed moments of cottage life, such as weekend free-play time. As comfort and rapport are established, parents can be invited to come into the cottage for progressively more structured activities in which they can both observe and begin to participate in a fuller parenting role with their child. The activities may include facilitating and partially overseeing the organization of a special event or everyday routine functions such as chore completion, dressing, and grooming tasks.

The variety of experiences in which a parent will participate depends upon the particulars of the residential program, the needs of the parent, and the creative energy of the staff. In general, parents will need help in learning how to get through an average day with their child. At times, parents also must learn how to use free time at home to play and have fun with their child.

Child care staff members are key elements in parental involvement programs because they deliver the bulk of the services. They are trained in behavior management and function more than other staff members as substitute parents. It is they who are most qualified to provide both the role modeling and the opportunity for parents to be monitored while they try to employ behavior-shaping interventions learned in parent education classes. Many parents have commented that they find it easier to relate to the child care staff than to social workers, whom they associate with the people who took their children away from them.

The Model in Practice

The following six case examples from our residential setting bring the theory to life. Two families received didactic intervention alone, two participated only in the experiential activities, and two received a combination of both programs. At three-year follow-up, none had experienced a disruption of their reunification.

Didactic Intervention

Case Example One: Mr. and Mrs. Williams had been married for 15 years and had been legally separated twice. They reported frequent loud arguments about the behavior of their four children, with each parent expecting the other to solve the problem. The two oldest boys, 11 and 13, had been removed from home after being arrested for vandalism, truancy, and petty theft. They were referred to residential treatment after a series of family foster care placements over a two-year period. Both boys were of average intelligence and in good health. The older boy, Joey, was diagnosed as having a conduct disorder and unsocialized-aggressive with schizoid features; the younger, Charles, as having a conduct disorder and unsocialized aggressive with borderline features.

Mr. and Mrs. Williams were reluctant to come into the agency and ashamed of having "lost" their children. They were unwilling to participate in cottage programming, but after some prompting they agreed to participate in the parent education group. This proved to be an excellent choice, since the family was quite isolated from the community and the parents reported no friends or social contacts. The parents responded enthusiastically to the group experience and became animated reporters of their efforts to use the suggested interventions on their weekend home visits with their sons. Joey and Charles responded competitively to their parents' involvement, vying with each other in welcoming their participation, wanting to see the material their parents were receiving, and making their own behavior modification charts for use at home based on the ones created for them in the residential cottages.

After four months in residence the boys' behavior on home visits began to improve significantly. Their parents chose to participate in a second parent education group at the agency and asked permission to have two of their neighbors attend the meetings with them. Since these neighbors were among those whose property had been vandalized by the two boys, the agency agreed to have them attend.

Mr. and Mrs. Williams felt that the social aspect of the parent group was more helpful to them than any other part of the program. Once they stopped being embarrassed about their inability to control their children, they were able to talk about it openly with other parents. The neighbors who attended the group developed an investment in the Williams' success, and began to function like supportive extended family members. The parents started accepting and incorporating new intervention skills with their sons.

It should be noted that in-home visits are a planned part of the program and are intended to reestablish family contacts in the home. Meetings with agency staff members following home visits reveal ways in which the family and child(ren) have changed since separation, and help the workers to assess what level of reconnection is most appropriate and optimal.

After 15 months the family was reunited and referred to an in-home services program to get some of the experiential learning they had previously been unable to accept. The Five Acres Home-Based services program seeks to prevent or minimize the trauma of parent-child separation by delivering immediate and direct support services to families in their own homes. Treatment teams help the family to identify and carry out actions to improve its situation and maintain a stable, nurturing environment.

Case Example Two: Mrs. Franco had a long history of emotional problems and was receiving disability payments following psychiatric hospitalization for a serious suicide attempt. She had married once, had two daughters, Barbara and Mary, and was now divorced. Her children had been removed from her care several times, but were always returned to her after a few months in each foster home. Mrs. Franco's attributed her suicide attempt, which followed the girls' last return home, to her inability to cope with their behavior. The girls, depressed and angry, were unmanageable in family foster care and were referred to residential treatment. They were both diagnosed as having dysthymic disorder with anxious mood. Both were of above average intelligence. They had not seen their mother for five months and longed to be with her, but they knew the court had ruled for permanency planning this time, and also knew that their mother was not capable of providing care for them.

Mrs. Franco stayed at home, suffering from depression, refusing to take her medication, drinking wine, and mourning the loss of her children. The agency social worker visited her at home and suggested that reunification could mean good contact and eventually visits, even though it would not mean living together in the foreseeable future. Encouraged, Mrs. Franco agreed to participate in the parent education group if the agency would provide transportation, which it did. The parent education group was selected because Mrs. Franco was too emotionally distraught to be in the cottage with many noisy children, and too suspicious and self-conscious to interact with her daughters in front of the child care workers.

Mrs. Franco attended the group but did not participate verbally the first four weeks. Then another participant, who lived near Mrs. Franco, offered to drive her home after groups. To everyone's surprise she accepted the ride. By week six she began riding both ways with her new acquaintance, and spoke in the group about her experiences in trying to manage her children. Two-hour monitored on-grounds visits for the family were begun in the main dining room. The girls' depression lifted, and their behavior improved dramatically. After six months they were transferred to a group home where they continued to visit one day a week with their mother and were doing well in school. Mrs. Franco continued to receive disability payments but stopped her alcohol abuse and participated in day treatment at an outpatient psychiatric clinic close to her home, where her depression and former isolation and alcoholism were treated.

This is a case example in which intervention helped the family and the staff to decide that full return home was not a desirable outcome. Still, based on an assessment of the intensity of attachment and connectedness in this family, an appropriate level of reconnection was accomplished and solidified, and regularly scheduled time together for mother and children became a part of their weekly routine.

The Experiential Component

Case Example Three: Mr. and Mrs. Greene had been married for 12 years. They had one child, a 10-year-old boy they had adopted as an infant. Sammy was neurologically impaired; had visual and motor perceptual deficits, low-average intelligence, and a poor memory; and was easily confused. His tantrums and general out-of-control behavior brought about a parental request for him to be placed in out-of-home care. The Greenes lived in a rural county, 400 miles away from the residential treatment center that accepted the referral. Sammy's diagnostic status was attention deficit disorder, generalized anxiety disorder, and pervasive developmental disorder.

The Greenes could visit only once a month because they lived so far away. The agency encouraged them to participate in an experiential learning program and arranged housing for them one weekend each month in an apartment on the campus grounds. They arrived on a Friday night, spent most of Saturday and half of Sunday participating in activities with their son in his cottage, and went home on Sunday evening. They were given printed material about behavior management to take home and study, and spent their time on campus assigned to a child care worker who coached them and encouraged them to work with and be with their son in new, successful interactions.

The first few visits ended in frustration for staff members and parents. Typically, Sammy would have a tantrum just before the visit was to begin. The staff would suggest that the parents first talk to Sammy about this and then begin their playtime together. Instead, the Greenes would arrive at the cottage with toys and gifts they had brought for Sammy and immediately hand them to him. After several such experiences, the staff was able to help the parents learn to offer direction and supervision when the child needed it, and later to offer rewards and special treats. After four months in the program, the Greenes were ready to take Sammy home for holiday visits. Ten months later they were reunited.

Case Example Four: Mr. Lopez and his second wife had been married for six months and were expecting their first child when he obtained custody of his 10-year-old son, Travis, from a previous marriage. Two months after the new baby (a healthy boy) was born, Travis began to act out in a bizarre and uncontrollable manner. He was assaultive, defiant, and destructive. He was placed in a psychiatric hospital for four months and then referred to residential treatment. Travis was assessed to be of dull normal intelligence with no special learning disabilities. His diagnosis was conduct disorder, undersocialized-aggressive.

Although Mr. Lopez and his wife were both English-speaking, they were functionally illiterate and concerned about being exposed as such. They refused to attend a parent education group but agreed to participate in experiential learning opportunities. Their first visit to the cottage ended abruptly. Upon entering the unit they observed Travis sitting in a group listening to a story being read by the child care worker; after 10 minutes Mr. and Mrs. Lopez silently got up and left. They later reported feeling tearful and overwhelmed by a sense of failure because they had never before seen the boy sit still and listen to someone for as long as 10 minutes. They interpreted his cooperation in the cottage as a statement about their own parental inadequacy.

The next two visits were arranged around meals in the campus main dining room. Following the meals Travis would demand that his parents take him home; when they refused he threw a tantrum, begged, screamed, flung himself on the ground, and tore up his clothing. The parents reported feeling guilty and embarrassed that Travis behaved well for the child care worker but was out of control with them. In a meeting with the parents the following week, the social worker was able to interpret the boy's behavior as his way of trying to gain control over the adults in his life. The parents understood and agreed to try one more time. Although each visit held the potential for another setback for them, they persevered. After four more visits their mood began to shift and instead of acting overwhelmed and helpless, they began imitating the child care worker's behavior with their son. Once progress began, it continued at a remarkable pace. Six months later the family was reunited.

The Didactic Intervention and Experiential Learning Components in Combination

Case Example Five: Miss James was a single mother. Her nine-year-old son, Anthony, a bright child, entered residential treatment from four months in a psychiatric hospital following a suicide attempt: he had tried to hang himself from the bedpost with his belt. He had been assaultive to his mother and school teacher, and had been suspended for making repeated sexual advances toward classmates. His multiple diagnosis was dysthymic disorder, overanxious disorder of childhood, and adjustment disorder with depressed mood. He was hypervigilant and conflicted about dependence/independence. In the residential treatment center he displayed no self-destructive behavior, but was quite combative, assaultive, and sexualized with staff members and peers.

Miss James, a well-educated professional, was a star pupil in the parent education class. She studied and memorized the material and was able to give sound advice to the other parents, but her interactions with Anthony did not improve. He continued to be assaultive toward her. When she began the experiential component, staff members were dismayed by her accusations about their care of her son; she said his hair and grooming were being neglected, his diet was not well-balanced, his activities were too restricted, and his school work was beneath his ability.

Following his mother's cottage visits, Anthony's sexualized behavior, generally very strong, became almost unbearably so. He giggled at ordinary conversations and interpreted them all as sexual in nature; he made overt sexual gestures toward peers and staff members; he stripped off his clothing, danced around naked, and refused to get dressed. All observations in family therapy sessions failed to detect any sexualized behavior between Miss James and her son, and no history of molestation was available.

On the mother's third cottage visit, however, the child care staff observed the following interaction between Miss James and another child resident. As Miss James entered the cottage, a 10-year-old boy yelled out to her, "Hey, foxy mama!" The staff's impression was that Miss James actually took the remark as a compliment; she brushed her hair to one side, blinked, and said, "Why, thank you." Further observation revealed that her behavior with the other youngsters was indeed quite sexualized. She spoke and used flirtatious mannerisms with them as though they were adult peers.

Feedback to the family therapist enabled him to use these examples to help Miss James be aware of her unconscious behaviors and to explore the possibility that her public display of sexualized mannerisms and responses to children could be a source of her son's sexual anxiety. Although her first response was shock, Miss James soon became an open and cooperative participant. She agreed to enter therapy to explore her desire for adult companionship. She monitored and changed her way of interacting and responding to sexual comments from the children. Her son's assaultiveness toward her diminished over a two-month period, and finally stopped altogether. His sexualized behavior in the cottage and at school also dropped to within what were considered normal limits. After 11 months in placement, Anthony was reunited with his mother.

Case Example Six: The two Mrs. Omnis, one a grandmother, one an aunt, had been taking care of eight-year-old Roland since his parents died in an auto accident when he was four. They were both affectionate and lenient toward him, letting rule infractions and other misconduct go on uninterrupted until "the last straw"; then they reacted with harsh and extreme disciplinary measures such as hitting him with a belt, locking him in a closet, and withholding food. On two different occasions, school personnel observed bruise marks on Roland from being hit with a belt; the protective services agency investigated and twice placed him in foster care. Each time he acted out severely in the foster homes, was remanded to the county shelter care facility for several months, and was then returned home. When the school reported a third abuse incident, Roland was placed in a group home. After extremely destructive behavior there he was sent to the county psychiatric hospital, where he spent six months before being discharged to residential treatment. His diagnostic status at admission was conduct disorder, socialized-aggressive, and borderline personality disorder.

The aunt and grandmother were enrolled in the treatment center's parent education and experiential learning programs. In the didactic group they argued about which of them was the more competent caregiver. Group leaders came to agreement about intervention strategies and presented a united front. In the experiential program aunt and grandmother argued with each other during the first three visits, and each time were asked to end the session and return the following week to try again.

During the fourth on-grounds visit the arguing ceased, and both aunt and grandmother began to participate in the program. They tried to intervene early and appropriately when Roland's behavior was unacceptable, but needed help to avoid being overly strict. For example, when Roland did not put his fork down between bites but instead kept stuffing food into his already full mouth, his aunt decreed, "Two hours sit time!" The child care workers at last had material to work with. They now could target specific interactions and help the grandmother and aunt to modify their approach so that it would be more consistent and fair.

Another example: As Roland was leaving to go on his first home visit, the child care worker checked his bags and found he had stolen several things from other residents. The worker told the grandmother to talk to Roland about this behavior and to remind him that he would be given restriction time upon return to the cottage after the visit. As they walked to the car the boy began crying and complaining about how unfair the program was. His grandmother then telephoned the worker to say, "I think he has paid enough for this already, he is really sorry and shouldn't have a restriction when he returns." The worker was able to use this reaction to help her understand the importance of following through with a reasonable consequence even when the child cries and says he is sorry. Roland rejoined his aunt and grandmother after 12 months in the program.

Implementation Strategies

In an established residential treatment center, implementation of a broad conceptual model of parental involvement, such as the one described above, is usually met by a mixed response from agency administrators, staff members, children, and families.

Opening up the campus to parents introduces an element of risk and challenges to the routines of the staff and the stability of existing programs. For example, having parents and children eat dinner in the staff dining room means that the kitchen staff will be interacting regularly with parents in unfamiliar ways. Parents may begin to comment on the quality, quantity, preparation, and serving of food. Heavier demands for tactful interactions will be made upon these staff members as well as on switchboard and reception personnel.

Having extra people around is frequently inconvenient. The front door may customarily be closed at five o'clock, for example, but with parents coming by during the evening hours, staff members sometimes will have to interrupt what they are doing to answer the doorbell.

Being constantly on display is exhausting, at least at the beginning when the staff feels pressure to perform rather than just go on about their daily routines. A period of desensitization is needed until everyone becomes relatively comfortable with parents coming and going at various times of the day and evening.

Activity therapists, who are accustomed to conducting their groupwork in an organized, preplanned, and orderly fashion, may find that the presence of parent-clients creates new dynamics requiring additional management skills, the ability to share control, and more flexibility about group goals; like any demand for change, this is sometimes uncomfortable.

Social workers, who previously were almost solely in charge of the messages parents received about the program and their child, may find, as positive transferences and relationships develop between parents and other staff members, that information is shared, ideas are suggested, and plans of action are developed at a pace and in a direction that are not always in concert with the original long-term plan. Case management becomes more pragmatic in some instances—that is, the best plan is the plan that is realistic and will work, even if it does not provide a close approximation of the ideal therapeutic outcome. The sharing of control becomes a delicate matter. Empowerment of parents may sometimes feel like disempowerment of the staff.

Sensitivity to all of these issues and adequate preparation to deal with them can substantially reduce the amount of resistance they might otherwise elicit. Although a comprehensive theory that covers both family system and organizational system resistance to change does not yet appear to be available, the working definition suggested by Anderson and Stewart [1983: 24] seems most appropriate to our purpose:

Resistance can be defined as all those behaviors in the therapeutic system which interact to prevent the therapeutic system from achieving the family's goals for therapy. The therapeutic system includes family members, the therapist, and the context in which the therapy takes place, that is, the agency or institution in which it occurs.

Brager and Holloway [1978] describe four phases of planned organizational change relevant to the worker who is trying to transform the service delivery of a residential treatment center to include an active parental involvement program: preinitiation, initiation, implementation, and institutionalization. Throughout their work they emphasize the need for the change-agent to gain the commitment of decision-makers as well as the continuing support of the workers who will actually be carrying out the change. In residential treatment, this team of persons will include parents, in addition to child care, social work, administrative, reception, kitchen, and maintenance staff members.

The following tactical interventions have been developed to put into operation an expanded model of parent education and involvement, drawing on these readings and on practice wisdom gained from field experimentation.

Administration

Funding is an important issue. Since no extra reimbursement will be paid to the agency by the public child welfare agency or other placement agents for this new and expanded model of working with parents, the agency will probably not want to pay extra fees to the staff for time or supplies used in conducting the program.

The responsibility of the change-agent is to develop a plan for reorganizing service delivery that will redistribute existing service resources without adding expenditures. Redistributing and rearranging, as opposed to adding and expanding, are key concepts here, at least in the short run.

Another question may center on utilization of the staff. Where will the time come from to perform the extra tasks of working with parents beyond delivery of traditional family therapy sessions? If time is found for new tasks, what current services will have to be sacrificed to accommodate the increased workload? Further, if no current services will have to be sacrificed, does this mean that agency staff time is currently being underutilized, and what are the implications of this for middle management?

A written plan of operation must demonstrate that, although additional staff time will be required, a plan for allocation of that time can be reasonably effected and its endorsement will be of professional benefit to the agency. From experience, the author found that an average of one hour per week per person will be devoted to providing the expanded model of parental education and involvement (including time for initial and continuing training). This time will have to be arranged by middle management and absorbed by the agency in terms of extra energy invested by the participating employees and some rearrangement of their usual tasks to accommodate the new responsibilities. Some of these tasks, such as doing the laundry and making up order lists of cottage staples, paper products, and cleaning supplies, can be done by the night-awake staff members, who will not be interacting with parents. Other tasks, such as decorating the cottage and bulletin boards for birthday parties, holidays, and seasonal changes, can be handled as group activities for the staff and done during meetings when environmental group living issues are being discussed. Again, on the basis of experience, it can be reasonably argued that although staff members who are involved in the project will have less time to spend with individual children, this loss of individual attention will be compensated for by the presence of parents who spend time in various activities both with their own children and with other youngsters.

Staff

Staff members in residential treatment often serve as surrogate parents to their child clients, modeling healthy adult interactions and providing the nurturance and support that children in care must have in order to benefit from treatment efforts. Many of these staff members may view parents as one more "child" to take care of, to monitor, to train, and to set limits for. Supervisors may wonder where they will find the time to schedule dual coverage when parents are on-grounds and extra management problems are to be expected with those children who do not have parents coming to visit. Child care workers may express fear that their control over the unit will be eroded by the presence of parents, that their work will be interfered with, and that their previous training has not prepared them for dealing with parents who have special needs of their own.

To deal with these legitimate questions, agencies must embark on a continuing program of both formal (e.g., staff meetings) and informal (e.g., lunchtime) intensive in-service education and preparation of all participating staff members. Sustained efforts must be made to help staff members understand the rationale and impetus for the new program, see how their own professional status will be enhanced through participation, and become familiar with and appreciate the view that parents must be true partners in the helping process. Staff members' opinions must be solicited and included at both the planning and implementation stages.

Children

When told that parents have been scheduled to come into the residential cottages to participate in birthday parties, meal preparation, leisure-time activities, and so on, some of the children may object, become oppositional, or develop somatic complaints. Others will be silent beforehand but defiant and rejecting when their parents arrive. Some may be passively resistant and ignore their visiting parents, or devalue any gifts they bring or any attempts the parents make to get deeply involved with staff members or other residents.

Some children genuinely fear for their safety because of past experiences at home. Others do not want their parents coming into the cottage to "poke around" and see firsthand how their child behaves under the supervision of other adult caregivers. It is difficult for children to sustain their rivalrous splitting of parents and caregivers (which often duplicates experience at home before placement) when parents and child care workers are face to face and united in their efforts to provide adequate parenting. It is not easy for children to convince parents on home visits that doing chores is unnecessary when the parents come into the cottage and see their children make a bed, set a table, unload a dishwasher, and such.

Once staff members understand what triggers a child's resistive behavior, it becomes easier to offer supportive interpretation and reassurance to relieve fear and anxiety. When children are able to see that the occasional presence of parents does not disrupt the orderly boundaries and rules for the safety and conduct of all residents, their anxiety is reduced to a level more tolerable for them and their resistance is considerably diminished.

Parents

Many parents have reason to mistrust the motives of helping agents, a mistrust that is exacerbated when a program change requires their additional presence and participation. The placement of children in residential treatment centers is not voluntary; the children have come under the custody of the court because of allegations that their parents were abusive and/or neglectful. Though many parents will want to engage in this new program to prepare themselves to parent their children more successfully, some will be suspicious that their performance will be reported to court authorities. Others may be more trusting of agency motives but still find it hard to believe that staff members can view them as capable, competent individuals who truly care about their children. Many will feel shy and rather embarrassed when they are in the presence of the child care staff or other parents in situations where they fear their weaknesses might be exposed.

As attendance at campus functions grows, some parents may express resentment that staff members are more successful in managing their children than they themselves had been when the children were at home. Somatic distress, night-blindness, car trouble, unexpected house guests, or sudden spurts of mandatory overtime work may be among the excuses that have to be dealt with and overcome. Other parents may attend without extra encouragement, but be openly self-critical, stating that they cannot compete with the agency now that their children have experienced its comfortable furnishings, sports equipment, swimming pool, and so forth. A few may appear to participate comfortably yet try to interact continually with other children rather than work with and, if necessary, confront their own.

To help parents feel comfortable and relaxed, their first meeting with the staff should be planned in a neutral area such as the campus library or main dining room. Initial on-grounds visits should be limited to a short period of time (one-half to one hour) to observe a leisure-time and minimally stressful event such as Saturday morning playground activity. The staff should be asked to encourage parents to telephone them during the week to check on how their child is doing, to walk down to the cottage after their child has had a home visit, to discuss the positive and not-so-positive aspects of the time they spent with their child, or to join the cottage group at mealtime. If shyness is a problem, staff members and children can meet the parents in the board room or staff dining area rather than at the cottage, where the presence of other youngsters might be too distracting for some families. All of these efforts, and more, can help parents feel respected, welcomed, valued, and competent.

As parents begin to be treated as "experts" on their child, an interesting change takes place: staff members are no longer just teachers providing information and role-modeling to parents, and parents are no longer just passive recipients of information. Parenting itself begins to be viewed as a discipline and the parents as useful and contributing team members. As staff members have more confidence in the parents, parents have more confidence in themselves, and the children begin to experience less anxiety and uncertainty both in the presence of their parents on campus and during their visits at home.

Following reunification, parents and children are invited to participate in weekly family meetings and multifamily group meetings at the agency. In the meetings the family's stability at home and their capacity to live together successfully can be supported and monitored and early intervention recommended if problems arise.

Conclusion

The model elucidated in this chapter has proven to be a manageable and practical intervention for reunifying troubled families whose children are in residential treatment. Two separate research studies conducted to measure its effectiveness yielded significant results [Carlo 1985; Carlo and Shennum 1989]. In both studies the data clearly indicated that separately applied, neither a cognitive (didactic) approach nor one that offers only experiential learning opportunities is as powerful as both conditions conjoined. Although there may be good reasons to begin with one or the other, the two components have a complementary value, and the effect of each is enhanced when they are together.

Although treatment agents may not be able to create the ideal family they would like their child-clients to have, legal and social policy realities such as Public Law 96-272 and the movement toward short-term treatment afford the creative practitioner a unique opportunity to produce new and effective program models that ameliorate family dysfunction in ways not previously available. Although it is true that financial constraints limit some very desirable options, the diversity of practical applications may be impeded more by lack of commitment on the part of agency administration and personnel than by funding problems.

Residential care providers for emotionally disturbed children can respond assertively to the political imperatives of permanency planning even when financial support for implementation of innovative services is deficient or lacking. They can initiate a reorganization of current delivery models to include an aggressive effort to reach out to the parents of children in residential care, involving them in the planning and delivery of services for their children. A more competent family unit, capable of being reunited and living together successfully, can emerge. Residential treatment can become a more usable and useful part of an overall child welfare service delivery continuum that has as its goal an appropriate, individualized, permanent living plan for each of the children under its care and jurisdiction.

References

Anderson, C.M., and Stewart, S. *Mastering Resistance: A Practical Guide to Family Therapy.* New York: The Guilford Press, 1983.

Arnold, L.E.; Rome, M.; and Tolbert, H.A. "Parents' Groups." In *Helping Parents Help Their Children*, edited by L.E. Arnold. New York: Brunner/Mazel, Inc., 1978, 114–126.

Brager, G., and Holloway, S. *Changing Human Service Organizations: Politics and Practice*. New York: The Free Press, 1978.

Carlo, P. "Evaluating Differential Provision of Didactic and Experiential Learning Opportunities to Parents of Children in Residential Treatment: Impetus to Family Reunification." Ph.D. dissertation. Los Angeles: University of Southern California, 1985

Carlo, P., and Shennum, W. "Family Reunification Efforts that Work: A Three-Year Follow-Up Study of Children in Residential Treatment." *Child and Adolescent Social Work* 6, 3 (June 1989): 211–216.

Dinkmeyer, D., and McKay, G.D. *Systematic Training for Effective Parenting*. Circle Pines, MN: American Guidance Service, Inc., 1976.

Finkelstein, N.E. "Family Participation in Residential Treatment." *CHILD WELFARE* LIII, 9 (November 1974): 570–576.

Ginott, H. *Between Parent and Child*. New York: Macmillan, 1965.

Gordon, T. *Parent Effectiveness Training*. New York: Peter H. Wyden, Inc., 1970.

Jenkins, S. "The Tie That Binds." In *The Challenge of Partnership: Working with Parents of Children in Residential Care*, edited by A.N. Maluccio and P.A. Sinanoglu. New York: The Child Welfare League of America, 1981, 39–52.

Knowles, M.S. "Innovations in Teaching Styles and Approaches Based on Adult Learning." *Journal of Education for Social Work* 8, 2 (Spring 1972): 32–39.

Knox, A.B. *Adult Development and Learning*. San Francisco: Jossey-Bass Publishers, 1978.

Krona, D.A. "Parents as Partners in Residential Care." *CHILD WELFARE* LIX, 2 (February 1980): 91–97.

Maluccio, A.N., ed. *Promoting Competence in Clients—A New/Old Approach to Social Work Practice*. New York: The Free Press, 1981.

Maluccio, A.N., and Sinanoglu, P.A., eds. *The Challenge of Partnership: Working with Parents of Children in Residential Care*. New York: The Child Welfare League of America, 1981.

Towle, C. *The Learner in Education for the Professions*. Chicago: University of Chicago Press, 1954.

Appendix A
An Outline for Parent Education/Support Groups

The following suggestions and program outline can be used as a guide for conducting the didactic component of a family reunification in residential treatment program.

1. Have snacks such as coffee, tea, and cookies available. Establish rules about smoking in accordance with group comfort level. Have ashtrays available if necessary.

2. Have someone serve as front-desk receptionist so parents are not kept waiting at the door.

3. Arrange chairs in a circle.

4. Introduce the leaders and explain the reasons for the group:

   a. To help parents to work together with the agency to help their children return home;

   b. To explain that the parents, not the agency staff members, are the real experts—while staff members have a knowledge base, skills, and training, parents have lived with their child longer than staff members have;

   c. To help parents share experiences and find out they are not alone;

   d. To teach parents to support one another;

   e. To offer parents an opportunity to express their feelings about what has happened in their families and begin to better understand how their feelings are connected with and affect their behaviors.

5. Concentrate on process: validate feelings, speak in the first person, present opening material as a guidepost but let discussion flow.

6. Help parents clarify their needs, express themselves, and perhaps explore their feelings a little; respond to their concerns about parenting children who have problems.

7. Encourage participants to define goals for the group and to report back along the way about the accomplishment of the agreed-upon goals.

8. Hand out printed materials on each topic for participants to take home.

9. Be alert for peripheral matters that will arise and have to be taken up in addition to the agreed-upon topics. For example:

   a. Controlling temporal aspects of behavior—the need for structure;

   b. Environmental conditions;

   c. Identifying the parameters of each event—time/place/expectations/rules/roles;

   d. Realistic expectations—not putting a child in a situation where he or she cannot succeed;

    e. Communication;

    f. Dealing with transitions; and

    g. Money issues—allowance, and so on.

10. Remember that guilt for inadequate parenting leads to understandable resentment toward those who more successfully take care of the children.

11. Build rapport: ask parents who their children are, establish common links.

12. Follow a format of agenda items such as that listed below.

Weeks One and Two: Orientation and First Topic

A. Begin with introductions, then:

1. Explain reasons for the group discussion.

2. Invite parents to share experiences with their children.

3. Validate parents' efforts and strengths and establish parents as "experts" on their own child.

4. Go over the ground rules for group discussion.

B. Discuss the importance of the parent-agency alliance.

1. Discuss feelings toward the system and the placement process.

2. Stress the importance of the agency as a treatment agent, not a judge or court monitor.

3. Discuss the importance of solving problems together.

C. Present an outline of topics you intend to cover; elicit parents' choice of topics to add to your list.

D. Present a discussion of values (focusing on self-awareness)

1. Ask what kind of persons parents would like their children to become (values imposition).

2. Conduct a values clarification exercise and discuss how the parents were reared and how they are trying to raise their children.

3. Offer alternatives to self-defeating beliefs—those ideas that parents hold dear that may be outdated or contribute to an unsatisfying family environment.

E. Discuss parental rights and children's rights.

1. Brainstorm with parents to create a sample list as an impetus to discussion.

2. Write sentence completion exercises on a chalkboard:

Good parenting _____

Poor parenting _____

3. Discuss the social equality of parents and children, emphasizing that both parents and children deserve respect.

Week Three: Understanding Behavior

A. Emphasize that all behavior has purpose. Describe the goals of misbehavior and the goals of positive behavior.

   1. Point out that the behavior of both parents and children has purpose and meaning.

   2. List ways to parent difficult children, acknowledging that endurance is an important parental quality.

Week Four: The Concept of Assertive Discipline

A. Discuss when to use assertive discipline.

B. Discuss caring enough about children not to let them misbehave.

C. List the components of an effective discipline plan:

   1. Communicate assertively.

   2. Back up words with action.

   3. Establish control and consistency.

D. Discuss ineffective responses:

   1. Nonassertive responses (begging, bargaining).

   2. Hostile responses (threats, name-calling, unnecessarily severe punishments, physical responses that release parents' anger).

Week Five: Behavior Management

A. Present behavior management techniques: structure, limit-setting, following through, presenting a united front, consistency. Discuss the agency's practices in disciplining children.

   1. Present principles of natural and logical consequences.

2. Develop definitions of punishment and discipline.

3. Explain the main differences between punishment and natural consequences.

4. Focus on building self-confidence and feelings of self-worth in both parents and children; indicate the difference between praise and encouragement.

Week Six: Feedback Session

A. Use this time for criticism/self-criticism.

1. Review process and content of group to date.

2. Elicit participants' reactions.

3. Prepare an agenda (revise if necessary) for the remaining three weeks.

Week Seven: Taking Responsibility

A. Focus on getting children to accept responsibility for their behavior. Discuss the problems of expecting too much or too little.

1. Discuss application of natural consequences, acting rather than reacting, and selecting the appropriate approach.

2. Explore alternatives for expressing one's ideas and feelings to children.

3. Explain active listening, "I" messages, and problem-ownership.

4. Present the steps in problem-solving.

Weeks Eight and Nine: Practicing Logical Consequences

A. Discuss common problems and how to handle them, emphasizing that there are no set responses or consequences. The group should brainstorm, using previous material as a reference, to come up with acceptable interventions for each problem discussed. Some typical problems that might be addressed are those in which the child:

Goes out without informing the parent

Argues

Engages in sibling rivalry

Won't clean his or her room

Acts out in public

Steals/sneaks food

Whines

Breaks curfew

Throws tantrums

Refuses to do chores

Has difficulty with homework

Acts out sexually

Week Ten: Review and End

The final session should include a summation, feedback, formal good-byes, and the voluntary exchange of parents' telephone numbers, as well as encouragement for them to continue to talk with each other in the future and to offer each other support.

Appendix B
Resources for Parent Education

Abidin, R.R., ed. *Parent Education and Intervention Handbook.* Springfield, IL: Charles C Thomas, 1980.
- A comprehensive resource on parent education, including research, work with special populations and special issues, and review of selected materials and packaged programs.

Arnold, L.E. *Helping Parents Help Their Children.* New York: Brunner/Mazel, 1978.
- Provides both an overview of parent guidance and practical ideas for working with parents and children with a range of special needs.

Dangel, R.F., and Polster, R.A., eds. *Parent Training.* New York: The Guilford Press, 1984
- A comprehensive collection of chapters on the behavioral approach to parent education, including theory, research, approaches, and issues.

Dinkmeyer, D., and McKay, G.D. *The Parent's Handbook: STEP* (3rd ed.). Circle Pines, MN: American Guidance Service, 1989.

Dinkmeyer, D., and McKay, G.D. *Parenting Teenagers: STEP* (2nd ed.). Circle Pines, MN: American Guidance Service, 1990.
- Both volumes offer self-instruction, including activities for parents, in the "Systematic Training for Effective Parenting" technique.

Glenn, H.S. *Developing Capable People Manual: Leader's Guide and Participants' Workbook.* Fair Oaks, CA: Sunrise, 1990.
- Activities and instruction for parent education groups using Glenn's approach to parenting.

Gordon, T. *Parent Effectiveness Training*. New York: Peter H. Wyden, 1970.

Gordon, T. *P.E.T. in Action*. New York: Peter H. Wyden, 1976.
  • Both volumes feature Gordon's strategies for improving communication between parent and child.

Harman, D., and Brim, O.G. Jr. *Learning to Be Parents*. Beverly Hills, CA: Sage, 1980.
  • A thorough guide to planning, implementing, and evaluating the results of parent education programs.

Haskins, R., and Adams, D., eds. *Parent Education and Public Policy*. Norwood, NJ: Ablex, 1983.
  • A macroperspective on parent education, including policy, research, and program issues.

Lamb, J., and Lamb, W. *Parent Education and Elementary Counseling*. New York: Human Sciences Press, 1978.
  • A good overview of various models of parent education.

Lot, L., and Nelsen J. *Teaching Parenting*. Provo, UT: Sunrise, 1990.
  • A practical, hands-on guide to planning and conducting a parent education course. The looseleaf format contains a range of resources, including exercises to use in conjunction with a number of parent education curricula.

7

Visiting: The Heart of Reunification[*]

Peg McCartt Hess and Kathleen Proch

Visiting is a planned intervention at the heart of reunification services. It maintains relationships when families are separated by placement; enhances children's well-being; helps family members determine whether they are willing and able to live together safely; and provides family members with opportunities to learn, practice, and demonstrate new behaviors and patterns of interaction. Without visiting, neither the feasibility nor the timing of reunification can be assessed accurately. In addition, a visiting plan that encourages a progressive increase in parents' responsibility for the daily care of their children sets the stage for successful reunification.

Visiting is not an intervention that stands alone. It is an integral part of the family's service plan; it takes place by plan and for specific purposes. The visiting plan, as part of the service plan, is always premised on case goals and on an assessment of family functioning and of the risk to the child.

Agencies should feel obligated to provide visiting services in sufficient quantity and quality either to support successful reunification or to reach a timely determination that a child's return home is not possible. Visiting serves further purposes when children cannot return home, including maintaining family connections in ways that support the permanency goal and the child's and

---

* This chapter includes material adapted with permission from *Family Visiting of Children in Out-of-Home Care: A Practical Guide*, by Peg McCartt Hess and Kathleen Ohman Proch (Washington, DC: The Child Welfare League of America, 1988); and from "Family Connection Center: An Innovative Visiting Program," by Peg McCartt Hess, Garth Mintun, Amy Moelhman, and Gayla Pitts (*CHILD WELFARE* LXXI, 1, January–February 1992: 77–88).

the family's needs. This chapter explores the role of visiting in achieving and maintaining various levels of reconnection, offers guidelines for developing effective visiting plans, and identifies the agency resources that are essential to an effective visiting program.

As it is discussed in this chapter, *visiting* means face-to-face contact between children and family members apart from family counseling or therapy sessions. Visiting should never be the only kind of contact between children in foster care and their families, however. Visiting can and should be supplemented by other forms of contact, unless they are negated by the child's age or concerns about the child's safety. These may include the exchange of correspondence, pictures, and gifts; telephone calls; and, when feasible, and especially when visits must be infrequent, the exchange of video- and audiotapes.

The Purposes of Visiting

Contact between children in placement and their family members serves many purposes. Planning visits that effectively accomplish the purposes described below is central to successful family reunification practice.

Visiting Maintains Family Relationships

None of us lives with all of the people who are important to us. We have family members and close friends who live far from us, and although we cannot live with them, they continue to be significant parts of our lives. We maintain our relationships with them by means of visits and other kinds of contact and feel a sense of loss if we are out of touch with them.

Families separated by placement are no different, despite the problems that necessitated placement. For the most part, feelings of love, need, and the security of familiarity predominate in children's attitudes toward their parents, and children's psychological health and sense of self are damaged if their relationship with their parents is not maintained. Moreover, only if relationships are maintained will there be a family to reunite.

Although much of child welfare practice centers on relationships and interactions between children and their parents, it is important to remember that children have other significant relationships, and that these relationships must also be maintained to protect the child's psychological health. Children are attached to their siblings and to others whom they know as "family," whether or not they are legally related. These relationships must be considered independently of the parent-child relationship. For example, even when children cannot visit with their parents, it may be important to continue visits between them and their siblings and other significant persons.

Visiting Helps Families Cope with Changing Relationships

Visiting helps family members cope with changing or ending relationships, when the goal is one other than the child's return home. This is true not only when the plan is adoption but also when it is long-term foster care. In such cases, visiting allows children to maintain relationships with parents, siblings, and others who can support them as they enter adulthood. The case of 11-year-old Carl, whose mother was diagnosed as paranoid schizophrenic, is one example.

Following the death of their father, who had been their primary caregiver, Carl and his older brother were placed in a foster home. After careful evaluation, caseworkers determined that the boys would not be able to live with their mother and that long-term foster care was the best plan for Carl. Carl was strongly attached not only to his mother but also to his older brother, who was soon to complete high school and planned to enlist in the military. Although his brother accepted the fact that their mother could not provide the care and supervision that the boys, particularly Carl, required, Carl could not understand why reunification was impossible, and he resisted all attempts by his foster parents to incorporate him into their family.

Through frequent visits with his mother—in her home, in his foster home, or in the hospital—Carl was able to protect and strengthen his relationship with his mother. At the same time, Carl came to recognize the seriousness of his mother's disability, the limits it imposed on her ability to care for him, and the stress caring for him imposed on her. As a result, he learned that he could continue to love and to see his mother while accepting the care his foster parents offered.

When the permanency plan is adoption, thoughtfully planned visits between children and their parents can be used to help children understand why they cannot return home and to help them experience, rather than deny, their feelings about the changes in family relationships. Visits in this situation also allow parents and children to say good-bye, facilitating the grieving necessary for healing and for successful adoptive placements.

Visiting Empowers and Informs Parents

Parents with children in placement experience not only the pain associated with separation from their children, but also painful negative self-judgments about their competence as parents [Jenkins 1981; McAdams 1972; Rutter 1978]. Preexisting low self-esteem and lack of self-confidence are magnified by the events surrounding placement. Parents can easily conclude that, because placement was necessary, they are incapable as parents in all ways. The hopelessness and sense of powerlessness felt by many parents can and do interfere with timely and successful reunification. Parents who feel they have no real control lose hope and stop trying to make the changes that allow reunification.

During visits, parents are reassured about their ability to act as parents and to care for their children at least to some extent. Parents can supervise their children and make decisions about their children's care. Interactions with their children reassure parents of their importance in their children's lives, which is essential to developing the strengths and confidence parents need to successfully reunite with their children.

Frequent visits help parents stay current with their children's changing developmental needs, increasing the likelihood that their responses to their children will be appropriate. Moreover, visits allow parents to identify their strengths and weaknesses as parents.

Visiting Enhances Children's Well-Being

Placement presents a child with a series of tasks—coping with the feelings created by separation, learning the rules of a new household, forming new relationships to have needs met [Littner 1956]. To cope with the stress of separation and placement, a child's personal resources are often diverted from normal developmental tasks. Attachment theory suggests that if attachment is maintained through visiting, separation distress will decrease, developmental progress will accelerate, and well-being will increase. Conversely, a child who is not visited may experience feelings of total abandonment and a decline in well-being.

Research generally supports the importance of contact to maintaining children's psychological health [Borgman 1985; Fanshel and Shinn 1978; Weinstein 1960]. Visiting reassures children that their parents want to see them and have not abandoned them, and helps children experience and work through feelings stirred by the separation, allowing developmental gains.

Visiting Helps Families Confront Reality

Visiting helps family members avoid developing either an overly idealized or an overly negative image of each other. Children's unrealistic expectations of a rarely visited "fantasy" parent, and the denial associated with that image, and parents' expectations of either the "impossible" or the "perfect" child both interfere with movement toward reunification.

Just as unrealistic expectations can interfere with reunification, they also keep families from confronting the reality that full reunification may not be possible or desirable. By the time placement occurs, family members are often confused, afraid, and ambivalent about their willingness and ability to make the changes necessary to live together safely. As visits increase in length and frequency, they may stimulate these feelings of ambivalence and confusion. This heightened sensitivity creates an opportunity for caseworkers to explore with family members the realistic options for the family's future [Hess and Folaron 1991]. Such was the case with Pamela, the mother of two preschool children in foster care.

> *Before dropping out of school, Pamela was enrolled in classes for the educable mentally handicapped. She was young and immature; her children had been placed in foster care because she left them alone for extended periods of time. Pamela insisted that she was capable of caring for her children. She cooperated with the reunification plan, struggling through parenting classes and trying to learn home management skills with the help of a homemaker. As visits with her children moved from the children's day care center to her home, and as she assumed more responsibility for her children's care and discipline, Pamela began to question her ability to care for the children and to express resentment over the demands the children imposed on her. Ultimately, she decided to surrender the children for adoption, a decision she could not have made if she had continued simply to play with her children at the day care center.*

Visiting Provides a Time and Place to Practice New Behaviors

As the family's service plan is implemented, visiting offers opportunities for building competence—learning, practicing, and demonstrating new behaviors and patterns of interaction. Family visits encourage a focus on the family as a system and on the nurturing available to the child within the family's relationships, rather than a focus on the treatment or change of any one family member. This is an important function of visiting, especially when a child is placed because his or her behavior is problematic.

During visits, family members increase their competence by testing and refining the skills they are learning in counseling sessions and other services. When family members are together, caseworkers, foster parents, homemakers, therapists, and others can teach child care and demonstrate ways of nurturing, communicating, and setting and enforcing limits. This allows family members to experiment safely with new behaviors as they try to change, and it allows them to receive immediate feedback from caseworkers and others who are supervising or participating in visits.

Visiting Promotes Accurate Assessment

Visits provide an opportunity for caseworkers to observe family interactions and to assess realistically whether family members have made the behavioral changes necessary to decrease the risks to the child in the home. The information gained in direct observation of family visits will support either a decision to reunify the family or a change in the permanency plan.

The most useful observations are those made in the family home or in another setting that allows for natural interaction between family members. Maluccio [1981: 14] emphasized the formulation of assessment as *competence clarification* and the importance of caseworkers being involved in the clients' own life space, "seeing and understanding through direct experience what is going on with the person in relevant ecological contexts." Assessments based on direct observations made during the visits—particularly visits in the family's home—assure reunification decisions that are not based solely on the family's compliance with the service plan or on family members' reports of readiness for reunification.

By observing family interaction during visits, caseworkers can gather information about the changes family members are making, the feelings that family members experience when they are together, and the problems that must be addressed and resolved before reunification can take place. In direct observation of visits in the home, caseworkers can also identify behaviors and situations that must be dealt with in planning for the child's protection upon return home. Moreover, caseworkers can assess not only the feasibility of reunification, but also when the children should return, whether all children should return at once or in sequence, and what services the family will need following reunification.

Visiting Provides a Transition to Home

Visiting plans that progressively increase the frequency and length of home visits provide the transition necessary for successful reunification. Typically, this progression moves from supervised parent-child contact to unsupervised daytime contact, then to overnight visits, and finally, to extended visits in the parents' home. This planned progression allows (1) parents to assume gradually the level and duration of caregiving that will be required of them when the child returns; (2) family members and caseworkers to identify and resolve problems that may occur only as family members are together for longer periods of time; (3) family members to adjust to the changes in the family system that develop as children reenter the family; and (4) foster parents and others to actively support the family as family members experience and identify the stresses of reunification.

Casework Visiting Activities

For visiting to facilitate successful reunification, caseworkers must complete a number of important tasks. They must develop a visiting plan; prepare the child, family members, and temporary caregivers for visits; coordinate visit arrangements; modify visit plans; evaluate, interpret, and document visit interactions and activities; and assist with the child's transition back to the family home. Each of these tasks is described here only briefly; a detailed discussion of the activities is available elsewhere [Hess and Proch 1988].

Developing a Visit Plan

Sound visiting plans are based on the child's permanency goal and service plan, and on case-specific information concerning the child, the family, and the child's temporary caregivers. To develop good visiting plans that correspond with service objectives, caseworkers must carefully assess interactions during visits and balance the often differing needs, requests, and expectations of those involved.

In planning visits, caseworkers must consider the child's age, requests regarding visits, reactions to visits, and developmental and therapeutic needs. Visits should take place frequently enough to sustain easily a child's memory of his or her parents and prevent a child from feeling abandoned; younger children, who have short-term memories, need more frequent visits.

Visiting plans must balance the child's need for protection and security with the parents' need to act as autonomously as possible during visits. The visiting plan is therefore shaped by those parental behaviors and abilities that must change before the child can return home and, if applicable, by those parental actions or inactions that endangered the child during previous visits. In addition, the caseworker must take into account the parents' requests, reactions to visits, schedules, and ability and willingness to cooperate with plans.

Relatives and foster parents can be important partners with the family and the caseworker in visiting. They can allow visits in their homes, help with transportation and supervision, and model appropriate methods of child care and discipline. Their willingness and ability to help children and parents with visits can have a major influence on visiting arrangements.

Preparing People for Visits

By actively preparing the child, family members, and temporary caregivers for visits, caseworkers maximize the family's movement toward reunification and prevent or diminish visit-related problems. Being prepared for visits empowers family members and temporary caregivers by enhancing their ability to manage interactions and feelings that arise.

Caseworkers should make sure that all persons involved in visiting have complete, current information about visiting arrangements and frequent opportunities to talk about their reactions to visits. Family members and temporary caregivers can prepare appropriately for visits if they have the chance to ask questions such as the following: What is the current visiting plan? How am I and others likely to react to visits? What is expected of me during visits? How can I handle problems related to the visit that might arise?

Volunteers, homemakers, and others often help with visits by transporting children or parents, or supervising all or part of a visit. Just as caseworkers must prepare children, family members, and temporary caregivers for visits, they must also prepare others who will be involved, particularly by clarifying the roles and expectations of each.

Coordinating Visit Arrangements

Logistically, visiting is enormously complicated. In addition to developing a visiting plan that supports movement toward reunification and preparing people for visits, caseworkers must attend to time, place, and transportation needs for each visit, and, if applicable, plan for supervision and for specific tasks to be accomplished during the visit. If the visit is to be at an agency site, is the room reserved? Who will transport the child to and from the visit? Do the parents need transportation? If the visit includes an appointment with a physician, teacher, or someone else, has the appointment been made and confirmed? The logistics become even more complex when several children in a family are placed in different homes.

The caseworker who is coordinating visits should meet frequently with all parties involved in the visiting plan to exchange information, identify and resolve problems, and revise the plan as needed. At a minimum, the visiting plan must be reviewed with all participants as part of each regularly scheduled case review.

Modifying Visit Plans

Because it is an integral part of the service plan, the visit plan should change over time to reflect the parents' improving ability to care for their child safely and independently. Although the need for and desirability of change in visiting plans over time seem obvious, all too often the first visiting plan for the family is the last visiting plan for the family; no changes are made to reflect and support improvement in family functioning [Proch and Howard 1986].

During the days and weeks immediately following placement, visits typically should be closely supervised, and the caseworker should carefully control the location and length of visits as well as the participants. This allows the visit supervisor to facilitate interaction among family members, ease the awkwardness of visits, and protect the children as needed. As the family's service needs are identified and the reunification plan is developed and implemented, visiting is used to facilitate change. During visits, family members apply what they have learned in parent education classes, in counseling, or through work with homemakers, home health educators, and others. As family members experience success within a particular visiting arrangement, changes in the arrangement should be made to promote further progress. If families do not experience success, or if their behavior worsens, caseworkers should determine whether a different visiting arrangement or different services could encourage improvement.

For example, a mother might first feed and bathe her child in the child's foster home with the help of the child's foster mother. After the mother has done this successfully, she might carry out these tasks without help or supervision, first in the foster home and then in her own home. If, however, the mother has difficulty feeding her child in the foster home, the visiting plan and tasks must be reevaluated. Is the difficulty the result of the mother's lack of knowledge, lack of empathy for the child, or discomfort in the foster home? The answer will in part determine what changes, if any, should be made in the visiting plan and perhaps in the service plan.

As families progress toward reunification, the primary responsibility for the child's care and protection during visits should gradually shift from the agency to the parents. Visiting plans should provide for visits that are progressively more frequent and longer and that take place in the child's home. The amount of supervision should gradually decrease. The following example illustrates how a visiting plan was revised to reflect a father's growing ability to care for his children.

William and Chrissy were placed in family foster care after they were found to be neglected. William was four years old at the time of placement, and Chrissy was 18 months old. At the time the neglect took place, William and Chrissy's parents were divorced, and the children were in the care of their mother, who was using cocaine and drinking heavily. Their father was living in the same city and occasionally visited the children. Although employed, he was not contributing to their support. According to the children's mother, the father was an alcoholic.

The initial permanency goal was to return the children to the care of their mother, but soon after the children were placed, she moved to another state without informing the agency either that she was leaving or where she was going. The permanency goal then shifted to return of the children to their father, who had expressed interest in gaining custody of the children and working with the agency toward that end.

Visits between the father and his children were initially scheduled for one hour a week in the agency visiting center. An agency volunteer transported the children to and from the visits, and the visits were supervised by the family's caseworker.

Because the father failed to keep several scheduled visits, the plan was changed to require that he call the agency by 9:00 A.M. on the day of a scheduled visit to confirm his intention to visit. In addition, because he arrived at several visits apparently under the influence of alcohol, the plan was changed to stipulate that if, in the opinion of the caseworker, he was under the influence of alcohol, the visit would be canceled.

Visits continued to be held in the office under these stipulations for several months; the father continued to deny his alcoholism. A change took place when, after being arrested for driving under the influence, the father entered a detoxification program. The children did not visit him during the three weeks he was in the program, but they talked with him by telephone.

After completing the detoxification program, the father began attending Alcoholics Anonymous. His visits then shifted to the children's foster home. The same stipulations concerning confirming the visit in advance and arriving sober remained in effect. The plan called for the caseworker to be present at the foster home before the father arrived and to be present at the beginning and the end of the visit. The father was not initially allowed to take the children out of their foster home, but he was allowed to spend some time alone with them.

The father continued in Alcoholics Anonymous, and he and his girlfriend successfully completed parenting classes. He maintained his sobriety and became more comfortable in caring for the children. In recognition of these changes, the visiting plan was changed to allow him to visit with the children for longer periods of time and to take the children for short periods of time to public places such as parks and fast-food restaurants. With the agreement of the foster mother, the caseworker no longer supervised all visits.

Visiting soon shifted to the father's home. At first, only William visited at home. The caseworker took William to the home for the first few visits, with full responsibility for transportation soon shifting to the father, who continued to visit both William and Chrissy in the foster home and to take them out alone briefly. After William had visited successfully at the father's home, Chrissy was included in the visits, with the caseworker once again taking the children to the visits.

When home visits began, the visiting plan required that the father plan activities and meals for the children during the visit and be prepared to discuss these plans with the caseworker. This requirement remained in effect as reunification neared and visits increased in length and included overnight visits. The plan for overnight visits further required that the children be allowed to call their foster mother if they wished to do so. As when visits moved to the home, William first visited overnight alone, and Chrissy was included in the visits later.

Evaluating, Interpreting, and Documenting Visits

Visits often stir strong feelings in family members. These feelings—especially when family members cannot verbalize their sorrow, anger, helplessness, and other common reactions to reunion and separation—often result in troublesome behavior. Caseworkers who have had extensive experience with visiting are familiar with the foster parent who complains that after a visit a child is enuretic, oppositional, or withdrawn. Similarly, they are familiar with parents who arrive for visits late or in the company of friends, who interact with their friends rather than their children during visits, who make promises to their children that they cannot keep, and who encourage their children to disobey their foster parents.

Caseworkers must carefully evaluate the participants' verbal and nonverbal reactions to visits. They must then interpret the reactions to foster parents and others and determine whether and what changes in visiting arrangements are warranted. The importance of carefully evaluating children's reactions to visits and interpreting these reactions cannot be overemphasized. Children's reactions that seem negative may actually indicate a strong and healthy attachment to parents. Unfortunately, caseworkers tend to respond to foster parents' concern about a child's negative behavior by decreasing the frequency of visits. Given the importance of frequent interaction to the development and maintenance of attachment [Ainsworth et al. 1978; Bowlby 1958, 1969; Fraiberg 1977], decreasing visits when reunification is the goal may significantly harm the child and ultimately reduce the chances for a successful reunification.

When a child has been removed from parental care, the agency staff, and typically a judge, must ultimately decide whether the child can or cannot return home, a decision that must always be justified. Family members' interactions during visits, and parents' compliance with reasonable and mutually agreed upon visiting plans are important—perhaps the most important—indicators of the feasibility of reunification. Therefore, caseworkers and others supervising visits must carefully evaluate and accurately document family members' compliance with the visiting plan and family interactions during visits.

Agencies can develop and use specific forms (see figure 1) to document visits. Forms are particularly useful when visits are supervised by homemakers or volunteers, who may not be sure of precisely what information to record.

Assisting the Child's Return Home

As illustrated in the case above, there are three critical junctures in visiting as the agency and family move toward the child's return home: (1) the point at which the child visits at home; (2) the point at which visits in the home are no longer supervised; and (3) the point at which the child stays overnight in the parents' home. Each requires that the caseworker carefully assess risks to the child while providing support to family members.

A date for return home should not be set until the family has safely completed the following steps: unsupervised visits in the parents' home; overnight visits; visits lasting several days spread over a period of time (two months or more); and, if at all possible, several extended visits (longer than one week). The importance of the shift to unsupervised visits in the child's home and to overnight visits cannot be overstated. Reunification can take place only after the family has had the opportunity to carry full child care responsibilities unsupervised and overnight and only after caseworkers and the family are confident that the child is safe in those situations.

Once it has been decided that reunification will take place and a target date has been set, visiting is used primarily to make the transition successful. Reunification can be just as traumatic as placement if it is not carefully orchestrated. An abrupt and unplanned reunification all too often leads to a return to foster care.

As reunification nears, visiting should promote maximum contact among family members; maximum parental responsibility for the child, particularly in situations where breakdown previously occurred; and evaluation of remaining problems. Visiting arrangements are successful if they either facilitate the child's successful move home or forestall premature reunification by identifying important unresolved problems.

A decision that will affect visit planning as reunification nears is whether the children in the family will return home together or in sequence. Visiting

FIGURE 1—SAMPLE VISIT REPORT FORM

Name _____ Case # _____

Date _____Time _____Place of visit _____

Persons participating in the visit _____

_____

	Yes	No
Parent on time and stayed for complete visit?	☐	☐
Parent clean and appropriately dressed?	☐	☐
Parent had appropriate activities planned?	☐	☐
Parent had appropriate snacks or meals planned?	☐	☐
Parent able to set limits?	☐	☐
Parent able to focus on child?	☐	☐
Parent greeted child appropriately?	☐	☐
House was neat and safe?	☐	☐
Child appeared clean, rested, and happy?	☐	☐
Child's affect was appropriate after visit?	☐	☐
Child went willingly/spontaneously to parent?	☐	☐
Parent promoted healthy separation at visit's end?	☐	☐

Comments regarding the visit: _____

_____

_____

_____

If the scheduled visit was canceled, who canceled it and what was the
explanation for canceling it? _____

_____

_____

Your name _____ Date _____

arrangements should carefully test the plan viewed as potentially most success-ful while protecting the self-esteem of all children in the family by making sure that each has individual time with the parents and that all siblings have time together. Throughout the placement, visit planning must be carefully tailored to the needs of each child in care.

Agency Supports for Visiting and Reunification

As staff members and foster parents begin to work with an agency, they quickly learn both the formal and informal rules of practice in the organization. Through their involvement in agency orientation and staff development, foster parent home studies, and written policy and practice guidelines, caseworkers and foster parents learn what is valued in the agency. If the agency values visiting, then its guidelines for foster parents and for parents with children in care will emphasize the importance of contact among all family members, including siblings, during placement, and its rules and regulations will mandate high standards of visiting practice and restrict actions that undermine visiting. During orientation and through in-service training and supervision, foster parents and caseworkers will be informed of their respective responsibilities, as well as the resources available to support visiting. If the agency values visiting, it will provide well-furnished space for supervised family visits, either in agency offices or elsewhere, and offer other supports such as help with transportation and a petty cash fund.

The degree to which visiting is an integral part of an agency's services reflects that agency's commitment to family reunification. The agency's written visiting policy, its placement practices, and its resource management and development can support or inhibit visiting. Without unequivocal agency support in policy, practice, and resources, visiting services will depend solely on the commitment of individual caseworkers or on court orders. Visiting will then vary from case to case in ways that do not reflect service plans, and may compromise not only families' rights to contact, but also the likelihood of successful reunification.

Written Visiting Policy

Several studies of visiting practice highlight the influence of agency policy on casework practice. Hess [1988] found through extensive interviews with caseworkers from five child welfare agencies that caseworkers in agencies having a minimum standard of visiting frequency developed plans that complied with the policy. In agencies with neither policy nor articulated norms governing visiting frequency, planned visiting frequency varied unpredictably. These findings are particularly important, since parents have been found to visit in accordance with the visiting plans developed by their caseworker [Proch and Howard 1986]. These researchers found that when there was no schedule, parents did not visit; when there was a visiting schedule, parents kept to it, especially if they had been involved in its development.

At a minimum, agency visiting policy should clearly emphasize the centrality of visiting as a service to families with children in placement, and should specify that the agency is responsible for developing a visiting plan for all children in placement, including those placed with relatives. The policy should further specify (1) how soon after placement visits should begin (within 48 hours is recommended), (2) the minimum frequency of scheduled visits (weekly is recommended as the base frequency), and (3) the preference for visits to take place in the child's home, except when precluded for reasons of safety.

Further, agency policy should require that visiting never be used either as reward or punishment. In other words, all changes in visiting arrangements should be directly related to assessments of risk to the child and of family progress in achieving case objectives. Policy should require that caseworkers inform family members of their right to appeal changes in visiting plans as required by Public Law 96-272. The appeal process should be clearly described in language clients can understand.

Planning for Visits. Agency policy should further require that the visiting plan be in writing and that it encompass visiting frequency, length, location, and supervision of visits; who will participate; what supportive services, including transportation, will be provided; planned activities, such as whether a visit is to include a doctor's appointment or a parent-teacher conference; and any conditions imposed on the visit, such as the existence of a no-contact court order or a requirement that a parent call the office to confirm a visit.

Moreover, agency policy should require that the visit plan be developed with the participation of all family members and reviewed as part of every administrative or judicial case review, and that copies of the plan be distributed to all persons involved in carrying out the plan, including foster parents.

Agencies can encourage adherence to their policy directives by developing and using a visiting plan form. The form can remind caseworkers what aspects of visiting must be considered and that they should change the plan over time to reflect improvement in the parents' ability to care for their children safely and to enhance progress toward reunification. In cases where parents are unable to assume child care, the plan should be revised to help the family achieve a level of reconnection other than the child's return home.

Visiting and Reunification. Recent research underscores the practice reality that without extensive visiting, the actual change achieved by family members and the continuing risk to the child in the home cannot be accurately assessed [Hess et al. 1989]. These findings suggest that agency policy should forbid returning children home until they have safely had unsupervised visits in their own homes, including overnight visits and visits lasting several days or more over a period of several months.

Expectations of Temporary Caregivers. Agency policies concerning foster parents and group care facilities also affect visiting practices. These policies should assure out-of-home caregivers' support of frequent visits. At a minimum, policies should require all foster parents and other child care providers to help prepare a child for visits and to accommodate themselves to reasonable visiting plans. Despite the serious shortage of family foster homes in most areas, foster parent applicants who are not willing to support visiting should not be licensed or used, because their unwillingness would undermine any reunification efforts. Moreover, policies should prohibit group care facilities from using visiting restrictions to punish children for misbehavior.

Placement Policy and Practice

Agency policy and practice related to the choice of placements for children have a powerful effect on visiting options. Federal law requires that children be placed in close proximity to their parents' home, consistent with the particular needs of the child. Written agency policy should reflect this requirement. When children are placed at a distance from their families, planning for visiting becomes more complex and visits consume more casework time. The same is true if siblings are placed separately. The result is a decrease in the frequency of visits and a greater likelihood that visits will take place in locations other than the parents' home [Hess 1988].

Standards concerning the number of children who are placed in a family foster home and the number of children with special needs who are placed in a home also affect visiting. Foster parents who are overburdened by the number of children in the home, or by the children's special needs, cannot be flexible in scheduling visits or in assisting with transportation. They cannot adequately prepare children for visits or respond to children following visits, and they cannot easily extend themselves as resources to parents during visits.

Resource Management

Most children are placed in out-of-home care under the authority of a court order, with the court typically vesting legal custody of the children in a public child welfare agency. In many jurisdictions, the public agency then purchases all or some of the services for the child and the child's family from other public and voluntary agencies. Just as an agency can purchase counseling, it may also purchase visiting services in some areas. Much of the discussion below reflects the knowledge gained through a contractual visiting program described in detail elsewhere [Hess et al. 1992].

Ideally, visiting services will be provided by the same agency staff members who provide other reunification services. This increases the likelihood that family visiting will be integrated with other reunification services, enhancing the validity of assessment and service planning, and resulting in a more timely reunification. It follows, then, that if primary services are being purchased from an agency, staff members in that agency should provide visiting services. If the agency with legal authority is providing direct services, however, staff members in that agency should be responsible for visiting services.

Regardless of which agency is the primary service provider, it is likely that volunteers and staff members other than the family's primary caseworker will be involved with visiting. When this occurs, it is essential that the primary caseworker retain responsibility for constructing and evaluating the visiting plan. It is all too easy for responsibility to become diffused. The result can be confusion, missed visits, and consequent delay in reunification. It is also essential that the primary caseworker observe some visits and talk directly with all the participants about events that arise during all visits, otherwise, valuable service planning information will be lost.

An effective visiting program, whether housed in a public or voluntary agency, requires a significant investment of agency resources. This investment is reflected in caseload size and in the availability of services during nontraditional hours, secure and comfortable visiting sites, assistance with transportation, reimbursement for visiting expenses, a qualified staff, and supervision and staff training.

Caseload Size. The agency resource in greatest demand is staff time—time to schedule and coordinate visits; time to supervise visits that have to be supervised; time to transport children and parents; time to prepare children, parents, other family members, and foster parents for visits; time to discuss reactions to visits with all the persons involved in the visits as well as with outside agencies involved in the case and giving other kinds of services; and time to record information concerning visits. As one caseworker noted:

> *It takes time and energy to plan visits and set up all the details. You can't just say, "Here's how it's going to be." Especially when children are first*

placed and you are supervising visits, you can spend hours planning and scheduling one visit. When you work with everyone's schedules, it seems no one is ever able to do it at the same time [as the others].

Because of the time consumed by visiting, staff members must have reasonable workloads. The higher the caseload and the greater the number of cases in which reunification is the goal, the less frequent visiting is likely to be, and the more likely it is that visits will be scheduled in the office rather than in the parents' home, since office visits invariably consume less staff time than home visits.

Nontraditional Agency Hours. Families identify agency hours as a major impediment to visiting. The hours of most agencies and the inflexibility of agency staff schedules often preclude visits in the late afternoon, during evenings, and on weekends and holidays—the times during which most children and family members are free from school and employment responsibilities.

To meet clients' needs, offices must be open for visits during nontraditional agency hours. Moreover, agencies must offer compensatory time and flextime to caseworkers to encourage and allow them to schedule visits according to clients' situations.

Secure and Comfortable Places for Visits. The majority of children are placed in out-of-home care due to parental actions or omissions that put them at grave risk, with reunification dependent on changes in the parents' behavior. Moreover, courts occasionally impose no-contact or restraining orders on some family members. The agency must therefore anticipate risk-management problems and select and prepare a physical site for visits that minimizes risk to children and to other visiting family members. A site with limited and controllable access and with waiting and visiting areas with separate entrances allows for safe entry to and exit from visits.

Effective visiting requires space that allows not only for security but also for privacy, and encourages natural interaction among family members. Comfortably furnished visiting rooms equipped with toys and games and, if at all possible, with facilities that allow parents to feed and care for their children, are essential if visits are to be used for meaningful assessment and for teaching. Moreover, rooms equipped with one-way mirrors can promote comfortable family interaction while allowing caseworkers and others to supervise visits unobtrusively.

It is also important to have a sufficient number of rooms to accommodate all the visits that must be held in the agency at any given time. One caseworker's observation emphasizes the need for adequate visiting space: "It gets to be a real cutthroat thing for visits during after-school hours. The supervisor has to decide which family and worker get the room for a visit."

Assistance with Transportation. To facilitate visiting, agencies must have staff members or volunteers who can take children to and from visits, in vehicles equipped with children's car seats. In addition, agencies should locate visiting sites near bus lines and provide easily understood maps to family members, foster parents, and others supplying transportation.

Reimbursement for Visiting Expenses. The agency can support visiting by reimbursing foster parents, volunteers, and others for visit-related expenses. Just as important, funds to help families with transportation and other expenses, such as providing meals for children during visits at home, also support visiting. Most parents with children in foster care are poor; many received AFDC before their children were removed from their care and may have no income for a time following placement. The financial burden imposed on parents by visits can be substantial, particularly visits that are held far from the parents' home, or longer visits in the parent's home that necessitate food and other purchases. This burden can and does interfere with reunification.

A Qualified Staff. Arranging and carrying out visits requires skill in making complex professional judgments. These judgments include assessing risk to a child; balancing the conflicting needs, requests, and expectations of all the persons affected by visiting; managing constantly changing plans; and coping with others' and one's own intense emotional reactions to visits. In addition to the knowledge and skills expected of all child welfare workers, caseworkers involved with visiting must be able to assess and manage risk and to cope with unpredictable situations. They must be personally flexible while possessing the ability to set and enforce firm limits on others' behavior. They must be sufficiently mature and self-aware to recognize and appropriately deal with the stress they and others experience as they help families visit. Perhaps most important, staff members must be firmly committed to preserving family relationships, even when those relationships are characterized by tension and trouble.

Supervision and Staff Training. Two other agency resources essential to effective visiting and successful reunification are often overlooked. One is good supervision; the other is training for caseworkers and for others involved in visiting. When visiting is conceptualized as an integral component of reunification services and as involving complex practice decisions, the critical importance of supervisory guidance and staff training becomes self-evident. Caseworkers, foster parents, and others can easily overlook and even subvert agency policy supporting visiting if they are not encouraged and challenged by their supervisors through new staff member orientation and continuing staff development.

Supervisors can assure steady progress toward reunification, and monitor any risk to the child entailed in visiting plans, by examining the degree to which the service plan, progress made by parents, and the visiting plan correspond. They can evaluate and encourage caseworkers' compliance with not only the content but also the intent of agency visiting policy. Supervisors also can challenge caseworkers to examine how their personal biases may affect visiting decisions, and help caseworkers recognize and respond to the intense stresses associated with visiting and other reunification decisions.

The development and implementation of visiting plans require that caseworkers, foster parents, homemakers, volunteers, and other service providers have a broad range of knowledge. The agency must therefore provide training and support staff attendance at workshops and other educational programs that increase knowledge related to visiting. Relevant topics include the multiple purposes of visiting, the importance of visiting to successful reunification, the various tasks associated with developing and implementing visiting plans, risk assessment, child and family development, the development of parent-child attachments, the impact of separation due to placement, and self-care. Without ongoing agency support for the development of knowledge and skills, staff members and others involved with visiting cannot be expected to manage this complicated component of reunification services successfully.

Conclusion

The agency's costs for visiting are high. The agency must have qualified staff members who can complete the complex and difficult tasks entailed in developing visiting plans that maintain and strengthen family relationships and facilitate reunification. Caseloads must be low enough to allow the time visiting requires. Additional resources to support visiting must be available. An agency committed to reunification must bear these high costs because visiting is essential to successful reunification.

A mother and a grandparent were asked to describe what it was like to have four children return home from placement. Was it stressful? Were there problems they had not expected? "It wasn't too bad because we got used to living with each other again in the visits. The visits made all the difference in being ready—all of us—to make it work."

References

Ainsworth, M.; Blehar, M.; Waters, E.; and Wall, S. *Patterns of Attachment: A Psychological Study of the Strange-Situation*. Hillsdale, NJ: Lawrence Erlbaum Associates, 1978.

Borgman, B. "The Influence of Family Visiting upon Boys' Behavior in a Juvenile Correctional Institution." *CHILD WELFARE* LXIV, 6 (November–December 1985): 629–638.

Bowlby, J. "The Nature of a Child's Tie to His Mother." *International Journal of Psychoanalysis* 39, 5 (September/October 1985): 350–373.

Bowlby, J. *Attachment and Loss: Vol. 1. Attachment*. New York: Basic Books, 1969.

Fanshel, D., and Shinn, E. *Children in Foster Care: A Longitudinal Study*. New York: Columbia University Press, 1978.

Fraiberg, S. *Every Child's Birthright*. New York: Basic Books, 1977.

Hess, P. "Case and Context: Determinants of Planned Visit Frequency in Foster Family Care." *CHILD WELFARE* LXVII, 4 (July–August 1988): 311–326.

Hess, P., and Folaron, G. "Ambivalences: A Challenge to Permanency for Children." *CHILD WELFARE* LXX, 4 (July–August 1991): 403–424

Hess, P., and Proch, K. *Family Visiting of Children in Out-of-Home Care: A Practical Guide*. Washington, DC: The Child Welfare League of America, 1988.

Hess, P.; Mintun, G.; Moelhman, A.; and Pitts, G. "Family Connection Center: An Innovative Visiting Program." *CHILD WELFARE* LXXI, 1 (January–February 1992): 77–88.

Hess, P; Folaron, G.; and Jefferson, A. *The Impact of Policy on Foster Care Reentry*. Indianapolis, IN: Indiana University School of Social Work and Indiana Department of Public Welfare, 1989.

Jenkins, S. "The Tie That Bonds." In *The Challenge of Partnership: Working with Parents of Children in Foster Care*, edited by A. Maluccio and P. Sinanoglu. New York: The Child Welfare League of America, 1981, 39–51.

Littner, N. *Some Traumatic Effects of Separation and Placement*. New York: The Child Welfare League of America, 1956.

Maluccio, A. "Competence-Oriented Social Work Practice: An Ecological Approach." In *Promoting Competence in Clients*, edited by A. Maluccio. New York: The Free Press, 1981, 1–24.

McAdams, P. "The Parent in the Shadows." *CHILD WELFARE* LI, 1 (January 1972): 51–55.

Proch, K., and Howard, J. "Parental Visiting of Children in Foster Care: A Study of Casework Practice." *Social Work* 31, 3 (May–June 1986): 178–181.

Rutter, B. *The Parents' Guide to Foster Family Care*. New York: The Child Welfare League of America, 1978.

Weinstein, E. *The Self-Image of the Foster Child*. New York: Russell Sage Foundation, 1960.

 **8**

Preparing Children for Reunification

Gail Folaron

Children's readiness to reunite with their families is often overlooked when preparing for reunification. Involving children in each phase of permanency planning—assessment, selection, and implementation—is critical to the plan's success. Even very young children can sabotage plans and threaten family security if they are not ready.

Social workers seeking to reunify children and their families must enlist the cooperation of each child whose fate is being decided. This chapter discusses the needs of children throughout the reunification process; denotes practice activities and strategies for engaging children, assessing commitment, improving communication, and developing a plan for protection; and sets forth practical interventions for maintaining family connections. Potential contributions of parents, social workers, and foster parents in preparing children to return home are reviewed and guidelines for action are illustrated.

Understanding the Placement

The traumatic effects on a child of removal from his or her family and the subsequent placement in out-of-home care are compounded by the general failure to inform the child about what is going on. Children are often left on their own to figure out what has happened, what will happen, and when. In their efforts to understand and thereby achieve some control, children often blame themselves and spend considerable energy trying to undo what they believe are mistakes they made that led to placement. Social workers skilled in removing these impediments to understanding can lessen anxiety, diminish stigma, and open doors to further questions from the children. The less energy children expend in trying to understand by themselves what has happened, the more effort they can put into adjusting to their placement and preparing for a new relationship with their own family.

Developmental Considerations

The capacity of children to perceive, remember, interpret, and communicate varies according to their developmental stage. Weinstein [1960] found that "foster children ages 5-6 were unable to define the word *foster* while the 7-9 year olds emphasized not 'belonging' to the people they lived with, and those children 10 years and older emphasized being cared for by people other than birth parents." Imagine the fear children may feel when they hear the terms *foster parent*, *adoption*, or *guardian ad litem* for the first time. For many children, these terms merely connote abandonment by parents and ownership by a stranger.

Children traumatized by placement are in particular need of skilled intervention because they often have a difficult time understanding abstract concepts, following conversations, and retaining information. Coupling verbal explanations with written ones or graphic illustrations or using toys or puppets to demonstrate concepts often helps.

Explanations, demonstrations, and illustrative activities vary with a child's developmental age. Infants and toddlers, for example, enjoy made-up songs and stories that teach placement-related vocabulary [Sharrar 1970]. Preschoolers and school-aged children can be engaged in play therapy or artwork. Preteens and teenagers can draw maps or diagrams to illustrate their placement experiences. All children benefit from bibliotherapy [Pardeck and Pardeck 1987], artwork, and lifebooks [Backhaus 1984; Folaron 1983; Aust 1981; Wheeler 1978], which illustrate the child's experiences, encourage questions, and provide clarification.

Explanations of circumstances leading to placement and the changes necessary within the family to enable a return should be given honestly but discreetly and should be geared to the child's developmental and intellectual level. Labeling parents as "mentally ill," "alcoholic," "retarded," or as "child abusers" should be avoided. Children can most easily accept explanations that are devoid of blame and highlight the feelings and behaviors that prevent the parents from parenting [Project Craft 1980]. For example, if a four-year-old child was removed because of abuse by alcoholic parents, the explanation might sound something like this:

> Your mother and father had some problems that they didn't always know how to take care of. Sometimes when their problems got so big that they didn't know what to do, they would drink some beer because they thought

that would help them forget some of their problems. Do you remember what happened when they drank a lot of beer? Sometimes when they would drink lots of beer they would hit you very hard. Well, your mother and father felt very bad about hurting you and they wanted to stop but they didn't know how. Since you have been in a foster home, your mom and dad have been working very hard to fix their problems so they won't hurt you anymore. They feel they are ready to try again and they want you to come back home.

Age-appropriate activities and explanations enhance children's understanding, diminish their confusion, and stimulate appropriate questions. Social workers also benefit from focused discussions by observing firsthand the child's capacity to understand his or her current situation and to participate in working to reconnect with the family.

Cultural and Religious Influences

To help a child understand and incorporate the various experiences resulting from placement away from home, the social worker must be sensitive to the child's cultural and religious heritage. Different ethnic backgrounds, socioeconomic groups, and religious affiliations carry alternative and even conflicting interpretations of the world, behavioral expectations, and rules for living. Expecting that foster children will adopt the values and beliefs of the foster family, often alien to them, can create internal conflicts for children and problems in adjustment following their return home. For instance, it may be difficult for children to incorporate new religious beliefs without judging their family of origin or worrying about their own and their family's salvation. As one former foster child explained:

For me, moving from home to home was spiritual abuse. I used to lie awake at night worrying that we would all be damned because we didn't go to church three nights a week. I couldn't close my eyes at night because I was afraid that if I did the devil would come and get me. I tried to talk to my mother but she only got mad. She wasn't interested in being saved. I feared for her.

Situations like this create conflict and fear for children who are trying to reconnect with their families.

Furthermore, different cultural norms and value systems are imposed on children as they move from home to home. It is often difficult for children to incorporate the varying beliefs they have found in their placements. Values are so strongly tied to emotions that it is not only difficult for children to verbalize their confusion about the conflicting sets of values, but it is often difficult to find a neutral person who can answer questions. The social worker should be aware of the foster family's values when a placement is chosen and begin a discussion of value differences with the child. This will give the child an outlet for exploring feelings and confusion and help the child to accept his or her own family, even in the face of other families' conflicting expectations.

Since ethnicity influences communication style, practitioners should be alert to each child's heritage, and know how to work within that set of norms. As Fahlberg and Jewett [1982: 20] emphasize:

> *A child's cultural background may play an important role in the ability to express feelings. Many Hispanic children may have been taught to repress strong feelings, both positive and negative. For example, one coping mechanism of many Hispanic families is the denial of problems. Accompanying this manner of coping is a repression of anger. A child raised in such a family, even for a few years, will incorporate that manner of expressing feelings. It becomes the adoption worker's task to assist the child in expressing negative feelings in a constructive manner. Because the Hispanic child has been taught to respect parental figures, direct expression of anger about the parent may be difficult.*

Workers can help both children and their families perceive the value conflicts created by placement and how differences have affected their view of each other, so that relationships can be rebuilt from a common base.

Denial

Children tend to minimize or deny the events that led to placement in an effort to protect family members and/or themselves. Exploring the child's understanding of the events leading to placement helps the child sort facts from fantasy and understand changes that are necessary for the child to return home. The social worker should expect loyalty conflicts and confusion, and should be aware of the child's need for defenses. The following explanation, given by ten-year-old Tommy, illustrates both his confusion and his protectiveness:

> *I don't know why I'm in a foster home. I was in the hospital because I got hit by a car. The day it was time for me to go home, my mom was coming to get me but she ran out of gas. I don't know how she ran out of gas because she filled her tank. Someone must have put a hole in her tank or something. Anyway, I waited for her to come and finally she called and said she couldn't come and get me. So the caseworker came and put me in a foster home. [PRAG 1989]*

Tommy had been removed from a neglectful home. No one had ever explained to him the circumstances leading to his removal. After he returned home, he worked around the neighborhood doing odd jobs for extra money. He also shoplifted and stole money from his neighbors. He did his best to protect his family and was very proud of his ability to bring in money. When Tommy was arrested and put into a juvenile detention center, he proudly explained that since his return home he had been able to give his mother a weekly allowance so that she would never run out of gas again.

Protecting the child's defenses, such as denial or avoidance, and pacing his or her disclosure of personal matters, particularly as they relate to family members, are important. If a child reveals too much too soon, the results can be countertherapeutic: the child may withdraw from further discussions with the worker or become unmanageable in the foster home. It often helps to allow children physical space to move around and hide, if necessary, while talking about their histories. The social worker should be gentle with defenses, honest with the facts, and respectful of the time the child needs to accept hard truths.

As Tommy's case illustrates, some children go to great lengths to remedy the problems they believe caused their removal; they may put energy into resolving a problem that does not exist, while real threats to safety go unattended. Other children feel personally responsible for their family's breakup and believe that placement is a punishment for disclosing what actually happened. These children may feel uncomfortable with the legal and therapeutic interventions required of the parents. The social worker must be sensitive to the child's understanding of events, initiate discussions of casework decisions and interventions, and explain the intended therapeutic benefits of each intervention for the child and family. Above all, the worker must be open to questions.

Exploring the past can be painful for both the child and the worker, but avoiding the subject leaves the child confused, afraid, and unable to resolve emotions [Jewett 1982]. The worker's help with remembering the past, correcting misinterpretations, and preparing for the future is essential for successful reunifications. Without this bridge to the past the child may not be able to prepare adequately for the future [Busch 1985].

Developing Communication Skills

Children under stress often regress in their behaviors and coping abilities, and may show their discomfort through unacceptable behaviors. They must be taught effective communication skills to help them deal with the many events that are a part of preparing for reunification. One important step is teaching children a "feelings" vocabulary, which enables them to communicate needs in a socially acceptable way. Further, by identifying feelings and helping children to label them, social workers communicate an understanding of the children's needs, normalize their experiences, and create an outlet for their confusion. Children will often feel relief when they discover that an explanation exists for their feelings and behaviors [McDermott 1987]. As they become more aware of their own feelings they can develop an understanding of, and patience with, their own functioning. A feelings vocabulary is an essential coping skill for all children in foster care—it enhances self-acceptance and lets the child play an effective role in working toward reconnection.

When practitioners acknowledge and identify a child's feelings, they demonstrate acceptance and create an environment for deeper sharing. They must keep in mind, however, that many dysfunctional families characteristically deny or misconstrue feelings; in these cases discussions have to be extended to the child's family as a whole. As all family members become more aware of their own feelings and needs, they are better able to appreciate the feelings and needs of others. The family system is altered in preparation for the child's return.

This approach to feelings can be incorporated into every worker-child (and worker-parent) relationship. Each interview can begin and end with both the child and the worker identifying their current feelings. Throughout the interview, the social worker can mirror, reflect, or interpret the child's feelings and seek clarification from the child.

Family Visits

The importance of family contacts in preparing a child for reunification cannot be overstated [see Hess and Proch, chapter 7]. Family visits, including varied and frequent sibling contacts, are essential to maintain connections with history and family and to ease the child's transitions back into the family. The loss of a shared history with other family members is one of the most significant losses for a child in foster care. Children cut off from their biological family, either temporarily or permanently, are without links to portions of their past, particularly to persons who can validate their memories. The following description, given by 16-year-old Rhonda, illustrates the effects of extended placement on family relationships and the challenge a child faces when reestablishing a place in the family:

> Things are really different from when I last lived at home. Mom has a different boyfriend living there. Two more kids were born since I first left home. The brother and sister I thought I knew had grown and changed.

> *I worry that mom, her boyfriend, and my sisters and brothers will never like me again. [PRAG 1989]*

Family Meetings

Visits in the form of family meetings can be used to fuse individual experiences into a single family history. The social worker can introduce the family meeting as a medium for sharing experiences and feelings, exchanging information, clarifying expectations, establishing family rules, and resolving conflicts. Parents can be encouraged to take the leadership in family meetings and to learn effective communication skills. When used as a preparatory tool, family meetings should begin before reunification takes place so that the changes in each individual's behavior can be tested in a safe environment. Without this reintegration, many families will resume after the reunion the dysfunctional patterns that restrict the sharing of information, feelings, and experiences. Rules prohibiting information-sharing may be explicitly stated, such as, "We don't talk about the past; today is a new day and a fresh start," or may evolve as a way of avoiding family tension. Children often remain silent about their feelings in an effort to avoid conflict. For example, Carrie, 16, describes her experience:

> *We weren't a family again. It was only people living together. It was only me, my mother, and my sister. My brother and dad weren't there anymore. I was really confused. I wanted everything to work out…My mom and I get along fine now as long as I pretend everything is fine. We don't talk about problems. [PRAG 1989]*

Children may need special preparation for family meetings, particularly if they have been taught not to express feelings or discuss family business in public. Workers can help children identify their needs and expectations before the family meeting and practice verbalizing them in discussions and role-plays. During family meetings, the worker's role should be secondary to the parents' role, and should support the parents' efforts and encourage children to share information and feelings. As a participant-observer, the worker can demonstrate effective communication and negotiation skills during stressful interactions.

Sibling Contact

Siblings who are placed together are often better able to adjust to placement and to be realistic about reunification. If a child is not placed with siblings, every effort must be made to maintain sibling relationships by arranging frequent visits and shared experiences. The child's age and sense of time strongly suggest the minimum visit frequency necessary to maintain relationships and sustain the memory of family members [Hess and Proch 1988]. Young children need more frequent visits; older children can bridge visits with phone calls and letters. Long separations with minimal contact can set the stage for dissolved loyalties and destructive competition when children are reunited.

Foster parents should be encouraged to bring siblings together for visits, joint therapy sessions, shared vacations, sleepovers, and special events [Hegar 1988]. Children in placement are reassured by the presence of a sibling [Heiniche and Westheimer 1965], and the sharing of experiences establishes a base of predictability and support when they return home. Nurturing sibling relationships throughout placement makes for a smoother transition period and better family adjustment after reunification.

The Support of Foster Parents

Many children in placement feel caught between two sets of parents and are unable to resolve the loyalty conflicts that having two families creates.

Unlike adults, who are generally capable of maintaining positive emotional ties with a number of different individuals unrelated or even hostile to each other, children lack the capacity to do so. They will freely love more than one adult only if the individuals in question feel positively toward one another. Failing this, children become prey to severe and crippling loyalty conflicts. [Goldstein et al. 1979]

It is part of the foster parents' responsibility to ease the child's transition back to the family of origin by visibly demonstrating acceptance of the child, the family, and the pending reunification. When children sense that their foster parents approve of their love for their parents, and support their wish to get back together, they feel less conflicted about their attachment to the foster parents, less defensive of their parents, and freer to develop a realistic awareness of their own family's problems. Children can then experience, rather than repress, anger toward their parents for making placement happen, experience sadness at the separation, and begin to resolve their grief [Hess 1981]. Encouraging children to express these feelings while in placement will hasten the resolution of issues and strengthen family connections, paving the way for a stronger commitment to the family following reunification.

Acceptance of Parents

Foster parents' acceptance of the child's family must begin the day the child is placed in the foster home. Acceptance can be visibly demonstrated by placing the parents' picture in a frame and hanging it on a wall or setting it on the child's dresser. If the child is literate, the parents' phone number may be written down in the foster family's directory or on a note pad near the phone. It can also be a relief for the child when foster parents initiate discussion of the child's parents. Even if the child does not respond, the permission to talk about the parents is heard and internalized by the child. An easy way to begin discussing the child's parents is to ask about favorite meals the parents liked to cook or activities the child and parents have enjoyed together.

Foster parents can further show support of the family by encouraging frequent contact with parents and siblings. Inviting family members to join in meals, parties, or special events is one way to demonstrate acceptance, ease tensions, and help the child create and maintain a shared history with family members. The importance of the foster parents' role in ensuring frequent visiting between children and their families cannot be overstated. The child's relationship with parents is "continued, strengthened, or established through thoughtfully planned visitation and other contacts" [Hess 1981]. The foster parents can help with visit scheduling and transportation arrangements, and by sharing information about the child's activities and progress since the last visit. Children generally favor a definite plan for visits: as the children put it, "Then a child won't be worrying about parents...[children] need security and a schedule" [Kufeldt 1984].

Many parents feel inadequate when their children return home because they cannot compete with the foster parents' ability to provide financially for their children, continue extracurricular activities, or afford experiences that compare with the foster family's. Choosing activities and experiences that reflect the child's background and involving the parents in decisions regarding the child's everyday life demonstrate acceptance of the family and respect for the child, and model child-centered parenting behavior for the parents. Which clothing to buy, whether or not to cut a child's hair, and how much allowance to give the child are all decisions that parents and foster parents can agree upon and that can lead to a smoother reunification. Schedules for bedtimes, chores, and dating may also be discussed with the parents so that the child can keep the same routines and schedules after reunification. Further, parents should always be consulted about and involved in medical appointments, school conferences, and religious matters.

Acceptance of the Child

Foster parents can help children understand their past and prepare for the future by helping them create a lifebook—a collection of pictures, drawings, and writings that depict major events in the child's life. The process of constructing it helps the child come to terms with events and losses. The mutuality of the experience allows the child to explore other people's reactions to his or her past, to ask questions about various events, and to clarify misunderstandings. Several authors have described the uses of lifebooks and explain how to construct one [Backhaus 1984; Aust 1981; Wheeler 1978].

Foster parents can help preserve the past by participating in collecting lifebook materials, such as school papers, ribbons, and report cards; pictures of the foster family, pets, and the house; pictures of the child; and school and medical records. Written anecdotes contributed by the child, parents, foster parents, and others are also invaluable contributions.

Foster parents can support the child's actual return home by ensuring that the child has ample opportunity to say good-bye. Although the child may wish to avoid painful terminations, without closure, he or she may have difficulty assimilating back into the family of origin. The foster parents may help the younger child plan for leaving by counting down: "You will be going home in three more bedtimes." The child should be encouraged to say good-bye to each member of the foster family, the relatives of the foster family, neighbors, friends, classmates, and pets. As each family member says good-bye, they should tell the child what he or she has added to the family's or the individual's life.

The role of the foster parents in the final stages of placement includes teaching the child survival skills, practicing a plan to protect against abuse or neglect, and supporting terminations. Foster parents can play problem-solving games, encourage talk about feelings and concerns, help the child identify unsafe situations, teach the child how to use the phone book and dial telephone numbers, encourage the child to identify (and name) potential supportive persons, and help the child verbalize needs. The ultimate means of empowering children lies in teaching them effective communication and problem-solving, and how to obtain their own resources to the extent possible for their age and developmental stage.

Foster Parent Support of the Reunified Family

The final supporting step is discussing with the social worker, parents, and child the kind of contact with foster parents that is acceptable following reunification. Some foster parents continue to support the family by providing respite care; others keep in contact by visits or phone. Many parents who have successfully reunited with their children credit foster parents who were available to help with problems, give advice, or "just be there when I needed someone."

Children's Readiness for Reunification

Children have the ultimate power to defeat reunification. Their feelings about it—good and bad—must be carefully explored; a plan to protect them from harm must be in place; and their willingness and ability to cooperate with the reunification plan must be assessed, along with the extent of their commitment to the family. Failure to solicit the child's support places the whole family at risk.

Involving children in the reunification decision by soliciting their opinions and informing them of the chosen outcome at the right time and in an age-appropriate fashion is essential. Children can express their feelings and needs, as well as crystallize and communicate their questions and concerns. Even young children can communicate a preference for a particular living arrangement when the worker takes the time to explore all options with the child. For even younger children, this may require the use of drawings or toys to ensure that both the worker and child are referring to the same family or living arrangement.

If children appear frightened about the idea of reunification but cannot verbalize their fears, the worker can help them express feelings indirectly. For example, younger children can demonstrate feelings with toys in a play-therapy setting, and school-age children can draw their "scary" thoughts and feelings. By responding to feelings as well as content, the worker clarifies meaning and probes for additional understanding. Once the worker has a clear understanding of the reasons behind a child's hesitation, he or she can decide how to proceed. Additional measures, ranging from educational efforts to increase the child's verbal and problem-solving skills to a delayed reunification or a change in the permanency plan, may be needed.

Preteens and teenagers can usually express concerns verbally, but if they experience difficulty identifying their feelings and concerns, artwork or role-plays are useful. If a teenager agrees to rejoin his or her family but appears hesitant, a written contract may be negotiated, keyed to the extent of each family member's commitment to reunification. It should include a plan for defusing tension, set forth family rules and expectations, and provide alternatives for the child if reunification goals have to be altered.

If a child is determined not to return home, or has unresolved anger toward family members, reunification may endanger the family's safety as well as the child's. Even young children can sabotage the chances for success and threaten family security, as illustrated in the case of seven-year-old Brent:

When Brent returned home he threatened to kill his mother with a butcher knife and burn the house down. He said he wanted to go back to his foster home. For several months, he told his mother and counselor he was going to burn down the house. Although everyone took Brent's warning seriously and his mother tried everything the counselor suggested, one day when his mother was at court and Brent was home alone with his grandfather, he started to set the kitchen on fire. His grandfather walked into the room just as the curtains burst into flames. Brent stood there and watched them burn. His grandfather had to pull him out of the house. Everything the family owned was lost in the fire. [PRAG 1989]

Better communication among court and agency personnel is one example of an approach that might have prevented such a tragic event [see Day et al., chapter 2].

Protection Plan

A protection plan is a contract between the family and the agency to protect the children from further abuse or neglect and to eliminate the need for further placement. The social worker can help the family create a protection plan by discussing situations or behaviors that have been problematic in the past, especially those that led to placement, identifying warning signs and developing guidelines for protection if a problem should arise after return. For example, a child who was removed after having been physically abused by a parent who was under the influence of alcohol may be taught to recognize alcohol intake as a warning sign.

With guidance from the social worker, parents should take responsibility for and demonstrate effective implementation of the reunification protection plan. Parental leadership in explaining to the children the circumstances of placement, the changes that have improved the situation, and the plan for protection give children permission to follow through with the plan, and is essential for its success.

After a plan for safety is created, the child should explain the plan as he or she understands it and demonstrate an ability to follow through with the suggested course of action. In cases involving an abusive parent, the child might name a friend or relative who would allow her or him to spend the night, and demonstrate an ability to contact the person. Some children may need help to carry out the plan. For example, it should not be taken for granted that a child—without being taught—knows how to use a telephone to get help, or that a child can identify a safe area in the home to get away from an angry parent.

The "What-If...." Game

The "what-if..." game does double duty by preparing children to return home and increasing their problem-solving ability. "What if..." refers to situations or problems that need solving and sounds something like the following: "Let's pretend for a minute. Imagine you come home from school and no one is home. You wait and wait but still neither of your parents comes home. Dinnertime passes and it starts to get dark. What will you do if your mom or dad still isn't home?" After the child responds, the worker can probe, summarize, or offer alternative suggestions. The child then takes turn creating a "what if" situation for the worker to solve. In this way, the practitioner can better understand the child's experiences and fears and the child has an opportunity to identify high-risk situations, as well as learn and practice problem-solving.

Conclusion

Preparing a child and family for reunification should begin when the case begins, as a planned sequence of interventions involving the active participation and commitment of the child, family, social worker, and foster parents. The complex and challenging tasks required to ready children and families for reunification demand that the persons who are most important to the child can demonstrate their capacity to be responsive, supportive, sensitive, and involved for as long as the child needs them to be to maintain a positive family reconnection.

References

Aust, P. "Using the Life Story Book in Treatment of Children in Placement." *CHILD WELFARE* LX, 8 (September 1981): 535–536, 553–560.

Backhaus, K. "Life Books: Tool for Working with Children in Placement." *Social Work* 29, 6 (November–December 1984): 551-554.

Busch, Joey. Lifebook workshop presentation in Indianapolis, IN, 1985.

Fahlberg, V.I., and Jewett, C.L. (1982). "Preparing Children for Adoption." In *Adoption of Children with Special Needs: Curriculum for Adoption Workers*. Athens, GA: The Office of Continuing Social Work Education, School of Social Work, University of Georgia, 1982, 20.

Folaron, G. *The Book of Me*. Indianapolis, IN: Author, 1983.

Goldstein, J.; Freud, A.; and Solnit, A.J. *Beyond the Best Interests of the Child*. New York: The Free Press, 1979.

Hegar, R.L. "Sibling Relationships and Separations: Implications for Child Placement." *Social Service Review* 62, 3 (September 1988): 446–467.

Heiniche, C.H., and Westheimer, I.J. *Brief Separations*. New York: International University Press, 1965.

Hess, P. *Working with Birth and Foster Parents: Trainer's Manual.* Knoxville, TN: Office of Continuing Social Work Education, University of Tennessee School of Social Work, 1981.

Hess, P.M., and Proch, K.O. *Family Visiting in Out-of-Home Care: A Guide to Practice.* Washington, DC: The Child Welfare League of America, 1988.

Jewett, C.L. *Helping Children Cope with Separation and Loss.* Cambridge, MA: The Harvard Common Press, 1982.

Kufeldt, K. "Listening to Children—Who Cares?" *British Journal of Social Work* 14, 3 (June 1984): 257–264.

McDermott, V.A. "Life Planning Services: Helping Older Placed Children with Their Identity." *Child and Adolescent Social Work Journal* 4, 3/4 (Fall–Winter 1987): 245–263.

Pardeck, J.T., and Pardeck, J.A. "Bibliotherapy for Children in Foster Care and Adoption." *CHILD WELFARE* LXVI, 3 (May–June 1987): 269–278.

PRAG. Excerpts from interviews of children and caseworkers conducted as part of a Professional Review and Action Group Project (PRAG), funded by the U.S. Department of Health and Human Services, Office of Human Development Services, Administration for Children, Youth, and Families. The project's purpose is to identify factors leading to disrupted reunifications and to suggest interventions for corrective action. The project is directed by Dr. Peg Hess, Associate Professor, Indiana University. The children were interviewed by Gail Folaron between 1989 and 1991.

Project Craft: Training in the Adoption of Children with Special Needs. Ann Arbor, MI: The University of Michigan School of Social Work, 1980.

Sharrar, M.L. "Some Helpful Techniques When Placing Older Children for Adoption." *CHILD WELFARE* XLIX, 8 (October 1970): 459–463.

Weinstein, E. *The Self-Image of the Foster Child.* New York: Russell Sage Foundation, 1960, 31.

Wheeler, C. *Where Am I Going? Making a Child's Life Story Book.* Juneau, AK: Winking Owl Press, 1978.

9

BELIEVING IN FAMILIES

Jeanne Zamosky, Jacqueline Sparks, Roger Hatt, and Julian Sharman

Reunifying families whose children have been placed in foster care presents unique challenges to all those involved. Many families separated by placement think of themselves as having failed in some way, or they resent those in the system who they feel harbor similar beliefs about them. Families have also undergone new experiences and changes during their children's absence. Children in placement have come to know other families; their experiences with those families must be incorporated into the biological family for reunification to succeed. A successful reunification effort must account for these divergent developments and must assist all family members in catching up with each other.

This chapter delineates and illustrates principles derived from the authors' experiences in an agency that provides in-home, intensive services to families who are having a child returned after foster placement.* The authors discuss how an underlying belief in the potential of all families to care adequately for their children, coupled with a "strengths" focus, is uniquely suited to reunification efforts. Implementation of a strengths approach is examined at four levels of service delivery: the individual caseworker, the supervisor, the family, and the larger child welfare system. Practice strategies are presented that can help agencies and individuals to convey attitudes consistent with a strengths focus

---

* The concepts described are those that guide practice at Familystrength, a nonprofit agency in New Hampshire that provides in-home intensive services to families that are at risk of having a child placed, or that are having a child returned home from foster care. Generally, family workers are involved with families for three months, but they may work with families for as long as six months. They provide a combination of services, including counseling, teaching, and community networking services.

for each level. In addition, the authors describe how to implement a strengths approach during each phase of reunification, from the beginning of the placement, to the child's initial weeks back home, to the successful integration of the child and the family.

A strengths approach develops out of both a philosophical and a practical base. Combining discussion and case example illustrates the inevitable mix of both these bases in strength-focused work. Tools to assess and challenge one's own beliefs are included, as well as practical guidelines for using a belief in families to enhance work in family reunification.

A Strengths Approach to Family Reunification

Several beliefs guide the strengths approach: empowerment of individuals and families is necessary for people to manage their own lives; families have strengths, can change, and can take charge of their lives despite difficult past or present circumstances; families should be full partners in a collaborative effort with helpers to achieve mutually established goals; and the family's extended social network and all involved helpers must be included in the process. A strengths approach:

- respects the significance of "family" to human beings;

- assumes an inner competence and logic behind everyone's behavior;

- embraces an underlying faith that all families have strengths;

- assumes that focusing on strengths will activate them as resources for solving family problems;

- highlights those qualities within the family and helping system that promote health, cohesion, and growth;

- acknowledges that the family's own constructive solutions to problems are the ones that are most effective and long-lasting;

- teams the biological family, the foster family, and the helping system to accomplish reunification goals;

- is both an attitude and a way of working.

These beliefs are consonant with a number of perspectives in the human services, including empowerment-based child welfare [Hegar and Hunzeker 1988]; competence-centered social work practice [Maluccio 1981]; and ethnic-sensitive clinical practice [Pinderhughes 1989; Solomon 1976].

A strengths approach embraces the idea that all families have both strengths and problems, and that the strengths are *keys to solutions to problems*. Family workers are encouraged to identify and bring into play the strengths they see—within the family, within the family's social context, within its helping system, and within the family members—to build a stronger family. A strengths approach assumes that the very act of adopting this posture will not only enable strengths to be identified, but will enhance the strengths themselves and facilitate their spread throughout the family and its helping network.

All Families Have Strengths

Family members, as well as helpers, frequently feel some discouragement about overcoming the many obstacles to successful reunification. It is common for parents to internalize a sense of failure, and for children to experience a sense of abandonment. Family helpers often have feelings of helplessness and failure, too. From society's viewpoint, a child's placement in out-of-home care is evidence that the primary role of the family—that of nurturing and socializing its children—has broken down. Because of this perception of failure, families and their helpers automatically enter the task of reunification from a deficit position.

How is it possible to find and highlight strengths in families where severe abuse or neglect may have occurred? How is it possible to view such families positively, or to see anything in the past as a positive experience? A strengths approach recognizes difficulties as only one side of the coin; a focus on the other side reveals new information. We may learn that the original placement was a solution that both the family and placing agency developed as an answer to an otherwise unsolvable and possibly dangerous situation. The possibility of severe physical injury to a family member, or the removal of several children at once instead of one, may have been present. In this light, the placement is seen as a reasonable choice, one that enables the family to eventually be stronger, not weaker.

If we believe in families we may see the abuse or neglect of a child as stemming from misdirected or blocked caregiving. The strength perspective invites the worker to listen for and understand the parents' story of how abuse and neglect came to exist in the family. This broader generational picture helps to redefine parents as survivors, and therefore as having strengths. An approach that focuses on ways in which the family's fundamental protective energy has been blocked or distorted avoids blaming individuals and often produces insight into ways to intervene.

As the time of reunification approaches, the family's and child's optimism in the face of many obstacles often emerges. One must then focus on the part of the family constellation that believes circumstances are different from those that existed at the time of placement, and that the past can give way to something new and better—the joyfulness that typically accompanies a family's coming together again, and the hopefulness with which they view the future. The strengths perspective enables one to view much of the work in reunification as hopeful and positive, even when faced with unique and often extreme difficulties. This reflects a conviction that, at its core, the family possesses a powerful and enduring tendency to survive and grow.

Strength Leads to Strength

Solution-based family therapists, such as Berg [1990], deShazer [1985], O'Hanlon and Weiner-Davis [1989], and White and Epston [1990] seek to identify and amplify strengths. In this kind of work, it has been noted that active discussion about strengths and using strengths has the effect of intensifying them.

This suggests that situations can be changed through a process of focus. Individuals and families are engaged in an ongoing identification of themselves by how they talk about and act out descriptions of their lives. When those engaged with the family begin to identify "unique outcomes," which are defined as previously overlooked behaviors or strengths that do not correspond with the family's view of themselves, those outcomes tend to be repeated [White and Epston 1990]. For example, simply noting what has gone well during a week more easily characterized by a child's daily temper tantrums tends to decrease the tantrums and increase what has gone well. Asking the parent how the child was able to pull himself or herself together, or how the parent was able to regain his or her equilibrium, puts the emphasis on strengths and invites the family to see themselves in a different light. By encouraging family members to engage in a "performance of meaning" concerning their unique outcomes—to talk about or do again that which succeeded—we increase the presence of strength and success in a situation previously saturated with problems and negativity [White and Epston 1990]. This subtle yet powerful shift is particularly helpful in altering the negative cycles and low esteem that stem from the legacy of failure in previously separated families.

Solutions Lie within the Family

A strengths approach assumes that the family has all it needs to solve its own problems. This is true even when families desperately struggle to survive or when obvious deficits exist in extended family or community connections. Believing that the family has the resources to develop its own solutions to problems does not mean that additional help cannot be provided or that others may not provide new information to help the family. When the emphasis is on unlocking and amplifying the family's own strengths, however, the result is a solution unique to the family, one that the family owns, and one that is likely to last.

How often does it happen that resources made available to a family go unused? How often is a "great idea" for how the family can get along better presented, only to be either politely or blatantly ignored, or to be changed so much by the family that it is no longer recognizable? Many explanations can be assigned to this fairly frequent occurrence in family work. For example, family members may be isolated from social support because they believe it is healthy to live in isolation, because they feel unworthy or too proud to ask for help, or because their poor economic conditions lower their ability to access resources. The worker can often mobilize a helping network that is effective for families whose economic or social constraints block full use of resources. But with families who view helpers as harmful, the worker must first create a context in which this belief is challenged. When the family members' view of themselves in relation to others is changed, they begin to make use of available assistance out of their underlying motivation to seek what is best for the family.

In these instances, the worker has paved the way for the family to chart its own course. The worker has succeeded in activating the family's way of dealing with problems and has not imposed a ready-made solution. It is generally not possible to know the many factors that go into the decisions individuals and families make, or their unique ways of operating in the world, nor is it always necessary. One must have faith in the family's unique expertise and self-knowledge and how these assets may be elicited and enhanced. In a strengths approach, this is accomplished by highlighting positive information previously overlooked and by creating situations in which a family's strengths and ideas for positive change can be further brought into focus.

The choices family workers make have consequences. How they think about a situation and the assumptions they carry into their work directly influence their actions and the outcome of their involvement. If they secretly assume that client families are, in most instances, unmotivated, resistant, uncaring, hostile, or any of the other terms used in conversation, in supervision, with colleagues, or even in official documents, they will draw out these kinds of responses in clients despite efforts to help them unlock and draw on their strengths. What is expected is what is found. What family members believe will be expected of them will, in part, shape their responses.

If, however, one chooses to look at both problems and strengths from a baseline belief in the family's ability to find solutions, then one can be part of creating a context in which the family can come to believe in itself and therefore be able to change in positive ways. This is the kind of therapeutic or healing communication that engenders hope and change for both clients and workers. Techniques may not always be on target, but no technique will be therapeutic unless the worker's belief in the client's capacity to work, solve problems, and grow is felt by the client.

Workers' Beliefs

Reunification work with families begins with the family worker carefully examining his or her own belief systems about families. Workers must first ask themselves whether they believe:

- that a family has a right to be together?

- that families are doing the best they can with the resources they can muster?

- that most families do not intentionally set out to harm their members?

- that families are capable of change and growth?

- that all families have strengths?

Family workers who answer yes to most of these questions must then consider whether these beliefs are accepted and supported by their supervisors, agency management and policies, the public child welfare system, the community, and the state government. It can be lonely and discouraging to find ways to put these beliefs into practice, only to find oneself just a small voice in the dark. The task of changing the system can seem overwhelming, but each individual worker holding these beliefs affects many colleagues, who can affect many supervisors, who can make changes in agency mission statements, and so on. The change can snowball and pick up momentum, but it has to start somewhere.

It is unfair to expect any one individual to be responsible for changing a system, or for changing a family, for that matter. Families are responsible for their change or lack of it. But workers are responsible for their own attitudes and beliefs and for recognizing the power their attitudes have. Believing in families can be contagious and can effect changes.

Implementing the Strengths Approach: Practice Principles

The Worker and Supervisor

Structuring supervision to focus on strengths and encourage belief in a family's ability to change is a crucial aspect of an agency's effort to maintain a strength-focused philosophy. Considering that workers encounter one difficult family situation after another, it is not surprising that even experienced workers can become discouraged about a particular family's ability to make changes. The worker may have difficulty identifying strengths in one family member or in several. It is up to the supervisor to help that individual regain a positive focus.

Mr. and Mrs. Smith have a boy of two and a boy of five. The boys were placed in a foster home following a report of abuse and neglect. The charges reflected concern about the parents' disciplinary methods as well as money problems that led to the family's eviction and homelessness. Feeling that the circumstances that led to being homeless were beyond their control and denying any abuse of the children, Mr. and Mrs. Smith were at first quite angry. Eventually they began to visit the children. After Mr. Smith found a temporary job, the couple moved into a new apartment, and the boys were returned home. Family-based counseling was provided.

The couple's initial happiness with the children's return soon turned to frustration. They complained that the placement had affected the children so that the boys no longer listened to them. The family worker suggested alternate approaches to discipline, but Mr. Smith was adamant that things were fine before the placement and he should not have to change. He insisted that the five-year-old boy was lying and purposely defying him. The worker became frustrated with the father's argumentative, hard-line approach. Mrs. Smith seemed desperate to return things to "normal" and willing to listen to different approaches. The worker spent extra time meeting individually with Mrs. Smith to discuss discipline. The worker found it easy to work with Mrs. Smith, who listened to her suggestions but seemed unable to carry them out against her husband's wishes. To make matters worse, Mr. Smith had begun missing work, which was jeopardizing his job and their new home.

A supervisor meeting with this discouraged worker can do three things to support the worker in dealing with the difficult situation: use his or her own focus on strengths to help the worker see new possibilities for family change; help the worker to adapt the worker's own strengths and skills, which have been effective in the past, to the new situation with the current family; or help the worker to acquire skills or knowledge through such means as training, consultation, and resource materials.

In the case described above, the family worker told the supervisor about her frustration with the family's progress, and stressed Mr. Smith's noncompliance. The supervisor expressed confidence in the worker's ability to be effective with this family and offered examples of similar family situations with which the worker had been effective in the past. The supervisor put forth her view that the father had an important part to play in helping the family to change and that the father himself was able to change. She asked the worker to describe the strengths she saw in the father, which were his desire to have his children returned and the persistence with which he had searched for a job and apartment; he was also a hard worker who wanted to support and take care of the family, and he had a desire to be in charge of the children, which often led to harsh disciplinary methods but which could be a potential strength.

The supervisor suggested a plan be devised with the worker to include Mr. Smith in the family meetings in a more productive way. The worker and supervisor agreed that the worker would spend the next meeting having Mr. and Mrs. Smith discuss the difficulties they were having with the children's behavior. The worker would not suggest any new ideas, but would elicit more discussion from both parents in the hope that they would come to an agreement on the need to set a goal involving discipline. The family worker also agreed to audiotape the meeting, with the family's permission, so that the supervisor could listen to the interaction.

This approach proved to be productive. Mrs. Smith asked her husband to try a time-out technique that the worker had discussed with her. Mr. Smith said he had to be especially hard with the children because of Mrs. Smith's inconsistency; he felt that she frequently ignored their bad behavior. The couple agreed to work on increasing their cooperation as a parental team in disciplining the children.

The supervisor was able to listen to the tape and to point out to the worker how she had acknowledged that each parent had something to contribute to resolving the discipline problems and that both needed to commit themselves to working together. The supervisor pointed out ways in which the worker had included both parents in the discussion. Since the tape had shown how the father still dominated much of the discussion, supervision included ways to achieve a better-balanced discussion in future meetings.

It is through a process such as this that supervisors can use a strengths approach in their work, that is, they can convey to workers their compassion and belief that the workers have the capacity to work toward solutions and grow.

The Worker and the Family

How do family workers form their first impression of the reunified family with whom they will be working? Most families will have been in the system for a long time and a thick file, typically containing an unflattering profile, will have accumulated. Words like abusive, neglectful, resistant, uncooperative, unmotivated, and hopeless jump off the pages, luring workers to adopt a similar impression of the family. Workers can make a choice: to accept what they have read and frame their interventions around that, or to develop a new framework. This first impression of the family lays the groundwork for a focus on strengths, not problems.

Words written in a file or court report are indeed powerful. Once the words are written, families are put in the position of disproving the labels. While a label may well have been true for a snapshot in time, it may no longer be applicable. Unfortunately, though, the written word often outlives behaviors. Further, the label used to describe a behavior may be different from the one the present worker or the family would use to describe the same behavior. For instance, a 13-year-old preparing meals for the family could be labeled "parentified" in one report, yet another worker—or the family—would view the behavior as functional.

Additionally, a family's inability or seeming unwillingness to follow through with a worker's directive may, in fact, be that worker's inability or unwillingness to devise directives that fit with the family's style of learning, culture, traditions, or strengths. For example, assigning readings on parenting to a family that does not value book knowledge would not be helpful; the family members may instead benefit from talking about their experiences and behavior, or from having a new skill demonstrated to them. They would not, however, necessarily lack motivation to learn more appropriate parenting skills.

In addition to reading the information in a file, a worker can ask questions of colleagues who have a history of working with a given family. The types of questions asked will begin to shape the picture of the family the worker is forming. Asking questions such as: "What resources does the Jones family have?" "What has gone well when Johnny comes home for a visit?" and "How does Mrs. Jones nurture Johnny?" begin to get at what the Jones's strengths are. But if the worker chooses to ask, "What problems did the Jones have when Johnny visited?" "Who will have most to lose when Johnny comes home?" and "Who will be most difficult to work with?" a different picture begins to form.

One can also learn about the family by asking the family directly, rather than obtaining information from the file and from colleagues. The worker's initial belief in the family is a resource that must be preserved. It is best to meet the family with a nearly clean slate; there will be ample time later to read assessment reports and evaluations. The family can be the first to provide the worker with current and accurate information about themselves.

Workers are responsible for the "baggage" they carry into their work with families, and its influence on the choices they make all the time about what information to accept, reject, or question. If one decides to focus on all that families do wrong, it will be simple to prove the labels in the files as correct; but one can choose instead to understand each family by focusing on its strengths. Just as a family needs a strong foundation on which to begin living as a unit again, a caseworkers needs a positive, strength-focused view. If workers start with an inherent belief in the family's ability to be together, they are obligated to search for positive signs, behaviors, and evidences of affection on which to build. Family workers have to feel confident about the way reunification visits are going and about a decision to reunite a child and family. Identifying and highlighting strengths will build the workers' faith in the family.

Families' Beliefs

Preparing for family reunification work by examining workers' attitudes and beliefs is a first step. An understanding of some of the general attitudes and feelings that reunification families hold for themselves is also needed, however. The following are common feelings among families working toward reunification:

- *Sense of Failure*. Families who have had a child placed in care have suffered a break in their family as they knew it. Any effort that the parents may have expended to keep their child at home was not enough—their child's removal from their care was a clear message that they were not getting the job done. Even parents who accepted or asked for the placement describe feeling that they have failed— a feeling that may be strong enough to discourage parents from making the effort to visit their child in placement and may therefore delay reunification possibilities.

- *Lack of Confidence*. Parents who feel that they have failed their children once will have difficulty feeling confident about their instincts or their ability to care for their children once they reconnect with them. If foster parents have been nurturing, feeding, disciplin- ing, and encouraging their children, biological parents tend to doubt that they can do as good a job. Parents have described needing to call their social worker during visits by their child to check out every decision they make regarding their child, constantly fearing that they are doing something wrong.

- *Anger*. Parents may direct anger at their child, the system, and/or themselves. Some families continue to disagree, rightly or wrongly, about the reasons for placement of their child. They believe they have had to "jump through the hoops" to have their child returned. This feeling of disempowerment can often turn to anger directed at the system that removed their child; at the child for "causing" the removal; or at themselves for allowing the removal to take place. Parents often wish they had fought harder to prevent the placement.

- *Mistrust of the System*. This feeling generally surfaces when a placement has continued for a long time and parents feel they have gone through the necessary steps to have their child returned, but to no avail. These families may tend to close up once the child is returned, for fear that revealing any difficulties may jeopardize their family.

While some may see the foregoing descriptors as negative, we prefer to view them as a necessary starting place. Who could experience the pain of separation from a child without feeling angry and scared? Anger often masks overwhelming sadness, humiliation, and fear. Mistrust may be a survival mechanism that should be nurtured and guided; feelings of failure are actually signs of accepting responsibility for the necessity of placement. A lack of confidence is normal and expected, and more importantly, it is something that can change with encouragement, education, and time.

Reunification families present many positive characteristics that make them exciting and challenging to work with, such as the following:

- *Feeling of Connectedness*. It is the exception rather than the rule to have a family separated without all members feeling a deep sense of loss. Although they live in separate places, their idea of family is of everyone together. A placement removes children physically, but not emotionally, from their families.

- *Perseverance*. Reunification families are typically motivated and committed families. Some have remained involved in their children's lives for years without being the primary caregivers; this agency's longest case involved a family separated for close to five years. Parenting in this way is extremely difficult and trying. Many parents end up wondering if they should just give up—if perhaps their children would be better off without them. At times, the system supports this message.

- *Increased Energy and Hopefulness.* The reunification process, beginning with visits and culminating at the point where a child can be returned home, can be an exciting, eventful, and positive time for the family. Parents and children may have changed in ways that allow them to feel emotionally closer to one another. The return of a child is viewed as a new beginning, another chance, and with that can come the resolve that separation will never happen again.

The Reunification Process

Reuniting children and parents is a complicated process requiring a structure to minimize the worker's chances of getting lost in the process and to maintain a focus. The process can be broken down into three phases, with tasks assigned to each phase. Although the process is described in figure 1 in a linear way, or as following along a continuum, it should be recognized that many families need to keep circling back, or never get to the end stage. It may be useful to teach families the different phases of reunification and its related tasks so that the process is demystified for them. With this knowledge and understanding, family members become true partners with the worker in facilitating their child's return.

A three-phase continuum is also an effective way to put a strengths approach into operation. Having a plan allows workers to interpret whatever strides or setbacks occur as a natural part of moving forward toward eventual reunification. Even if the child's return does not hold and re-placement occurs, all the parties have learned something about what changes a successful reunification would require. Obstacles can be identified within particular phases, and the time and focus of intervention can be structured accordingly. This is quite different from a plan that assumes successful reunification is, at best, a long shot, and that views setbacks as confirmation of the impossibility of the endeavor.

The three phases of the reunification continuum are *bridging, opening,* and *building.*

FIGURE 1–THE REUNIFICATION CONTINUUM

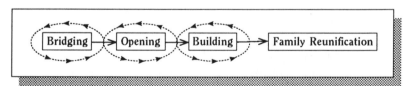

Phase 1: Bridging

This phase aims to create, if one does not already exist, a connection between the child's home and the foster family. Bridging helps families (and the helping system) modify the negative story family members believe about themselves based on separateness and allows everyone to construct a new story that joins two paths into one. This bridge phase serves the following purposes:

- *Preserving the Child's History.* A child's history should not be lost for the length of time he or she is in placement [see Folaron, chapter 8]. The child may have accomplished a new developmental task or may have gone from one developmental stage into the next. An intact family naturally records these events and incorporates them into their family history. Families who have a child in placement often miss these events and the corresponding emotions.

- *Informing the Child of Family Events.* While in placement, the child is engaged in the challenging task of being part of two families. The child expends much energy becoming part of a foster family, finding ways to fit in, to learn the rules, and to find his or her place. At the same time, the child is emotionally bonded to his or her family of origin and spends time wondering such things as, "Is my mom all right?" "Will my sister forget me?" "Will someone remember to feed the dog?" "Are other kids playing with my toys?" "Are they having fun without me?" and "Will they want me back?"

  If a bridge has been built between the placement setting and the home, the child will have the opportunity to get answers to such questions and to once again feel a part of his or her family.

- *Transferring Strategies.* Foster parents have often provided needed structure or implemented a behavior management technique that has successfully brought a child's behavior under control [see Hess and Proch, chapter 7]. This valuable information should be passed on to the biological parents. The two families should also discuss the child's daily routine, favorite foods, and so on.

- *Modeling Cooperation.* Seeing the significant adults in their lives cooperate offers children in placement many important lessons. Putting effort into developing and maintaining a working relationship can alleviate a child's need to choose sides and feel disloyal to either their parents or foster parents. If competition, quarreling, or uncomfortable silence between parents and foster parents can be reduced or eliminated, the child will be able to express emotions freely and honestly. Cooperation gives a child security, in much the same way as a united parental front does in an intact family.

Strategies and Tasks for Bridging. During the bridging stage the family worker facilitates the process by meeting with foster and biological parents separately at first, then arranging for joint meetings to transfer information from one home to another, and perhaps also to make the foster parents an ongoing resource for the biological parents.

Successful bridging requires some or perhaps all of the following strategies, depending upon the family situation:

- *Meeting with Foster Parents.* Spending adequate time with foster parents before they meet biological parents can be helpful. Preparation can include discussion of how the foster parents feel about the child leaving and their concerns about the home environment or parents' abilities. Foster parents can be asked how they feel the reunification process could be smoothed, and what they feel the child needs during the transition. They can be complimented about the strategies they employed that brought about a positive change in the child's behavior, and for the gains the child made while in their care.

- *Establishing the Biological Parent-Foster Parent Relationship.* Having foster parents describe methods of behavior management to biological parents can be tricky. The biological family is apt to feel threatened by the foster parents' expertise. Also, the foster parents may feel uncomfortable in the role of teacher.

  It may be most helpful to have initial meetings that concentrate on getting the two families to know each other, discussing how the child is doing, and bringing the family up to date on the child's accomplishments. Establishing this relationship can set the stage for biological parents to be open to soliciting and accepting information from the foster parents.

  Foster parents might be able to tell biological parents: "Johnny is very polite, you did a good job teaching him manners," or "Johnny told me that you used 'time-out' with him at home. That was a great idea, so I used that as well. With a timer he could keep track himself of how much time was left. He seems to accept the consequence more easily if he knows when it will be over." Identifying a strength while teaching new information can be a powerful tool.

Phase 2: Opening

Systems theory tells us that a family strives for homeostasis. Once a family member is rejected or extracted, the remaining members fight for survival, which means coming together and redefining themselves as a family. The placed child is excluded from this new definition. Although children are missed and probably longed for, their role or place in the family has most likely been taken over by one of the remaining siblings.

Creating an opening takes place at both psychological and physical levels. The family can be helped to first visualize and then discuss a way in which the child can be helped to fit into the family again. The family worker helps the family to remember events from the time before the child's departure. Family members are then encouraged to describe in detail pleasant memories of events or interactions that included the entire family. A strength focus at this stage helps the family resist returning to ways of operating in the past that were destructive. Attending at the same time to the child's new physical position in the home allows the family to actively create a new and more positive family structure.

- *Physical Space.* A tangible place to start is with the physical surroundings in the home. Does the family have a bed for the child? Is there a chair, and a place at the table? Is there space in the bathroom for the extra toothbrush? Where will toys and clothes be put? Encouraging family members to focus on these details opens the process of returning to the family. Visual changes around the home signal the returning child that his or her space is being readied.

- *Family Image.* Parents and siblings may have become accustomed to viewing themselves with one less member throughout the length of the child's placement. Their view, in a psychological sense, must begin to shift to include one more. The ecomap is a good place to start. Displaying the returning child's network and the family's network on one page illustrates the merging that has to be accomplished. Family meetings can also be a forum for members to discuss their hopes and fears for their reunified family, expectations for one another, daily routines, rules, chores, and consequences.

- *Social/Educational Environment.* An opening for the child must be created in the community as well as in the home. Parents can register their child for school and perhaps arrange for the child to visit the school before beginning to attend regularly. A walking tour of the neighborhood to acquaint, or reacquaint, the child with the community's resources can be a pleasant activity for a sibling to share with the returning child.

During this phase the family worker helps the family find out what will be necessary to make room for the returning child. Finding a task for each family member heightens the feeling of "being in this together." Even a very young sibling can make a special picture or clear a space in the closet for his or her returning brother. Families should be encouraged to be creative during this phase and to trust their instincts about what is important to their child.

Phase 3: Building

The majority of reunited families experience a honeymoon period after the return of a child from placement. Family members are excited about being together, and conflict tends to be minimal. It is unlikely that this can last; two to six weeks of this ideal state is typical. Then parents and children relax and more typical patterns of relating emerge.

The honeymoon presents a unique challenge for workers. Workers must highlight the family's togetherness, good will, and positive feelings; predict the typical course of events for reunification; and help the family prepare for what will come next. Family members can be encouraged to feel positively about what will happen when the honeymoon is over. Johnny's first fight with his mother could be interpreted as his trusting his parents with the real Johnny, or with all parts of Johnny. The difficult times, as well as the easy times, are part of being a family. Having disagreements and solving problems together, getting angry and making up, add richness to relationships.

This phase of reunification work involves helping family members to add to that richness, to strengthen relationships, and to mold their identity as a family. The following are tasks for this phase:

- *Family Meetings.* Teaching family members how to conduct regular family meetings can provide them with a way to express their feelings about the reunification and the ups and downs of living together again, negotiate household rules and chores, and share successes at school and work.

- *Recreation.* Providing the family with the opportunity to have fun and play together is as important at this stage as talking about the issues. Outings should be simple at first and carefully planned, so that they have a good chance of being successful. Having a relaxed, fun time together strengthens the family bond.

- *Traditions and Rituals*. Family members can discuss traditions they used to have and want to continue, as well as instituting new ones. They may decide to start "Family Day" in recognition of the day that their family was reunited.

During the building phase the worker is looking for opportunities to highlight the sense of family that is forming. Parents need encouragement and praise for their efforts. Many parents may hesitate to be parents fully because they do not trust the permanence of the situation. Their confidence has been shattered by their child's placement; their efforts at parenting may therefore be tentative at first.

A combination of education, family meetings, and recreation works well to increase family members' confidence in themselves and to reduce the anxiety that they are "not good enough." It helps to encourage family members to discuss expectations: will the family be what it was before, or will members automatically feel comfortable together? The adjustment to reunification will take time, much as stepfamilies have to take time to really blend.

The Social Worker and the Larger System

Throughout the reunification process, the worker communicates frequently with other service professionals. During the early bridging phase, the worker may perceive a need to connect the family to those who have become part of the child's system. For example, a child in foster family or residential care could have developed a strong relationship with a therapist, a guardian, or perhaps a Big Brother. The family may want to meet those who have had an impact on their child's life during the placement. Bridging can include enabling the court and other systems to catch up with what has transpired in the family since the beginning of placement. Once a child has been placed by the court, the court may put the case aside and move on to more pressing matters. When the decision is made to reunify the family, the court system is suddenly reactivated and must be caught up with changes that have occurred.

As the family creates a physical and emotional space for the child returning home, it may be necessary to widen the opening to include the child's new support system or "significant others." The child may not be prepared to sever ties with his or her counselor, Big Brother, or social worker. On the one hand, the task of the family worker is to help family members accept the fact that their child has developed supportive relationships with "outside" people. On the other hand, the worker may sense that it is the counselor and the Big Brother who are feeling a sense of loss as the child becomes less dependent on them and more excited about going home. In this case, the worker may want to introduce them to the family, creating an acceptance in their minds of the child's reunion with the family.

Once the child is moved home, the family worker must identify what additional supports are needed and help the child or family to connect with them. For example, it may be necessary to help the parents locate after-school care, arrange transportation, or enroll the child in day care. Outside activities such as youth groups, scouts, or religious activities might be looked into. Appointments with health care providers, such as doctors and dentists, are usually required. If the child is changing schools, the parents will want to meet with teachers, principals, and school counselors. Through such activities, the worker is attempting to link the family to larger systems and create supports. As noted earlier, using the ecomap can help the worker and the family to determine what services are needed.

The family worker joins an already existing group of helpers when called upon to assist in reunifying a child and family. The group usually includes child welfare workers, attorneys, guardians, therapists, school officials, and judges. In some cases it may be necessary to strengthen the relationships between the family and some members of this group.

Relationship with the Court System

There are several ways to use a strengths approach in building a bridge between the family and court-related officials. The first step is a strength-focused dialogue. Assurances to the family that everyone is acting in the best interests of their child may be met with initial disbelief, but they help to set the stage for a continuing strengths approach. Questions to professionals, such as, "What strengths do those parents have that can help them make this reunification a success?" begin to shift the conversation into a slightly altered, more positive frame. Blending strength-oriented statements into conversations about problems begins to change the conceptualization of the problems. Eventually, a bridge is formed between the family's views and the larger system's views, which once may have seemed miles apart.

Constructing an ecomap [Hartman and Laird 1983] can reveal hidden support networks that may otherwise go unnoticed and therefore unused. Strong connections to friends or community organizations are generally looked upon as strengths by courts and child welfare workers. These should be identified and made known.

Case Illustration

A district court judge reluctantly agreed to return five-year-old Suzy to her mother. His reluctance was due, in part, to his sense that her mother, Mrs. Sanders was overly dependent on her parents and perhaps not mature and responsible enough to parent her daughter properly.

Suzy's placement had occurred soon after Mrs. Sanders and her husband had separated. The husband had alleged that Mrs. Sanders was neglecting Suzy, and that the grandparents could not take proper care of her either. The judge remembered that the grandparents seemed uncooperative and he wondered about their motivation to change. The court had judged Mrs. Sanders to be an ineffectual parent, and the referral goals included helping her to become "less reliant" on her parents.

Almost a year went by before the court ordered a home-based agency to assist in the reunification process. During the assessment, Jan, the family worker, met several times with Mrs. Sanders and the grandparents. An ecomap revealed that Mrs. Sanders was far less reliant on her parents than she had been at the time of placement. In fact, she was now financially independent, had her own apartment, and was involved in several community groups and activities.

Thinking in the bridging mode, the worker wanted to connect the family to the court. One objective was to update the court on all that had changed for Mrs. Sanders over the past year. The worker's next step was to create an opening for a stronger relationship between Mrs. Sanders and the various professionals involved in the reunification process. Although this had already begun during the worker's initial conversations with everyone, it was agreed that face-to-face meetings would strengthen the bridge and open up further discussion about the reunification. Teaming together, the worker and the mother developed a service plan. Several goals were agreed upon, including one that was aimed at strengthening relations with the court system:

Goal #1. Jan will initiate separate meetings with the guardian and social worker.

The family worker role-played with Mrs. Sanders the meetings to help her feel at ease and reduce her defensiveness. The worker called the guardian and the social worker ahead of time and encouraged them to be receptive to the mother's initiative.

Goal #2. Mrs. Sanders will communicate more effectively with the court, the social worker, and the school.

Mrs. Sanders was armed with a new and stronger image of herself. She practiced communicating her strengths, her accomplishments, and her plans for reuniting with Suzy. The worker helped her to understand the system's views and how to talk with various members of the group.

Goal #3. Together, Mrs. Sanders and the family worker will construct a written report that will highlight and reinforce the progress made in parenting and independent living.

The system members were prepared to see Mrs. Sanders in a different way than they had a year ago. The worker had created an opening for them to see the changes, and their new view would be conveyed to the judge. Once Suzy returned home, the worker helped the family structure their daily activities and helped the mother to decide what outside activities would be in their best interests. Suzy's court-appointed Big Sister remained involved for many months following reunification.

Reunification cases tend to involve a multitude of social service professionals. The family worker should include members of larger systems in the bridging, opening, and building phases. Adopting a strength-focused approach involves choosing written and verbal language that brings the family and court system together in constructive ways.

Conclusion

The growing awareness of the importance of maintaining a child with his or her family has created a rapidly growing family preservation field. This, in turn, has led practitioners to look for strategies from social work, parent education, family therapy, and crisis intervention that can be effective in working with a diverse group of families when the goal is reunification of placed children and their families.

The approach described in this chapter emphasizes the importance of believing in the essential bonds of the family, in the family's ability to make change, and in the importance of focusing on a family's strengths to achieve reunification. A strengths approach is not only part of an overriding philosophy of how families change, but also a pragmatic aspect of day-to-day work. This approach with families is most effective when it is incorporated into all levels of the helping system. It must be part of ongoing supervision. The agency must promote this philosophy in its hiring, training, and daily operations; emphasize it in supervision; and encourage it in its interactions with the larger system.

The practitioners' belief that solutions lie within the family leads them to define their task as that of developing a partnership with the family in which strengths are identified, goals are defined, knowledge and skills are gained, and community resources are accessed. Only when this has been done will it be known whether family members can succeed in their efforts to reestablish their connections.

References

Berg, I.S. *A Guide to Practice: Constructing Solutions in In-Home Treatment*. Milwaukee, WI: Brief Family Therapy Center, 1990.

deShazer, S. *Keys to Solution in Brief Therapy*. New York: W.W. Norton & Company, 1985.

Hartman, A., and Laird, J. *Family-Centered Social Work Practice*. New York: The Free Press, 1983.

Hegar, R.L., and Hunzeker, J.M. "Moving towards Empowerment-Based Practice in Public Child Welfare." *Social Work* 33, 6 (November–December 1988): 499–502.

Maluccio, A.N. *Promoting Competence in Clients: A New/Old Approach to Social Work Practice*. New York: The Free Press, 1981.

O'Hanlon, W., and Weiner-Davis, M. *In Search of Solutions*. New York: W.W. Norton & Company, 1989.

Pinderhughes, E. *Understanding Race, Ethnicity, and Power*: The Key to Efficacy in Clinical Practice. New York: The Free Press, 1989.

Solomon, B.B. *Black Empowerment: Social Work in Oppressed Communities*. New York: Columbia University Press, 1976.

White, M., and Epston, D. *Narrative Means to Therapeutic Ends*. New York: W.W. Norton and Company, 1990.

PART THREE

Creating the Knowledge Base

10

EVALUATING FAMILY REUNIFICATION PROGRAMS

John Turner

Child welfare practitioners have a difficult task in implementing the public policy priority of reunifying children in out-of-home care with their families. To successfully achieve reunification, practitioners must determine accurately the changes that are needed in the family and the environment before reunification can take place, the services and practice methods that will effect and sustain these needed changes, the appropriate level of reconnection for the child and family, and the potential and/or actual consequences of reunification.

Currently, however, practitioners are in the unenviable position of having to make these decisions with minimal guidance from systematic evaluations of what constitutes effective reunification practice. Administrators and practitioners tend to rely on "rates of reunification" as the sole indicator of effectiveness. This measure—the number of children returned to their families—offers little insight into the effects of practice on children and families. More adequate evaluations of reunification practice and its results must become a routine part of programs to assure appropriate reconnection of children with their families, and to understand what characteristics of service best accomplish this goal.

This chapter aims to demystify evaluation research and thereby encourage practitioners to consider program evaluation as a necessary part of effective family reunification practice. In the first section, program evaluation is defined and its overall purposes set forth. A framework follows for organizing the types of questions and answers that might be sought about an agency's program. Finally, strategies for undertaking a program evaluation are discussed, including examples of current evaluation efforts in family reunification programs.

Program Evaluation: Definition, Purposes, and Framework

Definition

Program evaluation in the human services has been defined as the focus of necessary knowledge, skills, and sensitivities in the following four areas: determining the need for a program or service; determining if the program is offered as planned; determining if the service is sufficient to meet the need; and determining if the program actually helps the people who need it [Posavac and Carey 1985]. Others have more generally defined evaluation as the application of scientific methods to produce knowledge about program operations and effects [Tripodi 1983].

This chapter is based on the assumption that any thoughtful examination of program processes and outcomes is valid if it aims to improve family reunification services. Although rigorously scientific approaches that consider the general application of findings, for example, may be preferred, less rigorous approaches are useful to practitioners if they produce reliable evaluation data.

Purposes

This chapter focuses on the two types of program evaluation most commonly discussed: outcome evaluation and process—or implementation—evaluation.

Outcome studies examine the extent to which reunification programs are successful in accomplishing stated goals and assess whether programs are achieving desired client and case results. Relative to the status of clients, outcome evaluations provide information on changes in one or more of the following: (1) targeted behaviors; (2) available resources; (3) informal and formal support systems; (4) relationships between and among family members; (5) knowledge and skill levels; and (6) motivation. They also provide information on the status of cases, for example, the extent to which reunification programs are accomplishing the goal of the most appropriate level of reconnection between families and children.

Evaluations of process or implementation examine program inputs, operations, and outputs, providing information on (1) the types and level of resources invested in programs; (2) organizational arrangements, policies, and procedures; (3) service components of programs; (4) specific activities of practitioners; and (5) the intrinsic and/or perceived quality of service activities. Without this information, practitioners do not know whether there is a gap between what is intended and what actually occurs in reunification practice. Since gaps usually exist, it is the size of the gap that is most often of concern. For example, effective reunification programs make use of community services such as housing, employment, and day care to achieve appropriate reconnection between a child and family. It is likely that most programs intend to make extensive use of community resources, but there is evidence that a gap sometimes exists between intended and actual use of such resources in reunification practice [Turner 1984].

In the real world of child welfare administration and practice, the two types of evaluation are interrelated. In the case of family reunification, the ultimate aim is finding out what works to achieve a child's return home, or the highest possible level of reconnection for families and their children. Hence, so-called program evaluations focusing only on case outcomes, such as how many children are returned to their families, are clearly inadequate. They offer no information about whether children were returned to families willing and able to care for them, or about the services that helped to achieve the outcomes. Unfortunately, program staff members or administrators often attempt some form of outcome evaluation without first identifying and measuring the critical attributes of their programs. This approach is incomplete because, unless key implementation variables are specified and measured, program effects cannot be explained. Staff members cannot determine which program features contribute to desired outcomes, and should be enhanced and replicated, and which are inadequate, and should be modified or discarded.

Two temptations may result from the tendency to evaluate program outcomes without implementation information. On the one hand, if the results of an outcome evaluation indicate that a program is at least modestly successful, satisfied managers and practitioners may delve no further even though they cannot be sure which, if any, program features help to explain outcomes. On the other hand, if findings suggest that a program is not achieving the desired results, its personnel grumble about intractable families and children rather than grapple with program deficiencies. Neither of these responses is in the best interests of children, families, or effective reunification practice. Programs that routinely assess implementation factors as well as outcomes are less susceptible to these temptations.

Framework

A potential model or framework for evaluating a family reunification effort consists of the following seven program components: goals, inputs, operations, quantity of output, quality of output, and client and case outcomes. These are diagrammed in figure 1.

The diagram illustrates the major components of both process and outcome evaluations, and the relationship between program implementation factors and desired program outcomes. The specific components of the model that are

FIGURE 1–

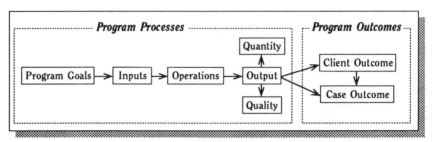

included in a particular evaluation will vary according to the information needs of each program. Generally, programs in early stages of development or those with major modifications require information on many implementation and outcome components. These programs benefit from an assessment of program processes before dealing with outcomes; this ensures that the program is being properly implemented before conclusions about its effectiveness are drawn. Programs with established and well-documented operations and services may conduct evaluations to discover which program outputs are most associated with intended outcomes.

Goals. Program goals are measurable statements of what the reunification program intends to achieve. Goals should specify intentions regarding implementation (i.e., to enhance staff productivity), as well as outcomes (i.e., increasing the percentage of cases in which an appropriate level of reconnection is achieved).

Inputs. Program inputs are the resources invested in achieving program goals. Typically, resources include dollar expenditures, staff time, materials, equipment, and facilities. Decisions regarding the level of program inputs are critical. Most child welfare practitioners will attest that inadequate inputs seldom produce adequate results.

Operations. Program operations are the organizational arrangements, policies, and procedures by which inputs produce service activities or outputs. Operations provide the context and guidelines for reunification practice, and directly affect the quantity and quality of service activities and outcomes. Practitioners are affected by operational issues such as whether or not organizational structures provide formal opportunities for them to influence policy. In the case of family reunification, an example of the role of program operations in achieving results might be the extent to which formal agency processes exist for the staff to manage and evaluate contracted services aimed at helping parents learn the parenting skills they need to resume full-time care of their children.

Outputs. Outputs can be measured in number and quality. The number of identifiable products generated by a program is generally measured by the number of units of service provided for a given time period (i.e., the hours of case management provided to a reunified family). It is useful to distinguish between the quantity of program outputs and the intrinsic and/or perceived quality of those outputs. The client-contact hours generated by a practitioner within a given month may or may not have resulted in timely, appropriate, and compassionate service. Given the huge caseloads of many involved in reunification practice, programs should be aware of the potentially inverse relationship between the quantity and quality of outputs.

Outcomes. Outcomes are program results. As previously noted, the results of reunification efforts are often measured simply by the ratio of children returned home to those still in foster care. Without more sophisticated measures of the effects of programs, concern will and should persist that the rate of reunification may at times be a measure of program ineffectiveness rather than effectiveness. High ratios may mean, for example, that a program is returning children who are immediately at risk because their families are not prepared for their return. For this reason, program effectiveness must be measured by assessing client as well as case outcomes. Evaluating client outcomes involves measuring changes in client conditions, problems, or functioning; case outcomes refer to changes in the service and/or legal status of clients [Magura and Moses 1986].

Strategies for Conducting Program Evaluations

Various outlines of the process of evaluation have been delineated [Weiss 1972; Tripodi 1983; Jennings 1978]. The following four-step process is used in discussing strategies for evaluating implementation and outcomes in family reunification programs: (1) planning the evaluation, (2) selecting program characteristics to measure, (3) determining evaluation approaches, and (4) reporting and using results. Theoretically, the steps are sequential. In practice, two or more steps may be addressed simultaneously.

Planning the Evaluation

In the initial phase of the process, agencies must answer two general questions: "Why are we conducting this evaluation?" and "What do we want to know about our family reunification program?" Once the overall purpose has been determined, it is important for staff members to identify the ways that study results will be used to improve the program and commit themselves to those uses. Will findings be used to revise goals and objectives? Will they be the basis for modifying staffing patterns or service activities? Evaluation studies are notoriously underutilized [Patton 1978]. If program staff members are not committed to specifically applying results, or if administrators are not committed to making the necessary changes in policy and program, the efficacy of conducting an evaluation should be questioned.

The types of questions practitioners and administrators want answered and their relevancy for program decisions are illustrated by Fein and Staff in chapter 11 and in a study undertaken by the Five Acres Boys' and Girls' Society of Los Angeles County. Administrators and practitioners in the latter program were interested in determining whether didactic or experiential learning opportunities for parents and children were more effective in enhancing the skills, sense of adequacy, and commitment of parents. Families were randomly assigned to one of three service components. Eleven families received experiential learning opportunities, ten received didactic learning, and ten received a combination of the two. Results demonstrated that families receiving a combination of learning experiences were more likely to be successfully reunified than the other families [Carlo and Shennum 1989].

During the planning phase it is also necessary to document the characteristics (inputs, operations, outputs) of the program and to assess the clarity and appropriateness of program goals and objectives. This planning step is often referred to as assessing the "evaluability" of a program [Rutman 1980]. Explicit program characteristics and objectives are preconditions for program evaluations, and must be attended to in the planning for them.

In planning a program evaluation it is useful to construct a model showing the components of the program. This concretizes and makes visible to all staff members the intended program inputs, operations, and quantity and quality of outputs. Figure 2 illustrates one approach to modeling reunification programs, and indicates some of the information such models provide. It also suggests possible variables to include in assessing a program.

Regardless of the developmental stage of a program, there are obvious advantages in staff members engaging periodically in the process of specifying intentions relative to program implementation. Clarity of program features and objectives is requisite to sound reunification practice, as well as a prerequisite for evaluation studies.

Finally, in planning a program evaluation, the evaluation budget and the leadership of the project should be established. The program staff should determine whether the study will be led by a program staff member or an outside consultant. Factors affecting this decision are the funds available for the evaluation; the availability of staff members with expertise in evaluation methods; and the extent to which the perception of a biased evaluation should be avoided [Rutman and Mowbray 1983].

Once these requirements have been met, programs can proceed to the second step in the evaluation process, the selection of program characteristics to be measured.

Selecting Program Characteristics to Measure

The selection of which program characteristics to evaluate is based on a number of elements. Chief among these elements are accountability to external reviewers, the key principles and components of reunification practice, and unique features of individual programs.

External Audiences. The Adoption Assistance and Child Welfare Act of 1980 (Public Law 96-272) established requirements for monitoring foster care cases and programs [Maluccio et al. 1986]. Court and civilian team reviews of cases are designed to make certain that appropriate plans are made for children in care, that plans are revised when needed, and that plans are acted upon. While the efficacy of these requirements continues to be debated and studied [Kadushin and Martin 1988], the requirements have had one effect: programs must account routinely to external bodies for some aspects of their efforts. Mandated reviews generally focus on the quantity and perhaps quality of selected program outputs, such as plans and activities for permanent arrangements for children. The reviews seldom attend to program inputs, operations, or comprehensive analyses of the quantity and quality of outputs. Although it may therefore be reasonable and necessary to evaluate program characteristics routinely accounted for to external audiences, studies limited to such factors are not sufficient.

Expectations on the part of funders and policymakers for quantifiable results may interfere with the selection of appropriate outcome measures. As mentioned earlier, most evaluations tend not only to ignore client outcomes, but also to measure effectiveness by two dichotomous case outcome variables: "reunified or not" and "reentry into foster care or not." The principle set forth in chapter 1 of this volume—that there are several forms or levels of appropriate reconnection between children and families—indicates that case outcomes are varied, and that these various levels of reconnection must be documented to arrive at informed conclusions about program effectiveness.

Key Principles and Components. As described in depth in chapter 1, and illustrated throughout this volume, a number of key principles and program components are essential to effective reunification. These can suggest which characteristics of individual programs might be selected for evaluation. For example, a program

FIGURE 2–DOCUMENTING A REUNIFICATION PROGRAM

Program Goals

- Efficient service delivery
- Effective service delivery
- Services follow prescribed policies and procedures
- Qualified and adequately trained staff members
- Achievement of client objectives
- Appropriate level of reconnection between families and children

Program Inputs

- Number of professional staff members
- Qualifications of professional staff members
- Number of support staff members
- Qualifications of support staff members
- Funding for training opportunities and materials
- Funding for professional journals, books, monographs
- Funding for program support materials
- Funding for transportation
- Allocation of office space
- Wages and benefits

Program Operations

- Ratio of clients to professional staff
- Ratio of supervisors to professional staff
- Ratio of support staff to professional staff
- Ratio of administrative staff to professional staff
- Intake operations and procedures
- Organizational location of reunification practice
- Decision-making processes
- Assessments of training needs
- Data collection and analysis procedures
- Case review procedures

Program Outputs

- Number of intakes processed
- Number and frequency of interagency team meetings
- Number and frequency of in-home pre-reunification contacts with children and families
- Number and frequency of in-office pre-reunification contacts
- Number of completed service plans
- Number of completed reunification plans
- Number of parent-child visits arranged
- Number and frequency of in-home post-reunification contacts
- Number and frequency of in-office post-reunification contacts
- Number of support groups and frequency of sessions
- Number and frequency of parent education sessions
- Number of collateral contacts
- Number and frequency of referrals to community services

Quality of Program Outputs

- Accurate and timely assessments
- Timely referrals
- Appropriate service plans
- Consistent pre-reunification contact with child and family
- Appropriate duration of pre-reunification services
- Appropriate duration of post-reunification service
- Appropriate use of community resources and social supports
- Consistent arrangements for visits between parents and children

Client Outcomes

- Percent of cases in which families improve parenting skills
- Percent of cases in which social supports for families increase
- Percent of cases in which relationships among family members improve
- Percent of cases in which problem-solving capabilities of families improve
- Percent of cases in which the majority of case objectives are achieved

Case Outcomes

- Percent of cases in which an appropriate level of reconnection between children and families is achieved emphasizing the principle of developing partnerships among parents, care-givers, social workers, and other service providers might examine elements that contribute to these relationships, such as the structure and timing of family meetings to discuss case progress. In addition, a review of what is known about effective programs and practice is an important starting place. Unfortunately, research to date on family preservation and reunification is too limited to warrant conclusions about cause and effect between service characteristics and outcomes. Available studies do provide, however, some guidance on key compo-nents of reunification practice.

Based on his review of research on family-centered, home-based services, Frankel noted [1988: 150] that the following service characteristics were consistently related to positive case outcomes: (a) service in the home rather than in the office; (b) concrete rather than soft or clinical services; (c) small caseloads; and (d) intensive services characterized by frequent contact between the worker and family.

Rzepnicki's [1987] findings on program and service characteristics related to foster care reentry suggest that the following factors may be important: (a) efforts to arrange visiting between children and families; (b) the planfulness of the reunification process; (c) the appropriateness, as well as the intensity, of pre-reunification services; and (d) the provision of aftercare services.

Hess et al. [1989: 5–6] have identified eight case management activities (outputs) requisite to achieving reunification, and are investigating program inputs and operations that affect implementation of these activities. Complete results of their study are forthcoming, and will help clarify the characteristics of effective reunification programs. The case management activities identified in the study suggest key components of good practice that should be assessed in implementation studies: (1) accurate assessment of family problems; (2) provision of appropriate services to the family; (3) coordination of services; (4) assessment of a family's progress and compliance with the service plan; (5) assessment of whether and when reunification should take place; (6) preparation of family members for the child's return home; (7) coordination of post-reunification services; and (8) monitoring of the child's safety following return home.

Established standards for family-centered casework services and intensive family-centered crisis services, such as those of the Child Welfare League of America, may also guide the selection of program characteristics for study. These standards prescribe caseload size, frequency of contact, service duration, and staff qualifications and training, among other program features[CWLA 1989: 50–51].

Unique Features. A program's evaluation should reflect its uniqueness; it will do so if program intentions are documented in the planning phase of the evaluation.

Some unique aspects of a program, however, might be more usefully studied than others; that is, some may be more directly related to the effectiveness of the program. For example, some family-based programs make extensive use of paraprofessionals to provide parent education, skills development, and role modeling. These programs vary on the tasks assigned to paraprofessionals and the extent to which paraprofessionals are teamed with professionals [Nelson et al. 1986]. The manner in which paraprofessionals are used would be valuable to include in a program evaluation.

To ensure that evaluations include the most relevant unique features of implementation, it is necessary to base the selection of study factors upon input from practitioners and clients. Practitioners can identify program inputs and operations that seem either to enhance or to impede service activities, as well as implementation issues related to the quantity and quality of outputs. Clients are a valuable source of information on the effects of specific program features. Programs that fail to include practitioners and clients in the evaluation process are likely to leave important evaluative factors unattended, and therefore limit the utility and efficiency of the study [Nauta and Hewett 1988].

Of equal importance to the involvement of practitioners and clients are the theoretical links between program strategies and desired program effects. These linkages guide the selection of both program implementation and client outcome variables. For example, the ecological systems perspective indicates that reunification practice should seek to strengthen the relationships, skills, and social, economic, and physical environments of families and children. All of these are important dimensions of client outcomes that should be included in evaluations. Each suggests certain intervention strategies that are theoretically effective in achieving desired outcomes. Counseling and case-monitoring activities are believed to strengthen relationships and facilitate adjustments, while income supports and housing strengthen economic and physical environments. Measuring outcomes must be based on theoretical linkages such as these.

Determining Evaluation Approaches

At this phase of the process, decisions are made about what information will be collected, from what sources, and how the results will be measured.

Evaluating Program Processes. Few reunification programs conduct process evaluations. Funding sources are most often interested in program outcomes, so there is little incentive for programs to assess operations and services. Also, as figure 2 illustrates, the numerous aspects of a program can make process evaluation perplexing. Nevertheless, neither the selection of program variables to include in an evaluation nor the collection of needed data is so daunting a task as to justify avoiding process evaluations. At a minimum, evaluations should include program factors that are believed to be associated with program outcomes. Figure 3 models a hypothetical program evaluation and illustrates factors theoretically related to reunification outcomes that could be included in an assessment of implementation. The selection of factors for any particular evaluation should also be based on the developmental stage of a program and the staff's concerns about certain aspects of program processes.

Common approaches to collecting data on program implementation are (a) examining existing records; (b) obtaining reports from program staff members and participants, and (c) observing selected activities. Records that are maintained routinely by reunification programs are a rich and credible potential source of evaluative data. With the exception of accounting to external bodies for certain activities, however, programs infrequently use existing records to assess program implementation. Case records and reviews, budgets, annual reports, and audits are examples of routinely generated information that can be used in evaluating whether programs are being implemented as intended. Most information on program inputs, such as funding levels for staff members, training, and materials, is readily available from such sources. Data on program operations of interest, such as caseload size and staffing ratios, are also maintained and reported on periodically. Mandated court and team reviews and required management information usually provide data on outputs such as the frequency and type of service, number of case contacts, and number of service plans completed and updated.

It is also important to get information from staff members and clients about key program features. Interviews and/or questionnaires can be developed to obtain information as needed on such factors as the adequacy of program inputs and operations and the quality of outputs. For example, clients could be surveyed on their perceptions of the timeliness, appropriateness, and usefulness of service activities.

Because developing instruments such as checklists, questionnaires, and service summary forms that record and measure selected aspects of program implementation is challenging and time-consuming, programs can, when appropriate, make use of instruments and measures developed and employed by others. For example, Casey Family Services, based in Connecticut, has designed a Daily/Weekly Activity Summary form that documents daily service activities associated with case plans [see Fein and Staff, chapter 5, for more information on this program's approach]. The instrument is useful in monitoring and evaluating the types and quantity of program outputs, and could be easily replicated by other programs. Nelson et al. [1986] developed a Family-Based

Service Inventory to collect data from workers on various measures of program performance, including workers' observations on program inputs, operations, and outputs. Portions of the inventory could be easily and usefully adapted by reunification programs for assessing implementation.

Finally, the credibility and potential impact of evaluation results are increased if multiple sources of data and several measures of the efficiency and quality of the program are used. Existing records may not always be complete or accurate, while interviews or questionnaires usually elicit recollections or impressions of the quality or consequence of an activity. Some memories are more reliable and some impressions are less biased than others. For these reasons, programs may occasionally use external observers, knowledgeable about reunification practice, as a source of objective information.

Evaluating Program Results. Choosing methods to measure client outcomes presents perhaps the greatest challenge to the practitioner. As Magura and Moses [1986: 2] point out, the field of child welfare continues to struggle with the fact that "precise measurement of a child's well-being and the suitability of the child's care have faced formidable conceptual and technical obstacles." They also note, however, that some consensus does exist on the types of problems besetting families and children who come to the attention of child welfare practitioners. They note that these problems generally are related to (a) activities performed by parents in their caregiving and socialization roles; (b) parental attributes and resources that affect the capacities of families to care for children; (c) behaviors of children in relation to their various roles (child, student, peer, sibling); and (d) the attributes of children that affect their capacities to perform roles. Magura and Moses [1986: 7–8] offer the following typology for organizing client outcomes: (a) parental role performance (b) familial capacities for caregiving; (c) child's role performance; and (d) child's capacities for performance.

Furthermore, they identify and critique 15 existing instruments (including their own Child Well-Being Scales and Parent Outcome Interview) appropriate for measuring one or more aspects of this typology. It should be noted, however, that no existing instrument provides a totally adequate measure of parental capability and its effects on children. Further research and development of outcome assessment are needed.

Validity and Reliability. Whether selecting from among existing instruments for assessing programs or designing their own, practitioners should ensure that the methods used to describe and measure program processes and outcomes provide accurate and pertinent information that is valid and reliable, or evaluations will have no utility or credibility.

FIGURE 3–MODELING A REUNIFICATION PROGRAM EVALUATION

Program Goals

- Efficient service delivery
- Effective service delivery
- Services follow prescribed policies and procedures
- Qualified and adequately trained staff members
- Achievement of client objectives
- Appropriate level of reconnection between families and children

Program Inputs

- Number of professional staff members
- Qualifications of professional staff members
- Funding for training opportunities and materials

Program Operations

- Ratio of clients to the professional staff
- Ratio of supervisors to the professional staff
- Assessments of training needs
- Data collection and analysis procedures
- Case review procedures

Program Outputs

- Frequency and number of in-home pre-reunification contacts with children and families
- Frequency and number of in-office pre-reunification contacts with children and families
- Number of completed reunification plans
- Number of parent-child visits arranged
- Frequency and number of in-home post-reunification contacts
- Frequency and number of in-office post-reunification contacts
- Frequency and number of referrals to community services

Quality of Program Outputs

- Appropriate service plans
- Consistent pre-reunification contact with child and family
- Consistent post-reunification contact with child and family
- Appropriate duration of post-reunification service
- Appropriate use of community resources and social supports
- Consistent arrangements for visits between parents and children

Client Outcomes

- Percent of cases in which families improve parenting skills
- Percent of cases in which social supports for families increase
- Percent of cases in which relationships among family members improve
- Percent of cases in which problem-solving capabilities of families improve
- Percent of cases in which the majority of case objectives are achieved

Case Outcomes

- Percent of cases in which an appropriate level of reconnection between children and families is achieved

Validity, the most critical aspect of a data-collection method, refers to the degree to which an instrument actually measures what it claims to measure. If a program wishes to measure clients' perceptions of the quality of services, it cannot validly do so by merely asking clients whether services were rendered. It should obtain data on client satisfaction with indicators of quality such as the timeliness, accuracy, and comprehensiveness of services. *Reliability* refers to the consistency and stability of measurements. For example, a checklist to describe and measure case activities, such as in-home contacts for a particular time period, should produce the same results if two or more persons apply the checklist to the same case for the same time frame. Further, programs using reliable and valid measures of program processes or outcomes can most convincingly document the changes in their clients over time if they apply the measurements at least once before services are provided and again at the time cases are closed. Without baseline data on the functioning of families and children before their involvement in a program, it is difficult to document objectively that changes take place. At a minimum, therefore, programs should evaluate outcomes by using a "before-and-after" evaluation research design, in which client functioning is measured before, and after, program intervention.

Truly experimental designs are generally viewed as the most rigorous for attributing client change to program intervention [Tripodi 1983]. They involve randomly assigning some clients to an experimental group receiving the intervention to be evaluated, and others to a control group not receiving the intervention. Because the groups are formed randomly, they are assumed to be equivalent on important attributes (i.e., age, class, skills, attitudes) that might rival program intervention as the explanation for changes occurring over time. Such experimental designs usually involve serving some clients more adequately than others. The ethical implications are obvious and important. These designs may be most appropriate for large-scale, well-funded studies from which findings will be generalized to other reunification programs. The focus here, however, is not on evaluations for the purpose of generalizing results and recommendations to other programs and settings. Rather, it is on providing practitioners with accurate information on the effects of their efforts.

A few programs already are using evaluation approaches that attend to reliability and validity issues. The Kent County Mental Health Center in Warwick, Rhode Island [see Boutilier and Rehm, chapter 4], has found the Child Abuse Potential (CAP) Inventory [Milner 1980] and the Child Behavior Checklist (CBCL) [Achenbach and Edelbrock 1986] useful for measuring client progress. The CAP Inventory used by Kent County is a series of statements that describe parental feelings, attitudes, and values (i.e., "I do not trust most people," "I sometimes act without thinking," and "Children should never be bad"). Parents indicate whether they agree or disagree with each statement. The CBCL consists of 118 behavior-problem items that are organized into separate Child Behavior Profiles for males and females in three age groups (4 to 5, 5 to 11, and 12 to 16 years). Each behavior-problem item (i.e., "refuses to eat," "easily frustrated") has three potential responses: "not true," "sometimes true," or "very true or often true." The instrument can be filled out by parents, other caregivers, or practitioners.

Casey Family Services, mentioned earlier, uses the Family Risk Scales [Magura et al. 1987] and the Parent Outcome Interview [Magura and Moses 1986]. The Family Risk Scales measure a child's risk of entering foster care. The scales consist of 26 items covering such elements as "suitability of living conditions," "financial problems," "adult relationships in household," "family's social support," and "parent's physical and mental health." Each item has four to six levels or response categories, ranging from adequate to inadequate performance on that factor. For example, "financial problems" has four levels of performance: 1 = "no continuing financial problems," 2 = "constant financial problems, but scraping by," 3 = "family deprived of some necessities and/or can't repay debts," and 4 = "financial difficulties imminently resulting in serious consequences." Workers are asked to record their factual assessment of each item. The Parent Outcome Interview obtains information from parents on both outcomes and agency services, and is intended to be administered by workers at the conclusion of service. Structured and semistructured questions are used to obtain the parents' assessment of services received and changes in such areas as "housing and economic conditions," "physical child care," "discipline and emotional care of children," "children's conduct and academic adjustment," and "victimization of children." The instrument is useful for studies of implementation and outcomes.

The Family Connection Project (FCP) of the Children's Bureau of Los Angeles and Boysville of Michigan's Family Reunification Program are using the Family Assessment Form (FAF) recently developed by the managers and practitioners of the FCP [McCroskey and Nelson 1989]. The instrument obtains workers' assessments of family functioning in the following areas: (a) physical, financial, and social environment; (b) personal attributes and child-rearing capabilities; (c) interactions between and among caretakers and children; and (d) development and behavior of children. Five responses are possible for each item, ranging from an above-average level of functioning to problems that are sufficiently serious to endanger the child's well-being. The FAF is based in large part on practitioners' judgments about the key components of in-home services; practitioners had a significant role in designing, testing, and implementing the instrument, and are reported to be delighted with its utility [McCroskey and Nelson 1989].

Reporting and Using Results

If an evaluation is well planned and well conducted, most issues related to this final phase in the process will have been anticipated and handled in earlier phases: the purposes and uses of the study will be clear and potential resistance to changes based on findings will have been identified and dealt with. Sustained commitment to using results is most likely if staff members are involved in all aspects of the evaluation process. This increases their confidence that pertinent factors are being studied, that appropriate methods are being used to measure those factors, and that the analysis and report of the information collected will accurately document the program's accomplishments and deficiencies.

The distribution of an evaluation report can also affect the use of results. The report should be widely disseminated among reunification program staff members, as well as predetermined external audiences. Reports can be used to document the need for additional resources or policies to effect changes in the program. To avoid presenting a blemished program to external audiences, it is advisable to discover and act on program shortcomings before evaluating and reporting program outcomes.

The report itself should (1) reiterate the methods used in the study, (2) document the reliability of those methods, (3) note any discrepancies between goals/objectives and achievements, (4) recommend improvements, and (5) applaud the program's accomplishments.

Conclusion

Changes in public policy have resulted in an increasing number of children in out-of-home care returning home [Kadushin and Martin 1988]. Few programs, however, are systematically documenting the changes in families and children that occur before or after reunification. Few document that services are being implemented as intended or identify the most effective program strategies for reconnecting families and children. If reunification practice is to be responsive and responsible to families and children, agencies must evaluate the implementation and consequences of practice. Effects of programs on the circumstances of families and children should be assessed, as well as effects on the rates at which children are reunified or helped to reconnect with family members at other levels. Evaluations for the purpose of program improvement should be reasonable to conduct, technically correct, and ethical, and should yield information needed by child welfare practitioners, administrators, and public policymakers.

References

Achenbach, T., and Edelbrock, C. *Manual for the Child Behavior Checklist and Revised Child Behavior Profile*. Burlington, VT: University of Vermont Department of Psychiatry, 1986.

Carlo, P., and Shennum, W.A. "Family Reunification Efforts That Work: A Three-Year Follow-up Study of Children in Residential Treatment." *Child and Adolescent Social Work* 6, 3 (Summer 1989): 211–216.

Child Welfare League of America. *Standards for Services to Strengthen and Preserve Families with Children*. Washington, DC: The Child Welfare League of America, 1989.

Frankel, H. "Family-Centered, Home-Based Services in Child Protection: A Review of the Research." *Social Service Review* 62, 1 (March 1988): 137–157.

Hess, P.; Folaron, G.; Jefferson, A.; and Jennings, P. *Decision-Oriented Program Evaluation*. Austin, TX: The University of Texas at Austin School of Social Work.

Kadushin, A., and Martin, J. *Child Welfare Services* (4th ed.). New York: Macmillan Publishing, 1988.

Magura, S., and Moses, B.S. *Outcome Measures for Child Welfare Services: Theory and Applications*. Washington, DC: The Child Welfare League of America, 1986.

Magura, S.; Moses, B.S.; and Jones, M.A. *Assessing Risk and Measuring Change in Families: The Family Risk Scales*. Washington, DC: The Child Welfare League of America, 1987.

Maluccio, A. N.; Fein, E. and Olmstead, K.A. *Permanency Planning for Children: Concepts and Methods*. London and New York: Routledge, Chapman and Hall, 1986.

McCroskey, J., and Nelson, J. (1989). "Practice-Based Research in a Family-Support Program: The Family Connection Project Example." *CHILD WELFARE* LXVIII, 6 (November–December 1989): 573–587.

Milner, J.S. *The Child Abuse Potential Inventory: Manual*. Webster, NC: Psytec Corp., 1980.

Nauta, M.J., and Hewett, K. "Studying Complexity: The Case of the Child and Family Resource Program." In *Evaluating Family Programs*, edited by H.B. Weiss and F.H. Jacobs. New York: Aldine de Gruyter, 1988.

Nelson, K.; Landsman, M.; and Hutchinson, J. *Family-Based Services Inventory*. Iowa City, IA: National Resource Center on Family Based Services, The University of Iowa School of Social Work, 1986.

Patton, M.Q. *Utilization-Focused Evaluation*. Beverly Hills, CA: Sage Publications, 1978.

Posavac, E.J., and Carey, R.G. *Program Evaluation, Methods and Case Studies*. Englewood Cliffs, NJ: Prentice Hall, 1985.

Rutman, L. *Planning Useful Evaluations: Evaluability Assessment*. Beverly Hills, CA: Sage Publications, 1980.

Rutman, L., and Mowbray, G. *Understanding Program Evaluation*. Beverly Hills, CA: Sage Publications, 1983.

Rzepnicki, T. "Recidivism of Foster Children Returned to Their Own Homes: A Review of New Directions for Research." *Social Service Review* 61, 1 (March 1987): 56–69.

Tripodi, T. *Evaluative Research for Social Workers*. Englewood Cliffs, NJ: Prentice-Hall, Inc., 1983.

Turner, J. "Reuniting Children in Foster Care with Their Biological Parents." *Social Work* 29, 6 (November–December 1984): 501–505.

Weiss, C.H. *Evaluation Research: Methods of Assessing Program Effectiveness*. Englewood Cliffs, NJ: Prentice Hall, 1972.

11

The Interaction of Research and Practice
in Family Reunification

Edith Fein and Ilene Staff

Research in a practice setting can discover the factors associated with success-ful service provision and client outcomes. In chapter 10, Turner delineated a framework for evaluating family reunification programs. This chapter eluci-dates the interactions of research and practice that occur, and the potential benefits of embarking on research in family reunification programs. The Family Reunification Project of Casey Family Services (described in chapter 5) is used as illustration; preliminary findings are presented and implications of program evaluation for policy and practice are discussed.

Practice Research

Research is "systematic, controlled, empirical, and critical investigation of hypothetical propositions about the presumed relations among natural phenom-ena" [Kerlinger 1973: 11]. In conducting research, an investigator will typically define the phenomena under study and hypothesize a relationship among them, hoping to find a correlation that approximates cause and effect. In examining reunification programs, for example, one hypothesis to investigate might be, "Families that participate in a multidisciplinary program designed to educate and support them will have fewer incidents of abuse than those who do not participate." Another hypothesis might be, "Families that participate in a multidisciplinary program will have a more integrated family life than those who do not participate."

After the formulation of a hypothesis, experiments are designed to produce data that will lead to the acceptance or rejection of the relationship stated in the hypothesis. These experiments require the following conditions:

1. The presence of control or comparison groups, with random assignment if possible. (By the luck of the draw, some families would be assigned to participate, others not to participate.)

2. The constant application of the experimental condition. (In the example above, participants would have to receive the same amount and kind of treatment.)

3. Measures that are both valid and reliable, that is, that actually measure what they purport to be measuring, and, when repeated, prove stable and dependable. (An integrated family life must be assessed by instruments in whose results there is confidence.)

These requirements for rigorous research hint at the difficulties in conducting careful studies in human services. Problems occur in defining the variables embraced by the hypotheses, finding measures that are technically acceptable, having the subjects "hold still" while the experimental condition is applied, denying the treatment condition to the comparison group—a sticky ethical situation, and dealing with various administrative elements, such as program changes due to decreased funding or political interference in the selection of participants, that militate against the control and stability that is the essence of experimentation.

To meet these challenges, program evaluation techniques were developed, stemming from the antipoverty programs of the 1960s, adapted to the demands of real-life programs delivering services to people in the ordinary course of their lives. The rigorous scientific method described earlier was adapted to make it appropriate for use in analyzing programs. By 1967, a research analog was created that described evaluation as "the process of stating objectives in terms of ultimate, intermediate, or immediate goals; of examining underlying assumptions; and of setting up criteria of effort, performance, adequacy, efficiency, and process" [Suchman 1967: 71]. In applying the definition, analysts typically gather program information in one or more of the following areas [Bander et al. 1982]:

• What effort is going into the program? How many people are delivering what kind of services, at what cost?

• What is the efficiency of the program planning? What is the relationship between the objectives and what is actually occurring?

• How adequate is the program in relation to the particular community's needs? For example, are the 100 families served by reunification services the total population of those requiring services or only 10%?

- What is the effectiveness of the program? Is it achieving its goals?

Evaluation studies can be classified as formative or summative [Patton 1978]. Formative evaluations examine ongoing programs and produce results that can be used to improve the programs. Summative evaluations are based on completed programs and are used to determine program effects, usually for funding or other planning decisions.

Program Example

Purposes of the Research Effort

In the reunification project used here to illustrate the interaction of research and practice, the research component of the program was of the formative type, and it was designed, as all evaluation efforts ideally should be, in conjunction with the program planners [see Turner, chapter 10]. The evaluation sought to understand the needs of identified groups of children and their families and to discover the factors associated with effective service provision and successful outcomes.

The goal of the reunification program in this voluntary agency was to reunify children in public agency foster care with their biological families, or to assure the children permanency with an adoptive or long-term foster family if reunification was not possible or in the children's best interests. The children had all been abused or neglected. Services were delivered at three agency sites, one serving abusing families, one serving neglecting families with children up to age 5, and the third serving neglecting families with children up to age 14. Client populations of abused or neglected children were separated to shed light on whether the reason for entry into care influences service course and outcome. Research has shown that the reasons for entering care have little effect on functioning while in care [Fein et al. 1990], but it was hypothesized that the kind and level of reunification achieved would depend on the characteristics of the biological families and how they coped.

The project's social workers were interested not only in whether reunification occurred, but also in whether outcomes for the children were good. Some wanted to know more about the comparative functioning of abusing and neglecting families. Others were concerned with how social workers and paraprofessional family support workers provided services. Everybody was curious about whether the goal orientation concept of the program was viable. Many meetings were held between the research and program staffs to ensure that the program's focus and goals, measurement variables, and recordkeeping forms were the product of a consensus that amalgamated evaluation and service delivery objectives [McCroskey and Nelson 1989].

Thus, in line with the interests expressed by staff members and administrators, the research effort was designed to produce information in the following areas of client characteristics and program operations: differences between abusing and neglecting families, kinds and amounts of service provided, goal orientation as a theoretical basis for service delivery, outcomes for children, and family functioning. Because the program being evaluated was a demonstration program, decisions would have to be made about future funding, whether services should be modified, who should be served, and other management questions.

Evaluation Plan

The evaluation plan in figure 1 is a tabular depiction of how this formative evaluation was planned. The first column—Research Issues—displays the areas of information-gathering. The first issue—"Which children and families participate in reunification services?"—evaluates questions of efficiency and adequacy, as described earlier in this chapter. The second issue—"What services are provided?"—is an evaluation of effort; the third and fourth issues—"What outcomes ensue?" and "What changes take place in children and families?"—involve assessment of effectiveness.The second column—Related Questions—gives a little more detail about the research issues and ties them to the services that are the focus of the program and the evaluation. The third column—Data Sources—lists the instruments that will provide the information to the research team.

Graphically portraying the evaluation plan encourages understanding of the overall direction of the evaluation effort and stimulates questions from practitioners. This interaction has the happy effect of increasing social worker participation in the evaluation, thereby amplifying the probability that results will be used.

Preliminary Findings

At the end of the first eight months of the program, 36 families had been referred to it; 19 were accepted, six did not meet program eligibility criteria, and 11 were still in assessment. Two families had been reunified. Services to five families had been terminated without reunification, and new permanent plans for these children were then established by the state agency. Most of the children referred were Caucasian (65%) and under five years old (65%); 55% were boys.

FIGURE I—REUNIFICATION SERVICES: EVALUATION PLAN

Research Issues	Related Questions	Data Sources
Which children and families participate in reunification services?	• Can families be distinguished by their presenting diagnosis (abuse, neglect)? • What are the participants' demographic indicators (age, race, sex, etc.)?	• Case records • Family Risk Scales
What services are provided?	• What are the specifications and generalities in case plans? • What are the perceptions of each of the principals about the need for services, their adequacy, and their usefulness?	• Case records • Daily/weekly summary • Monthly goal rating • Interviews: Children, parents, and social workers
What outcomes ensue?	• What outcomes occur? • How are outcomes related to: case plans; demographics; family process (biological family), or foster family (child's success in placement)? • Reactions of the professional staff?	• Case plan • Daily/weekly summary • Monthly goal rating • Parent outcome interview • Interviews: Children, parents, and social workers
What changes take place in children and families?	• Can particular phases in reunification be defined dynamically? (Before child is returned; immediately following return; post-honeymoon) • What critical events trigger or postpone each phase? • What services or supports characterize each phase?	• Interviews: Children, parents, and social workers • Case plan • Daily/weekly summary • Monthly goal rating • Case records

As indicated in figure 1, the Family Risk Scales developed by Magura and Moses [1986] were used as an assessment tool. (See chapter 10 by Turner for a concise description of these scales.) Ratings at intake indicated that the families had financial difficulties, troubled relationships among the adults, and few or no persons ready to help during a crisis. Primary caregivers showed a history of substance abuse, a lack of knowledge about child care, and low motivation toward the return of their children. The goals for work with these families encompassed striving for financial stability, helping parents understand their children's needs, dealing with substance abuse problems, setting limits for children through appropriate discipline methods, and making use of resources in the community.

At this point in the life of a project, when insufficient data have accumulated to answer the questions posed about program operation and decision-making, the benefits of a formative evaluation become evident. As mentioned earlier, the overriding advantage of a formative evaluation is its use of preliminary findings to sensitize workers to important issues, modify program practice, and alert evaluators to areas of further investigation. In contrast, summative evaluations require a neutral stance until all data are collected and information analyzed. In this project, the interaction between the research and program staffs led to the identification of several issues early in the course of the program that significantly affected program modification and the conceptualization of reunification services in general. These are discussed below, along with certain general themes that emerged in the course of the evaluation effort.

Paperwork and Program Design. As suggested in chapter 5, record-keeping and program design are intimately connected, particularly in a goal-setting orientation. Recordkeeping forms should encourage and reinforce goal and plan formulation. This synergy is best achieved when staff members are closely involved in the interaction of program formulation, record design, and paperwork. In this project, the research staff consulted with the program staff to come up with the original paperwork formulations that would support the program being envisioned. Pretests of the instruments, revisions based on staff critiques, and further revisions in the early stages of the program led to forms that were the best compromise among the needs of administrators, researchers, and service delivery staff members. There is no question that the forms also influenced practice: the staff's cognizance that their day's work would need to be captured on particular recordkeeping forms structured how they formulated and focused their interactions with clients [see Fein and Staff, chapter 5].

As would be expected in implementing any extensive recordkeeping process, the Casey Reunification Project experienced some difficulties with paperwork, both with the program's forms and with the more standardized Family Risk Scales. Social workers, like most service providers, are more comfortable with doing than with writing; their priorities when time is short are to deal with crises and client concerns rather than records; and their orientation is to people rather than paper [McCroskey and Nelson 1989]. Tension arose between the recordkeeping needs of the program design and the workers' perception of their primary tasks. For example, some workers felt that the goal and plan record-keeping was too time-consuming, too difficult for them and the families to understand, and did not reflect the quality of the casework. Others felt that the Family Risk Scales did not offer enough choice points on some scales, focused too much on the present situation, or were not appropriate for young children. The following strategies, however, helped to achieve a high level of cooperation on the part of practitioners:

- including the practitioners in formulating and pretesting the recordkeeping instruments, and being willing to change the forms in response to their comments;

- keeping forms as simple as possible while still communicating necessary information;

- allocating work time for writing records;

- training in record-keeping to assure the maintenance of standards;

- demonstrating the value of the records through their use with families and by supervisors [Maluccio et al. 1986].

Use of Service Agreements. Although service contracts or service agreements have been an integral part of permanency planning in child welfare practice for many years [Maluccio et al. 1986], the timing of service agreements—when in the course of the case they are formulated and signed—has not been the subject of study. Generally, parents are asked to sign an agreement with the child welfare agency, specifying the expectations and responsibilities of each of the signatories, at the time service is undertaken. For a child to be returned, the parents must agree to work with the social workers in a variety of more or less distinct areas. In the best of situations, the expectations are clearly set forth, with plans for how the client will meet them and what the social worker will do.

What does all of this mean for the vulnerable client receiving reunification services? Who knows the parents well enough at the beginning of service to create specifications that will proceed in productive steps until success is achieved? How can the parents be engaged in formulating the goals and plans for service when the service agreement must be signed before the engagement can take place? In the worst scenarios, clients feel constrained to sign general agreements formulated by others, with no sense of power over their own lives.

Researchers learned that at various times the three Casey program sites under study had different solutions to the use of service agreements. This information would not have surfaced without the data collection. One early approach was to have clients sign a preliminary agreement before the case plan was formulated and another agreement later that included the plans. Later, the agreement to work together at the beginning was designed as an exploratory verbal agreement; the more formal service agreement was signed only after a study and negotiating period that was to last, on average, 30 days. Timing is one of several problem areas in the use of service agreements. Others include what they mean to the client and what strengths clients feel they have in the negotiating process.

Goal Orientation. The optimum number of goals that should be set at the beginning of service delivery—a balance between a small number that enhances motivation and a complete set of goals that represents reality—is discussed in chapter 5. In this project, the average number of goals set at the beginning of service was five. Correlation of the number of goals with client outcomes is not yet available at this writing, but it can be seen that the number of goals used is a complex function of client motivation, client problem-solving style, and worker comfort with the use of goals.

Goal-setting as a way of structuring reality and implementing the work ethic is also alluded to in chapter 5. The element of coercion—imposing the child welfare orientation of planning for the future on parents whose lifestyle is inimical to a goal structure—creates conflict for some workers, who may be committed to a family systems approach in which respect for the family and empowerment of its members are of paramount importance. Social workers may feel reluctant to confront this difference between the way they organize their own lives and a client family's ways.

The conflict is a significant theoretical and philosophical issue [Hancock and Pelton 1989] and was highlighted by the research structure of tabulating much of the data by goal and plan. Raising the questions led to the articulation of a practical resolution, that is, for practitioners to focus on the child in the situation. The youngster's need for protection and permanency becomes the decisive factor, giving less weight to satisfying the parents' right to freedom of choice and empowerment. New programs should expect controversy about this, particularly if they operate on a family systems-family empowerment model.

Foster Families That Abuse and Neglect. When children are removed from their biological families to protect the youngsters from abuse or neglect, it is not expected that they will be put at similar risk in their foster homes. That danger, however, exists. Abuse by foster families occurred in four of the first 19 cases accepted through the first eight months of the program. Reunification services, in their intensive work in the home with caregivers and children, are apt to uncover risk situations in foster care that are not exposed in the ordinary course of placement supervision. The reunification worker then faces several dilemmas. First, removal of the child from the abusing or neglecting foster family protects the child but initiates another placement, with its attendant separation, loss, and adjustment problems for the youngster. Avoiding subjecting the child to another foster placement creates pressure to return the child home as the lesser of two evils. Yet the family may not be ready for reunification, and premature return may sabotage the long-term effort. Finally, the lack of a satisfactory resolution is further exacerbated by the shortage of appropriate foster homes and the inability of state social workers with immense caseloads to monitor placements that do not present emergencies.

Anticipating this situation, the Casey program, with the agreement of the state agencies, originally had arranged that the foster families would continue to be served by state workers and that Casey would work only with the biological families and their children. Eventually, however, some work with foster families by Casey was necessary to meet the needs of the children, and the evaluation forms had to be changed to accommodate this additional service. Other programs may need to include this reality in their allocation of workers' time.

Substance-Abusing Families. The role of drug abuse in modern family life is well documented [Fink 1989; Gelles 1987]; the situation is particularly acute in abusing and neglecting families. In the Casey project, substance abuse was a consideration in the majority of cases. Most reunification programs, including this one, will not work with families where active, untreated substance abuse is present, as seen in the negative experience of family preservation programs [Mitchell et al. 1988]. In many substance-abusing families, however, reunification services are undertaken because a recovery process is under way, and there is no body of practice wisdom to predict when children can be safe in their homes.

As might be foreseen, in some cases (five of the first 19 in the Casey program) reunification was delayed or not achieved when parental attempts at recovery failed. The evaluation instruments permitted the monitoring of progress in these cases; more important, the evaluation uncovered a serious concern deeper than the treatment disappointments that might have been anticipated: the conception of family life reflected in the substance-abusing family. Care and nurturing of children, particularly among neglecting families, proved to be less of a priority than satisfying the addiction. Motivation to work for reunification became dependent on the condition of the addiction. Given the prevalence of substance abuse, this changing conception of parental responsibility in family life has profound implications for children's well-being and should be a prime consideration in designing service delivery [Wells 1991].

Implications for Future Research

Research on reunification services has been minimal [Frankel 1988]—not surprising in so new a service. There are general issues on which research must be conducted, such as the following:

- What outcomes result for particular children and families as a consequence of different patterns of service delivery?

- How can we deal effectively with the variety of unsettled programmatic questions, of which the use of service agreements and dealing with abusing foster families, discussed earlier, are examples?

- Can we learn more about such fundamentals in reunification service delivery as the treatment of substance-abusing families and the provision of goal-oriented services for non-goal-oriented clients?

Second, as discussed below, more particularized service components, such as the child's well-being, criteria for decision-making, program success, and home-based services, must be examined.

The Child's Well-Being

What is happening to the child while the family is being readied for reunification? Some evidence exists that children whose return to their biological families is unsuccessful and who go on to a subsequent out-of-home placement have a better adjustment than youngsters for whom the reunification attempt was never made [Fein et al. 1983]. For many youngsters, however, especially the very young, their urgent need for permanency clashes with their parents' need for more time in which to rehabilitate themselves.

In the Casey program, six months was set as a time guideline for reunification. The first two reunifications took place within the guideline; two other cases went beyond the six-month period without a decision concerning reunification. No conclusive data yet exist on the appropriateness of this time span, which typically becomes a judgment based on preestablished program criteria or workers' assessments. Research and program staff members struggled unsuccessfully to codify the elements involved. New reunification services should decide in advance whether permanent placement of the child or family integrity is the highest priority. That a choice is necessary is unfortunate, but for some families, workers need that guidance to structure their service planning.

Criteria for Decision-Making

The bases for accepting cases for service, reunifying families, and closing cases have been well investigated [Gambrill 1977; Gambrill and Stein 1983]. Criteria have been specified and various guidelines developed to clarify the judgments that must be made; in most cases decision-making is founded on the explicit or implicit causal connections between social work activities and family outcomes [Stein and Rzepnicki 1983]. Some critical thinking, however, rejects the causal-explanatory approach to human behavior in favor of a humanistic-interpretive approach, in which the meanings or interpretations ascribed to behavior are the most significant elements [Smith 1989]. The rigorous research method of isolating and connecting specific input and outcome variables may not be as fruitful as interactive investigation of the complex processes that affect children and families [Fein et al. 1990].

The Casey Reunification Project is an example of the interplay of the causal and interpretive perspectives, proposed currently as the most promising direction for research in the human services to take [Smith 1989]. Criteria for decision-making are specified (see figure 1), but they are enlarged by the qualitative information obtained from the case plan and social workers' interviews. This view responds to the understandable quest of practitioners for useful knowledge and guidelines to structure their work and optimize outcomes for families.

Program Success

Reunification services would seem to have a built-in criterion for success: are the families physically reunified? This measure of effectiveness is deceptively simple, however; as discussed in chapters 1 and 10, reunifying families can take a variety of forms that stop short of physically returning to the home. It is natural, however, for service providers to commit their energies to the stated goals of a program; a program entitled "reunification" emotionally engages them in efforts to ensure a family's physical integrity.

Although termination of parental rights or long-term foster care that includes family connectedness without shared residence may be the optimum outcomes in particular cases, workers may consider such outcomes as falling short of the program's mission. The stresses inherent in time-consuming home-based services—the intensity of contact and closeness of relationship with a small caseload—can then be exacerbated by disappointment in outcomes, a major ingredient of staff burnout [Edelwich and Brodsky 1980]. Program supervisors and administrators might well be sensitive to this possibility, and evaluators also have a responsibility to present data with an awareness of their potential for increasing or ameliorating burnout.

Home-Based Services

The relative success of family preservation programs, that is, placement prevention, has led to a proliferation of their principal design element—home-based services [Whittaker et al. 1990]. The rationale for providing services in the home is admirable; workers see family members in their own environment and thus are in the best position to understand the family's stresses, to have contact with multiple family members, and to model techniques and skills that will promote problem-solving. Yet social workers entering the home also may be perceived as investigative or intrusive [Hancock and Pelton 1989]. Their presence may counter client empowerment—one of the goals of home-based services—that is, enabling clients to feel "masters of their own fate" [Hegar 1989: 377].

Some writers even question whether empowerment is an operational concept in child welfare [Rothman 1989]. Programs typically try to deliver services sensitively, but beyond evaluations of client reactions to service [Mitchell et al. 1988], family attitudes toward home-based services have not been well studied. Such an assessment is an important assignment if the elements of control or coercion are to be eliminated from reunification services and the concept of family empowerment respectfully implemented.

Conclusion

This chapter presented information on the interaction between research and practice in family reunification. There is no question that evaluation of reunification services is vital if program planning and implementation are to be carried out rationally. As suggested in this chapter's examination of a particular project, a research effort is essential to account for the variety and variability of client characteristics, social conditions, and program processes. Although decisions on implementing, maintaining, or expanding programs may be based, in reality, on emotional or political instincts, those instincts are best informed when a solid information foundation exists. Data can originate from evaluation studies of effort, effectiveness, efficiency, and adequacy, as described in this chapter, or from more rigorous research studies. These investigations should take advantage of the wisdom accumulated by practitioners, as well as the body of knowledge already extant, and should be solidly founded in practice.

Practice-based research has the advantage of accumulating information on the real world of service delivery rather than a carefully controlled but then impossible-to-implement experimental condition. The unanticipated effects that occur in all service delivery become included in the investigation, and the connection between the evaluation and the reality is enhanced, strengthening the foundation for utilization of results. Utilization is further increased when studies are designed to consider variables and measurements that are not only rigorous, but also sensitive to the serendipity and flexibility that characterize human interactions. This kind of evaluation orientation has the maximum potential for building the knowledge base in child welfare and supplying information of the greatest usefulness for developing policy and practice.

References

Bander, K.W.; Fein, E.; and Bishop, G. "Evaluation of Child Sexual Abuse Programs." In *Handbook of Clinical Intervention in Child Sexual Abuse*, edited by S.M. Sgroi. Lexington, MA: Lexington Books, 1982.

Edelwich, J., and Brodsky, A. *Burnout*. New York: Human Sciences Press, 1980.

Fein, E.; Maluccio, A.N.; and Kluger, M. *No More Partings: A Study of Long-Term Foster Family Care*. Washington, DC: The Child Welfare League of America, 1990.

Fein, E.; Maluccio, A.N.; Hamilton, V.J.; and Ward, D. "After Foster Care: Outcomes of Permanency Planning." *CHILD WELFARE* LXII, 6 (November–December 1983): 485–560.

Fink, J.R. "Effects of Crack and Cocaine upon Infants: A Review of the Literature." *Children's Legal Rights Journal* 10, 4 (Fall 1989): 2–10.

Frankel, H. "Family-Centered, Home-Based Services in Child Protection: A Review of the Research." *Social Service Review* 62, 1 (March 1988): 137–157.

Gambrill, E., and Stein, T.J. *Supervision: A Decision Making Approach*. Beverly Hills, CA: Sage Publications, 1983.

Gambrill, E. *Behavior Modification: Handbook of Assessment, Intervention, and Evaluation*. San Francisco: Jossey-Bass, 1977.

Gelles, R.J. *The Violent Home*. Beverly Hills, CA: Sage Publications, 1987.

Hancock, B.L., and Pelton, L.H. "Home Visits: History and Functions." *Social Casework* 70, 1 (January 1989): 21–27.

Hegar, R. "Empowerment-Based Practice with Children." *Social Service Review* 63, 3 (September 1989): 373–383.

Kerlinger, F.N. *Foundations of Behavioral Research*. New York: Holt, Rinehart and Winston, Inc., 1973.

Magura, S., and Moses, B.S. *Outcome Measures for Child Welfare Services: Theory and Applications*. Washington, DC: The Child Welfare League of America, 1986.

Maluccio, A.N.; Fein, E.; and Olmstead, K. *Permanency Planning for Children: Concepts and Methods*. London and New York: Routledge, Chapman and Hall, 1986.

McCroskey, J., and Nelson, J. "Practice-Based Research in the Family Support Program: The Family Connection Project Example." *CHILD WELFARE* LXVIII, 6 (November-December 1989): 573–578.

Mitchell, C.; Tovar, P.; and Knitzer, J. *Evaluating the Bronx Homebuilders Program*. New York: Bank Street College Division of Research, Demonstration Policy, 1988.

Patton, M.Q. *Utilization-Focused Evaluation*. Newbury Park, CA: Sage Publications, 1978.

Rothman, J. *Client Self-Determination: Untangling the Knot*. Social Service Review 63, 4 (December 1989): 598–612.

Smith, M.B. (1989). "Scientism in Psychology: A Critical Retrospective." *Readings: A Journal of Reviews and Commentary in Mental Health* 4, 1 (January 1989): 13–16.

Stein, T.J., and Rzepnicki, T. *Decision-Making at Child Welfare Intake*. New York: The Child Welfare League of America, 1983.

Suchman, E.A. *Evaluative Research*. New York: Russell Sage Foundation, 1967.

Wells, K. "Eagerly Awaiting a Home: Severely Emotionally Disturbed Youth Lost in Our Systems of Care: A Personal Reflection." *Child and Youth Care Forum* 20, 1 (Spring 1991): 7–17.

Whittaker, J.K.; Kinney, J.; Tracy, E.; and Booth, C., eds. *Reaching High-Risk Families: Intensive Family Preservation in the Human Services*. Hawthorne, NY: Aldine de Gruyter, 1990.

About the Authors

Co-Editors

Barbara Pine is Associate Professor of Social Work at the University of Connecticut School of Social Work, West Hartford, CT, where she chairs the Administration Concentration. She received her Ph.D. at the Heller School, Brandeis University, and has taught and written on social work administration and family and children's services. Her work in child welfare has focused on ethics, policy, special-needs adoption, foster family care, and the preparation of adolescents for independent living.

Robin Warsh is Director of a project, "Preserving Families through Reunification," at Boston College Graduate School of Social Work. At the time of preparation of this volume, she was Curriculum Specialist at the Center for the Study of Child Welfare, University of Connecticut School of Social Work, West Hartford, CT. She earned her M.S.W. at the University of Connecticut, and was formerly director of a national project on foster parenting adolescents. She has taught and written on independent living for adolescents in out-of-home care and on family preservation, and conducts workshops for Head Start staff members, parents, and children.

Anthony Maluccio is Professor, Boston College Graduate School of Social Work, Chestnut Hill, MA. At the time of the preparation of this volume, he was Professor of Social Work and Director of the Center for the Study of Child Welfare at the University of Connecticut School of Social Work. He earned his D.S.W. at Columbia University and has taught and written extensively on family and children's services, particularly on such topics as permanency planning, family preservation, family foster care, and the preparation of adolescents in out-of-home care for independent living.

Contributing Authors

Linda Boutilier, M.A., M.S.W., is Clinical Social Worker, Bradley Hospital, East Providence, RI. She was formerly Program Director, Kent County Parent-Child Reunification Program, Kent County Mental Health Center, East Greenwich, RI.

Katharine Cahn, M.S.W., is Director, Northwest Resource Center for Children, Youth, and Families, University of Washington School of Social Work, Seattle, WA.

Paul Carlo, Ph.D., is Director, Center on Child Welfare, University of Southern California School of Social Work, Los Angeles, CA. He was formerly Director of Residential Treatment, Five Acres, Altadena, CA.

Pamela Day, M.S.W., is Director, Family Preservation Services, Child Welfare League of America, Washington, DC.

Edith Fein, M.A., is Research Director, Casey Family Services, Hartford, CT.

Gail Folaron, Ph.D., is Assistant Professor, Indiana University School of Social Work, Indianapolis, IN.

Ann Hartman, D.S.W., is Dean, Smith College School for Social Work, Northampton, MA.

Roger Hatt, M.S., is Regional Director, Familystrength, Concord, NH.

Peg McCartt Hess, Ph.D., ACSW, is Associate Professor, Columbia University School of Social Work, New York, NY. She was formerly Associate Professor, Indiana University School of Social Work, Indianapolis, IN

Paul Johnson, M.S.W., is Project Coordinator, Northwest Resource Center for Children, Youth & Families, University of Washington School of Social Work, Seattle, WA.

Anthony N. Maluccio, D.S.W., is Professor, Boston College Graduate School of Social Work, Chestnut Hill, MA. He was formerly Professor, School of Social Work, The University of Connecticut, West Hartford, CT.

Barbara A. Pine, Ph.D., is Associate Professor, School of Social Work, The University of Connecticut, West Hartford, CT.

Kathleen Proch, Ph.D., is Professor, University of Denver Graduate School of Social Work, Denver, CO.

David Rehm, M.S.W., is Executive Director, Hospice Care of Rhode Island, Providence, RI. He was formerly Assistant Executive Director, Kent County Mental Health Center, East Greenwich, RI.

Julian Sharman, M.A., is Regional Director, Familystrength, Concord, NH.

Jacqueline Sparks, B.S., is Regional Director, Familystrength, Concord, NH.

Ilene Staff, Ph.D., is Research Associate, Casey Family Services, Hartford, CT.

John Turner, Ph.D., is Associate Professor, Department of Sociology and Social Work, Appalachian State University, Boone, NC.

Robin Warsh, M.S.W., is Project Director, Boston College Graduate School of Social Work. She was formerly Curriculum Specialist, Center for the Study of Child Welfare, School of Social Work, The University of Connecticut, West Hartford, CT.

Jeanne Zamosky, M.S.W., is Treatment Director, Familystrength, Concord, NH.

From the Child Welfare League of America

A SOURCEBOOK

Edited by
Robin Warsh, Anthony N. Maluccio, Barbara A. Pine

Teaching Family Reunification: A Sourcebook contains curriculum models, handouts, and a bibliography intended for use in training service providers working with families toward reunification. It provides the conceptual tools to rethink family reunification; setting forth the range of competencies required for effective practices.

This book is an excellent companion to *Together Again: Family Reunification in Foster Care,* edited by the *Sourcebook's* authors. Together, the books enhance appreciation of family reunification theory and practice, in addition to providing training opportunities.

1993/paper/0–87868–511–1/Stock#5111

To order: **CWLA** c/o CSSC
P.O. Box 7816 • 300 Raritan Center Parkway
Edison, NJ 08818
908/225–1900 • Fax 908/417–0482

Please specify stock #5111. CWLA pays shipping and handling for prepaid U.S. orders. Bulk discount policy (not for resale): 1–49 copies 15%, 50 or more copies 20%. Canadian and foreign orders must be prepaid in U.S. funds by international money order.